CASTING
THE
CIRCLE

A Women's Book of Ritual

By Diane Stein

BCE
Before the Common Era

The Crossing Press • Freedom, California 95019

For Sue Fink

I would like to publicly thank several women for their input in the creation of this book. First among them is Shekinah Mountainwater, for all that she's taught me over many years about ritual and Women's Spirituality, and for the parts of her work she has allowed me to include here. Thanks go also to Nett Hart, Morgana Davies, Tanith and Elaine Movic for their editorial comments and suggestions: Nett for general editing, Morgana and Tanith for educating me about traditional wicce, and Elaine for her suggestions on herbs and incenses. I thank her too, for her help with the chapter on candle magick.

Library of Congress Cataloging-in-Publication Data

Stein, Diane, 1948-
    Casting the circle : a women's book of ritual / by Diane Stein.
      p.   cm.
    Includes bibliographical references.
    ISBN 0-89594-411-1
    1. Ritual. 2. Women--Religious life. Goddess religion--
Ritual. I. Title
BF1623.R6S74 1990
291.3'8'082--dc20
                             90-40400
                             CIP

Contents

altar set up [28-29]

Women and Ritual

We create ritual because we are restless inside. We call this 'searching' or 'seeking enlightenment' but we know what we seek is within us. We are aching for wholeness. Our restlessness, our spirit reminds us that 'what is' is not at all that of which we know ourselves to be capable. We are charged in our tolerance, even acceptance, of limitations. We are coaxed on by our memory of the time when we were not bound—when we were/are whole.

When we say we create energy we mean we transform the energy around us into creative energy.

Ritual as an aim in itself is absurd but ritual as the outward sign of inward action is in one form or another natural and necessary to human creatures. It releases religious energy and both expresses and stimulates transcendental feeling.

Evelyn Underhill, 1933

From Lee Lanning and Vernette Hart, *Ripening, An Almanac of Lesbian Lore and Vision* (Minneapolis, Word Weavers, 1981).

Chapter One

———————○———————

Women, Ritual and the Goddess

The Goddess movement is growing, vital, viable spirituality practiced primarily by women. An outgrowth of the activist climate of the 1960s, traditional positive witchcraft (wicce) and the ongoing feminist movement, Women's Spirituality, Feminist Wicce or the Goddess is the fastest developing world religion since the start of Christianity. Embodying the feminist values of peace, freedom, earth awareness, personal and global responsibility, and multicultural respect, its practice puts into spiritual and religious context the ethics and political messages of the women's movement. When feminists in the late1960s discovered that 'the personal is political,' they also discovered that the personal is Goddess and that in women's values they themselves are the Goddess-within.

With a simple series of moral standards and individual ethics based on natural law, Goddess movement wicce embraces women's values in only a few short rules and redes. Foremost is the original women's wiccan root of the Golden Rule, "Harm none," and the second, "What you send out comes back to you, multiplied three (or ten) times." A world that followed the first law would have no use for nuclear weapons or any weapons, or for the military industrial complex, or for apartheid. A world that followed the second rule would perhaps send out food and medicines instead of incentives to burn the rainforests and overthrow governments. It wouldn't tolerate child abuse or incest, homelessness, homophobia, world hunger, rape, environmental pollution, misogyny or racism, and certainly not any form of imperialist intervention or aggression. There would be plenty of money to research a cure for AIDS and no more abandoned AIDS babies or adults. A third wry adage, more an adage than a law, is "Be careful what you ask for, you may get it." This statement shows the power of individual will and thought and cautions using them wisely. The fourth, less verbalized but most important, is, "What you do has consequence in the world."

Central to these ethics is the idea of a female deity, the Goddess. In virtually every world culture before the advent of Judaism, Islam and Christianity, deity was female. She was a Goddess worshipped under an infinite number of names and forms in countless languages, cultures and places. The Goddess was (and is) black skinned in Africa, brown skinned in India, yellow skinned in Asia, red skinned in Native America, and white skinned in Europe. Her artifacts are 30,000 years old or older.[1] Her cultures were woman-oriented with all that implies. She stood for peace, healing, communal living, and reverence for the earth and all life.Under the Goddess cultures, civilization was initially developed; the women's work skills made survival of tribes and humanity possible. These woman-originated skills included food gathering, agriculture, weaving and basketmaking, pottery, cooking, animal domestication, healing and midwifery, building, tools and clothing making. Religion, timekeeping, the alphabet and the arts began here, also. These skills made survival of tribes and humanity possible.

In a Goddess culture, creation of the universe was seen as happening by birth from the vagina or other creative action of the Goddess. This was the beginning of all religion. Women as birth-givers and nurturers were the images and embodiments of the Goddess and creators of life on earth. They were the creations of individual life as the Goddess was the creator of the universal, of all species and life as a whole. With this idea implicit in society, women were in the position of initiators and leaders of culture and politics, the creators of their families and tribes as earthly representatives of universal form. Women were therefore people of consequence in the early tribe or state — they were mirrors of divinity. What they did had meaning and political/personal influence and power.

Then it changed. As near as archeology can now determine, the changes began in approximately 15,000-12,000 BCE and continued to completion by 2400 BCE.[2] At this time in succeeding migration waves, northern hunting tribes moved south, conquering the Goddess matriarchies and destroying them. They brought the order that we know today — patriarchal world culture with its misogynist male god and biases against women, who were the images and form of the conquered Goddess. The Era of Great Purity, as it was known in China, the age of peace and women's autonomy, the age of the Goddess, was over. While no artifacts of weapons have been discovered in any of the Goddess archeological sites on several continents, the northern invader tribes had metal, weaponry, horses and war chariots. The destruction was eventual and total. By the time written history as we know it began in the Middle East and Asia, only distorted remnants of these civilizations remained. Early written exhortations to suppress women were warnings to suppress the Goddess, lest she rise again to reclaim her own lands and cultures.

The patriarchal takeover was perhaps the first and most profound of world wars, the greatest world revolution of any time. Traces of the struggle remain, for women who seek to find them. The artifacts are powerful and provocative. They are finally being interpreted by archeologists who are women, who have no vested interest in patriarchy. Emerging with the clay and stone figures of large-breasted, pregnant Goddesses is the realization of the female as divine, and of a woman-oriented, peace- and life-oriented world order that's been lost.

History in the meantime has been a series of invasions against the female. Once the leaders of civilization, women became breeders and housekeepers without autonomy or voice, isolated from each other and from the workings of society. Some patriarchal countries and religions even denied that women had souls. Women worldwide were kept uneducated and dominated while their thousands of years of culture were taken over by male establishments or lost altogether. Female learning and herstory were systematically destroyed, as evidenced in the burning of the libraries at Alexandria and other places, and in the burnings later of women themselves, nine million or more in Europe from the thirteenth to the seventeenth centuries. Once women were decimated, the slave trade, colonial and missionary movements continued the process of destruction in the remaining Goddess cultures. The takeover was universal, but somehow women have survived, along with women's peaceful, life-oriented values, and the women's divinity, the Goddess.

Goddess women were the healers, counselors, midwives, and scientists. They have continued in these roles despite the oppressions of the patriarchal order. The wiccan religion went underground, becoming highly secret, with groups and members separated from each other, but it continued and survived. Slaves abducted to the New World from Africa brought their religion with them, and, though forbidden to practice it, they did so underground or fused it with the Christianity that was forced upon them. Native American religions continued in the same ways. In China, a women's written language survived for thousands of years, known only to women and used in great secrecy. Women in all cultures taught their daughters the old ways, often at great risk and kept the Goddess and women's values alive. The remnants of the Goddess matriarchies remain in folklore, literature, archeology, mythology, healing and in women's oral traditions. Too much has been lost and distorted, but much remains.

Women today are reclaiming the Goddess as a way of regaining their own identities, Be-ings whose lives and actions have autonomy and consequence. A punishing male god and the patriarchal system give women no role models, or at best, distasteful ones. The Judeo-Christian-Islamic gods of war and judgment are quite foreign to women's ways of looking at the world or to their vision of what the world should be. Herstory has been written out of history, and what's been missing is the Goddess.

The modern feminist movement, beginning with the First Wave in 1848 and rising again in the late 1960s, returned to women their personal power and identity. This movement has known clearly from the beginning that women's values, however patriarchally denigrated, are the values that make continuing civilization and human survival possible. These values are vitally necessary now to save the planet from destruction by wars and environmental breakdown. Women have the power to manifest anything in the world that they choose, and they have learned what to ask for responsibly. Being the mothers of all living, they know about harming none. They send out peace and healing, much needed to return tenfold. They know the need for an end to the oppression of women and of any other group of people. Women work for universal civil rights and freedom, and the end of the abuses of patriarchal power-over gone mad. Recognizing the need for the embodiment of feminist ethics by all, they have reclaimed and returned the Goddess and developed the Women's Spirituality/wiccan/Goddess religion. Rapidly, in less than fifteen years, it has become an international movement.

The Goddess means a variety of things to a variety of women, but what she is *not* is the changing of the male god to a female body. The Goddess is the eternal feminine, the embodiment of female ethics and values. For most women in the movement, she is the creative life force of the universe in all of its expressions. She birthed the universe, moon, earth, and all the species of life from her body. As a birth-giving, all-nurturing mother she has much in common with every woman. As an embodiment of the universe, she is usually seen as immanent, as the earth herself, and as present in every living thing from a blade of grass or a crystal to a wolf or a woman doctor. The Goddess *is* the earth and universe and everything that lives. She is present in all things and all living Be-ings are the Goddess-within, containing divinity in themselves. Anyone who is Goddess-within has consequence in the world, and that is everyone.

The Goddess is cycles within cycles. She is the changing moon, the rotating earth, and the turning of the seasons. In her earth aspect, she has (as the land has and as life has) her designated times for being born, growing up, maturing and experiencing sexuality, giving birth, growing old, and dying. In her moon aspect, the form she is most often likened to, her cycle is similar but shorter, and she is the Maiden, Mother and Crone. The all-giving mother is also the all-taking mother, in a cycle that moves through the ages of life.

These cycles within cycles are turning wheels with no endings. While an individual lifetime goes through the stages from birth to death and the life ends, the species and all life continues. There are deaths but there are also new births to carry life forward. Most women in the Women's Spirituality/Goddess movement believe in reincarnation, that the death of the body is not the death of the soul or spirit, which returns again and again to live a series of incarnated lives. In the turning of the cycle from birth to death to rebirth, every aspect of the process is valued and honored. This process is symbolized in the changing of the seasons and the moon phases. In the Goddess movement, all the ages of women are honored, from the newborn to the Crone: they are all manifestations of the Goddess and her Wheel and are all to be celebrated.

For most women, the Goddess is a real entity, but for some she is a symbol or thought-form only. The Goddess has had her own name in thousands of cultures, with aspects and archetypes that are worldwide. The all-nurturing mother aspect has the name of Isis in Egypt, Kwan Yin in China, Yemaya in Yoruba, West Africa, Spider Grandmother in the Navaho and Hopi cultures, Sarasvati in India, Chalchiuhtlique in South America, Tonantzin in Mexico, and the Virgin Mary in the Christianized West. The all-taking mother aspect is Kali in India, Oya in Yoruba, Nephthys in Egypt, Sedna in the Inuit culture, Hecate in Greece. The all-nurturing aspect does not exist without the all-taking one, without death there is no birth/ rebirth. Both are part of the Wheel of Life. As a Moon Goddess, three forms, faces, or ages are often seen, as in Diana, Selene and Hecate. For some women, the Goddess is individualized and personified in one or more of her names, ages, or cultural aspects, and she is as real as milk and as close as looking within. For other women, she is only an ideal, an idea rather than a manifest Be-ing, of the feminine and higher self within each woman.

The concept of Goddess-within and of consequence is an important and basic one for Women's Spirituality. In the patriarchal system, god is somewhere out in the stars or clouds, ruling from above but not present on the earthplane. The rewards of living are also not found on the earthplane but must wait until after death, when the soul returns to the god it's been separated from. In Goddess spirituality, with its concept of immanence, the idea is much different. Divinity is the earth herself and is present as the life force within each individual. The rewards of living are attained during life on earth, and the woman-as-Goddess has consequential power in herself to create her life. As she moves through the life cycle, she creates what her life is by her own chosen actions and thoughts. After death her spirit continues, and she returns to earth to live and create again. In her Be-ing and Becoming as a woman through the life cycle, she is Goddess.

In effect, these concepts have given women back themselves. In the patriarchal system and religions, women have no consequence since they are not god. Only men are "made in god's image," a male image, and even men find god only outside themselves. Male dominance and its complementary abuses are the result, since not finding divinity within, they find it by dominating and playing god over others. They have consequence by right of rulership and force, not by right of Be-ing. In returning to the Goddess, however, women (and men who choose it) find deity/divinity within themselves and present in every aspect and part of living. Abuse of another is abuse of the Goddess, and since Goddess resides within, it's also abuse of the self. Abuse of the earth is abuse of the Goddess and the self, and abuse of perfection. Every woman is Goddess, a Be-ing to honor and worship. Every living thing is Goddess. In worshipping deity as female, a woman worships her own divinity, herself as Goddess-within.

Up to twenty thousand years of patriarchal rule have left women with erased self-images, little herstory, and only discredited or historically ignored role models. By adopting the Goddess, women also adopt the concept of Goddess-within self-image. Each woman who sees herself as deity finds and becomes her own role model, raising her personal self-worth immeasurably. If Goddess created the earth, moon, and universe, and if she *is* the earth, moon, and universe, and if women are Goddess, too — there is little an individual woman cannot accomplish. When women discover that they have personal power, have consequence, they discover that they can autonomously direct their lives as well as change and correct the problems of the world. Using the laws of harming none, sending out only what is welcomed in return, and being responsible for what is created, women learn who they are, their strengths and abilities as Goddess-within and as people of consequence. This is something new in the patriarchal world.

The actual practice of Women's Spirituality wicce does not return to what was done thousands of years ago; the remnants of knowledge from ancient times are too fragmented for that. Instead it goes forward to what women need for living in a patriarchal world and for reclaiming their self-image and consequence today. The movement uses a number of skills and practices, learned from salvaging women's past knowledge and also from new work. Much of the learning is done orally, taught by woman to woman as it must have been done in the matriarchies of the past. Some of the skills include healing, herbalism, bodywork and midwifery; divination with tarot, I Ching, Table of Ifé, crystal gazing and runes; gemstone, crystal and color work; meditation and psychic development; research into ancient Goddesses and cultures; activism and networking; and ritual. Because women have diversified interests, ritual is probably the skill and activity that most have in common.

A purpose of ritual is to teach women the skills of discovering and using their Goddess-within/consequence. The cast circle is a safe space, a space for women to be who they are. In it women enact themselves as Goddess-within, creating a universe of their own design, and using that universe to manifest their needs and/or discover the magick that emerges. Ritual space is a microcosm on earth of the cosmic Goddess universe. By creating it, women become the designers and directors of what happens in a model world. The symbols of the ritual are a reduction of universal elements to manageable size, a reduction of the planetary order to something available for use and touch. By learning to work with the symbols and with the self as deity in the safe microcosm of the circle, women learn the skills for working magick/consequence in the day-to-day real world. Using Goddess-within and the few natural laws, they discover personal power and learn to develop and depend on it.

Ritual is a training ground to end the patriarchy, and to learn to work together. In the drama and energy-weaving of a ritual, women (together or alone) state what the world should be, and they create it. Then they take that vision and creation into the patriarchal world and manifest its energy there, a very different form of energy than that which presently exists. In taking the rules of harming none, sending out only what is welcome to return magnified, and manifesting/asking for responsibility, something new is brought to an order that has lost its values. That something new is very old, very whole, coming from respect for life, for others and the planet — and such new/old ideas inevitably catch on. A ritual acts out the mythos of what should be, what could be, and what was, and manifests it as now.

Beyond the manifesting and training, there is an individual and collective change in consciousness, for making ritual is also making an action into habit. By creating the precedent for Goddess-within personal power in the cast circle, women doing ritual learn to use that power in daily ways. Using power-within/consequence becomes a habit, a way of life that changes the woman using it, changes the women who watch her using it, and changes the reality and consciousness around them. When Goddess-within values become a habit, and women's self-image as Goddess becomes a habit, the world as we know it will truly have changed. When women come together to make and create these changes, a new society is born. The Goddess returns to civilization and civilization returns to a peaceful, respectful, woman-valued way of doing things. The time for this change is long overdue and only women of consequence have the awareness to make it happen.

Luisah Teish, in an interview with Patrice Wynne, puts it this way. Her name for Goddess-within is the African word *aché*:

> *Aché* means power, not power to dominate anybody, but the power to run your body, to think, to create, just the power to be. Ritual is primarily done for this purpose by pulling *aché* from the universe, having guidance on how to use *aché* and then to give that *aché* back to the universe. To circulate, renew, use, attract and commune with power is the primary reason for all rituals. Ritual is stylized in order that it become a habit. If I can get in the habit of getting up in the morning and drinking a glass of spring water as a ritual to Oshun I remember how precious that stuff is. Only 2 percent of the water on the Earth's surface is sweet water . . . That's a habit.[3]

Oshun is the Yoruba tradition Goddess of love; she is the sweet river water that runs down to the sea.

Habit as ritual is so familiar in everyday life that it usually goes unnoticed. How a woman proceeds to get dressed or undressed everyday is a ritualized habit for most of us, which we don't even think about. What comes off or goes on first? Second, etc.? Most women do the task in the same steps every time. Only if the ritual/habit is interrupted, does it become at all conscious. There is a moment of confusion until the gap is filled. Animals create habits as rituals, too. When you come home from work, watch how a dog or cat greets you. Children jumping rope, the routine of blowing out the candles on a birthday cake and singing "Happy Birthday" are rituals. When rituals are consciously created, new habits are created with new potentials for tapping into Goddess-within, consequence or *ache*. Rituals created with conscious awareness of habits and personal power have the potential to change a culture and a planet.

Women living in patriarchal life are not often in the habit of creating such consciously crafted rituals. In the Goddess movement, however, women are becoming aware of the possibilities of such creating. They are experimenting with ritual and with reclaiming their consequence in the circle and in the world. As more and more women enter the Women's Spirituality movement, the discussions about, concerns with, and exchanges of ideas and information on the subject of ritual increase. It has become the overriding topic of more than one Goddess conference weekend and many an evening's discussion at home. As more women reclaim their personal power, more seek to understand just how to use it, what it means, what its potentials are. And the training ground for answering those questions is in ritual itself.

But women's consequence and self-image is an uncharted land, the maps lost 5,000 to 20,000 years ago with the patriarchal invasions of the Goddess matriarchies. Women have been isolated from each other and from consequence and the Goddess for that long. How do women learn ritual? How do they reclaim the communities in which to work ritual or how do they discover it alone? How do they find the lost information? Women learn from each other in small groups and at large festival circles. They learn alone from the available woman-oriented books, like Starhawk's *The Spiral Dance* (San Francisco: Harper and Row, 1979), Z Budapest's *Holy Book of Women's Mysteries, Volumes I and II* (Los Angeles: Susan B. Anthony Coven No. 1, 1979 & 1980), from my own *The Women's Spirituality Book* (St. Paul: Llewellyn Publications, 1987), and now from this book.

And most vitally and importantly, women learn ritual by experimenting, by doing them with groups and alone. Books are a beginning, an aerial view, but no book can truly teach ritual or should be used as a this-way-only map. Books, discussions, and others' ritual outlines chart the beginning of the way, but the way to doing ritual is a very individual one chosen by each woman or each working group. It is in the creating and doing of individualized, self-designed rituals that women find their Goddess-within fastest and make their own maps to having consequence. There is no right or wrong way.

One of the strongest things about the Goddess movement, and about feminism as a whole, is its essential lack of hierarchy and dogma. What is right is an individual thing, and even the few laws and rules of women's craft are open to interpretation. There is no single answer to most questions. When you ask six women what the Goddess means to them, there are six different answers, and when you ask six women what makes a good ritual there will also be six answers — or more. And all of them are right. The lack of rules beyond the basic ethics leaves Women's Spirituality work highly open to creativity and exploration. It makes women think, makes them look within to find what works for them as people of consequence and manifestations of divinity. And since divinity manifests in each in different ways, women who plan rituals together learn to work together to find common ground, common consensus or agreement, for what they design.

This diversity and individuality is the reason that Goddess spirituality has grown so rapidly and is growing so strongly. The patriarchal religions lost their creativity and concern for the individual long ago. They have the Church, Bible, and Koran to tell people how to live, how to think, what to do every step of the way. Contact with divinity (which is out there somewhere) is available only to the ordained. In the Goddess movement, divinity is within and contact with deity is constant and implicit. Women take the active roles. Immanence and creativity make Goddess clear and present and women touch Goddess and Goddess-within at will. There is no Women's Spirituality Bible or book to say that "This is the only way to do it," though some women's covens develop a Book of Shadows (a ritual book). Instead there are many books and many women and many ways in every step of the process of women's ritual.

Rituals in the women's craft come under a number of categories and types. Moon phase rituals, at least the ones in this book, focus on the quickly changing month cycle of women's bodies and emotions, the 28-1/2 day menstrual/lunar cycle. By ritualizing the happenings of the Goddess-within at the high energy points of this cycle, women come into closer touch with their own selves. Patriarchy has separated women from their bodies, and celebrating the moon cycle is a returning. In the Wheel of the Year, the rituals are different. By celebrating the eight Sabbats in ritual, women move throughout the changing year, acting out the times and ages of the seasons which are also women's life cycles. In ritual there is an acting out, a mythologizing of the process to honor, affirm and welcome the changes.

Rites of passage rituals follow basically the ages and seasons of life, too, but are individualized to each woman's own times of life. The rites of passage are designed to specifically honor and validate what's happening in a woman's growth from birth to death, marking the occasions that are peaks of experience along the way. This category of ritual has lost much of its meaning in the patriarchy, but its traces remain in the Christian sacraments, and in weddings, bat mitzvahs, and birthdays.

Other rituals are ritualized habits of daily life, designed to make something happen or make something sacred — to bring the Goddess and Goddess-within consequence to the everyday. While moving into a new home or apartment would not be as significant as say, the bonding of a love relationship or memorializing a death, such daily events are still important. By ritualizing them, the new apartment becomes a sacred place. This is a valid and important thing to ritualize. And lastly in categories, candle magick is a simple-to-elaborate form of sympathetic magick to induce something to happen, like finding a job or banishing depression. These short rituals add energy to earthplane activities and focus a woman's will and consequence. Candle spells can be done as mini-rituals with a simplicity that makes their power surprising.

These are the types of rituals discussed and exampled in this book. While the rituals here are given in full detail, they are not carved in concrete, but are given with the intent that women using them change and adapt them, agree with parts and disagree/throw out other parts. The rituals are my own Book of Shadows, and they may or may not be yours.

The ceremonies in this book are also *rituals*, rather than *celebrations*, though the words are often used interchangeably.[4] When women celebrate, they come together socially to enjoy and share an event, like someone's birthday party or the Fourth of July. They come to be together and to party, to eat and drink, talk, have community and perhaps dance, drum, or listen to music. When women do ritual, however, they are working to make a change in consciousness, creating a microcosm world in the cast circle to effect Goddess-within/consequence in the participants. They are creating the sacred, rather than the social. This may be done by re-enacting myth, by creating a sacred atmosphere that makes action safe, or by becoming in the ritual what they choose to be and then taking that power out to the larger world. Ritual, therefore, has focus and intent, while celebration is an unstructured gathering. Ritual has sacredness whereas celebration has sociability. Many women's rituals end with celebrations, after the design of the ritual is completed and the circle is opened.

This is not to say that celebrations are fun and rituals aren't. Though rituals have serious intent, they are not always solemn occasions. If there is no joy in a ritual, something is very wrong. There is also no reason to leave humor out, as long as the humor harms none and has respect for the occasion, the Goddess, the earth, and for others. Play is just as sacred as drama, and has as much or more consequence. In a society and community where often women have not learned to play, to have fun, to validate and to honor the child-within, fun and humor in ritual has an important and needed place. In creating sacred space to do ritual, women are also creating a safe place to let the child-within come out and play. And when that happens, it is Goddess, too.

Along with play, women in ritual include the arts of all sorts. In creating a microcosm of the universe as it should be, women create a space of great beauty and creativity. All the arts are involved, according to the women's skills and interests. If someone is a poet, use her poetry in casting the circle or doing invocations, or anywhere else it fits. If a woman is a dancer, she can dance the ritual or parts of it. Add drums, rattles, flutes, or synthesizer music, and women's songs and chants. Use artwork. Design and decorate the ritual space to make it beautiful and match each season or purpose.

Involve as many of the senses in each ritual as possible, too. The changes in awareness and consequence that occur in ritual occur through the senses and all of them can be stimulated to advantage. Inner work, inner change, and transformations are what Women's Spirituality rituals are all about. Every way in which the inner self, the subconscious, is opened makes the effect of the ritual more powerful. It is important to create an atmosphere, a setting, to use soft lighting and flowers, fragrant incense, music and candles and colors, tastes, motions, and sounds. The Goddess-within is only slightly interested in words; she wants to be delighted by images and symbols. Reaching that subconscious, that Goddess-within, is made easier and more powerful through using the senses in the most artistic ways.

Women in ritual work both alone and together, and in working together they work in small intimate groups and in larger communal ones. All three of these ways are important. Working alone, a woman develops her sense of consequence in the most intense ways, and this is often the first step for women beginning in the Goddess craft. A Women's Spirituality working group, a coven or circle, is harder to find or start. In it a few or as many as thirteen women (the number is traditional and practical) come together to develop the ritual and the group mind. They learn to work together, to make collective decisions and choices that validate and satisfy everyone. Trust and closeness develop in such a group. At its best a women's coven becomes an extended family, sharing deeply in ritual work as well as in daily life. Like any relationship it takes time to grow. The number of members is usually small to allow that closeness to develop.

Community rituals are larger group gatherings, sometimes hundreds of women, and they happen primarily at the women's cultural festivals and conferences. The National Women's Music Festival offers a yearly Women's Spirituality Conference along with its high quality women's music performances and other special events. Presenters teach workshops and there are sometimes large rituals, like the one Starhawk led in 1986 for 500 women. Smaller ones happen either in workshops or spontaneously. The Michigan Women's Music Festival, held yearly in August, is a camping-out festival with an attendance of 6,000 to 10,000 women, about a fourth of them interested in spirituality. A variety of workshops and large and small rituals happen there daily, both planned and spontaneous, led by women from all over the world. The Women's Spirituality publication *Of A Like Mind* sponsors a yearly Dianic Wicce Conference with a featured big ritual, and Womongathering is also a spirituality-focused women's festival event that happens yearly. These are somewhat smaller events.[5]

In all the sizes and types of ritual the question of who will lead them arises. All women are priestesses in Goddess wicce and all are potential leaders, but some make good high priestesses (leaders of ritual) and some do not. Ideally, a high priestess is a woman with experience in group ritual, having a psychic sensitivity for channeling energy and monitoring the group mind. She has the ability to design and lead a successful ritual of her own, or to lead one written collectively by the group. In some women's covens, the high priestess is a rotating position, a different woman acting the role each time. Traditional nonfeminist wiccan covens have an initiated and trained high priestess who is the sole mother and leader of the group, the ritual leader and teacher for every coven activity. Women's movement values and wicce declare all women equal, all are Goddess-within; they believe in sharing the glory and the work, but Women's Spirituality ritual leaders often lack traditional wicce's thorough training.

In a small women's group, all the members train as high

priestesses. They take turns leading rituals or divide rituals into parts for everyone to share in. Sometimes a woman chooses not to lead at all and her wishes are honored until she changes her mind, but everyone is encouraged to share the leadership. It can happen in some new groups that there is one woman who has more experience and becomes the coven's high priestess by default, or by the others refusing to work. This is best discouraged, with the more experienced woman using her skills to involve everyone and to teach. Consequence is for everyone, not only for one star in the group, and ritual is a training ground for consequence.

Norma Joyce, founder of Women In Constant Creative Action in Oregon, calls her organization's high priestesses the HPD — the High Priestess of the Day. In this rotating role, the woman who leads the ritual has full responsibility and full glory for its success. The next time, however, the HPD is some other woman. Newer groups need to be non-judgmental about the HPD. Women come to leadership with varying degrees of expertise and learn much of it by doing. Ritual critiques that are constructive can be helpful to all, but critiques that are unloving do much more harm than good. A circle is a safe space where women are free to be who they are, and that means free to be who they are safely. As long as the leader is doing her best work, women will care for her and support her.

Occasionally in groups there are problems around the issue of leadership. A lack of balance can develop especially in newer groups. One woman tries to lead all the rituals, not by group choice, and wants everyone to think she is the only one who can do it. Remember that women are reclaiming their power and consequence for the first time in 20,000 years. Members should be gentle with her while at the same time not allowing her to continue. Her ego will balance out in time, or she will choose to leave the group. Another woman may lack the self-confidence to lead at all, and this is the other side of the same issue — women's need for consequence and knowledge of Goddess-within. Both women need the love of the group and the safety in the group, and they should be encouraged to reach balanced roles.

Leadership is a major issue in the women's movement. The emphasis on equality of all women has sometimes been interpreted to mean that no one can be a leader at all. This becomes more of an issue in larger groups and community rituals than in small, private groups where the women work together regularly and grow into priestessing from the beginning together. The fact is that some women are more talented at leadership and/or ritual priestessing than others. Some women devote their lives to it. While one woman may make a very fine high priestess, another woman may be superb at teaching healing or reading tarot or facilitating meetings and planning sessions. Different women have different skills and all skills are valuable. A high priestess is no more valuable (or less valuable) a group member than the woman who makes a great split-pea soup. She has a special skill that the group validates and makes use of.

Sometimes in the politics women forget that all are Goddess and the results can be hard to live with for everyone. In some large group gatherings, no one wants to accept the role of high priestess or HPD at all. Accepting the job means putting oneself under attack for star-tripping, or being subject to overly harsh criticism no matter how well the ritual goes. It takes strong skills to lead large group rituals. If a woman has this particular skill as a leader, she has a right to expect validation and caring from the community for her work. The lack of caring that happens at times is evidence of the harm that patriarchy has done to women and women's consequence. Some women are too insecure to accept and validate others' leadership. When the critiquing of a ritual causes hurt to the woman who has led it in good faith, the critique has gone too far. And it's gone too far when women are afraid to lead for fear of censure. This is not to say that such imbalance is universal, only that it happens at times. The women's movement and Goddess movement are very young, and women are growing fast.

What it comes down to is that in most cases *someone* has to lead the ritual or there won't be one. Groups settle the question with the knowledge that all women are Goddess-within, that all women have leadership potential, and they work to develop it in everyone. When a woman has a particular skill, whatever it is, it should be encouraged and validated. When women share the role of high priestess, all learn and develop in leadership and consequence. Whoever is high priestess or HPD needs the rest of the group's support and caring to feel safe enough to lead. Taking leadership in a ritual or anything else is a very scary place for women just beginning to find themselves. Practice love and understanding while everyone's abilities grow. The goal is that every woman discover her own leadership ability and realize her potential. And the group goal is for successful, magickal rituals that empower all.

Planning the ritual is another group discussion issue, again with a number of possibilities. Some covens plan the ritual as a group, each woman adding her ideas and input to the process. Agreement on a topic or idea is usually by consensus, by discussing and working with an idea until it is agreeable to everyone involved.

Some ritual circles with larger membership pick a committee to plan the coming event, or less often one woman who is also to be the high priestess designs the ritual. (Often this is the case in large community rituals where it is harder to organize the group.) Sometimes a woman with a germinal idea presents her idea and plans a ritual around it with the group's consent. In some groups, women take turns presenting rituals that they plan and lead individually or with only a few members. They do rituals often enough to give everyone a chance to be involved.

In most circles, the women meet together for ritual planning at least once before the ritual date, or plan the ritual in the last group meeting before it is to happen. The meaning of the ritual is discussed first. If it is a Sabbat, what does this Sabbat mean? A focus is necessary for the ritual. What effect, action or myth is to be enacted? What ideas and changes are women to bring away from it? With the purpose of the ritual firmly defined, the how-to becomes much easier. If a Hallows ritual is to focus on the old age of the year and the life cycle, the women choose aspects of that to use and validate. If the choice is to focus on the Crone, how can the group use symbols and actions to present and validate the Crone, and what are her positive aspects? Wisdom and experience might be the theme here, or birth and rebirth, or foremothers and grandmothers. With these in mind and the general structure of ritual in place, the plans begin to emerge.

When a group plans the ritual together as a whole, all the women present ideas, or there is some brainstorming from which the most interesting ideas are taken for development. Every woman has input and if the group likes an idea they include it. When some want an idea and others don't like it, there has to be a way of coming to agreement. Usually this is a process of discussing what doesn't work for someone and rethinking the idea until all are comfortable with it, or until the dissenting woman decides she can accept it. If someone feels strongly against a particular idea and cannot resolve the difference, the group using consensus drops or changes it. Everyone agrees, if choices are made by the consensus process, and it can take some time to come to that agreement. Each step in the ritual is developed in this way. The process can happen quickly by consensus or can grow slowly.

Once the ritual is planned, the women decide who will lead it. If there is a rotating high priestess system, it may only be the one who is next on the list. If there is no definite list, it may be a volunteer or a woman who likes the ritual and wants to be more involved. If the women lead it together, they then determine who will take what parts. These issues settled, the next question is what props or tools are needed for the ritual and who will bring what items. What color will the candles be for the altar (they usually match the season or event), what decorations, what objects are needed in the working of the planned ritual? Is there to be a potluck dinner afterwards or a giveaway blanket or skills sharing? Will there be flowers? Who will bring what?

Obviously this is a lot of discussion and work, and it's not good generally to wait till the evening of the ritual to do it. When the ritual is planned in advance and everyone knows what is to happen, what she is to do in the ritual, and what she is to bring, things go more smoothly. Mixing the earthplane work of consensus and planning with the astral/magickal work of the ritual itself holds back the effect of the ritual considerably. When women come to the ritual ready to go, the ritual begins actually as they gather and anticipate it. All of the ritual planning, however, centers on determining the purpose for having a ritual in the first place.

If a member misses the planning, the group has a policy on how or whether to include her. In many groups the women agree to be present for every meeting and/or ritual planning session, but this is not always possible for everyone all the time. If a member in good faith misses a ritual planning, the group can tell her later what has been decided. They may choose to simply carry her, to tell her what to do the night of the ritual, but to minimize her active role. Some groups exclude women from the ritual who do not participate in the planning. Some groups have the rule that if a member misses too many meetings she is dropped from the group — a policy to consider only with caring and applied to the individual. As a group bonds, missing meetings becomes less of an issue than at the beginning; nonserious members drop out. Any rule a group decides upon is developed by consensus and administered with flexibility and awareness of individual situations. If a woman shows a consistent lack of commitment, doesn't come often or take part in group work regularly, her membership may be in question with the group.

In rituals done alone, the same woman plans, leads and participates and she does all of the steps and readying process herself. The planning happens more quickly than in a group, as she has only herself to please. Working alone, she might be willing to take more emotional risks than she would be with a group. On the other hand, with more women to share the planning, group rituals are often more involved and more structured. In doing rituals singly, a woman develops a good basis for magickal skills, probably more than she realizes. Many women want to work in groups but have no access to them, so many more women do rituals on their own. If there is one place to start to do ritual, solitary rituals are the place.

In doing ritual with groups there is the potential for great sharing and intimacy among women and that is the basis and reason for a coven. In starting and building a circle, women not only learn craft and ritual skills but learn group interaction and processes. This is another way of developing women's skills and consequence. Groups develop slowly and pass through processes of their own. Most groups start with an open meeting of interested women, and there may be quite a lot of them. After a few such meetings, many of the women do not return, having decided that the group is not best for their needs. The women who remain discuss what they want from the group, what they are willing to give to the group, and then they may plan their first ritual together. After a few months of meetings and plannings, the group can undergo changes in which more members drop out. The remaining women become the core group and the work of building a coven and building an intimate working relationship begins in earnest.

As women's situations change the group may change — someone moves, a couple separates, someone else asks to join. At some point most groups close to new members, and entrance after that becomes more difficult. The process of group bonding has begun, and the group is ready to work seriously together. Many women's covens are limited in term, but some remain active and whole for many years, the members becoming a chosen family. Often such a coven becomes a teaching group at festivals or for other new covens. Sometimes a group becomes so large that it divides into two, or a divergence of interests causes it to divide.

Community ritual groups are large but short-term covens. The women gather together at a festival or conference. They live in different cities and perhaps have ritual groups of their own at home. They come to the ritual not knowing each other or knowing each other only slightly, and they come together to work one ritual or a few rituals over the weekend, and then they separate. In these situations it may not be possible to plan the ritual by consensus or to choose a high priestess by rotation. Often the festival chooses the woman that is to lead the ritual, or a small group of women meet beforehand to plan a ritual for the rest. Most of the women of the group are not the ritual's planners, and they participate under the direction of the high priestess or committee. If the planning involves active participation of all the women, the ritual has a much better chance of meeting its goals and the women's needs. It is also the responsibility of each woman participating to follow the priestess's directions and take part in the event. To hold back is to slow the energy and endanger the success of the ritual for everyone. In planning a large group ritual, the high priestess works at activating a group mind rather than at individual transformations (which happen from it, too). The individual has consequence in being a part of the whole.

A major issue in the planning of small or large group rituals is the idea of safe space. An estimated half of all women are survivors of incest, rape or abuse, and a third are in alcohol or addiction recovery. Another large segment of the community lives with some form of physical disability. These women's needs must be met and their presence in ritual and in the group validated and honored. No woman should feel unsafe emotionally or physically in a ritual; the very nature of ritual is to create sacred, safe space where women are free to be who they are and to be honored as Goddess-within. No woman should be excluded from ritual because of physical-access barriers, like stairs or rough ground for the woman in a wheelchair. She should not feel physically endangered by the group's forgetting her needs. No woman should feel uncomfortable because alcohol is served or there are drugs present. These are all issues of respecting the Goddess in each other.

Women who are incest or rape survivors may feel very threatened by physical activity and involuntary intimacy. While a group hug feels good to most women, it can cause a great deal of fear to one who has been abused. Some women feel highly uncomfortable where there is much physical movement around them, as in women dancing or doing a spiral dance. These women have been hurt by the very patriarchal abuses that Goddess spirituality works to change in the world, and in a ritual they need nurturing, protection, and safety. Women in recovery do not want to be faced with the substance from which they are battling so hard to be free.

Many women have disabilities, whether they acknowledge them as such or not. The woman who broke her leg as a child and walks with a limp may have a hard time keeping up if there is rapid movement in the group. She may fear being knocked over if there is dancing. A woman with a bad back may have difficulty sitting on floors or standing for long periods, while another woman may have trouble seeing and moving around in the dark. Some women have allergies to incense smoke, or to the perfumes and soaps other women in the group are wearing. A woman who is blind may need a sighted guide or a ride to the ritual, while a deaf woman needs enough light to read lips or see a signer. Some disabilities are visibly evident and others are not. Some women talk about their disabilities and others do not. Everyone, with or without disabilities, has special needs.

The women's movement and Women's Spirituality movement have done more for emotional and physical disability awareness than perhaps any other segment of the Western population. Real effort is made at most women's events to make the space accessible and safe for anyone who comes. While the level of awareness is not as high as it could be, the intent is there, and great progress is being made. Most of it becomes a matter of caring about others and of common sense.

Women who work together in a small group come to know each other well. As women become comfortable working together it gets easier for a woman with special needs to make them known, and her coven will have the caring and respect to listen to her. If incense discomforts her, she says so, and the group works out other ways to do ritual purifications. If she has difficulty moving around in the dark, the group keeps its rituals more lighted or less physically active. If she is in a wheelchair, rituals are held in places that are accessible, and the group asks her what she needs to make sure she can be there.

In larger groups and community rituals the issue becomes more difficult as the women don't know each other as well and there are many more of them. It is impossible to ask each woman in a festival what her needs are, although she can talk about them to the high priestess or ritual planners beforehand. It is just in such large groups that access and safe space issues become the most important. Where women's needs are unmet, a crowd of women either leaves the ritual or gathers outside the circle to watch but not participate. Everyone loses with this — women who want to participate are excluded and the rest feel "watched" and inhibited from fully enjoying the ritual. So what to do?

One solution, developed over several years of experimenting at the *Of A Like Mind* Dianic Wicce Conferences is to make a safe space area within the circle. This may be around the altar in the center or at one of the directions, and includes some chairs and floor pillows. If a woman feels threatened at any time by the intimacy or movement, or if her physical disability requires her to stop for awhile or not take part in a portion of the ritual, she comes to the safe space in the center. As she is right in the middle of the action, she remains a part of it, but removes herself from what may be discomforting her. In a ritual where there is drumming, music or a circle or spiral dance, the women in the center can take up drums or rattles and participate that way if they choose to. The space is there, for anyone to use it at any time.

When there is physical intimacy at a ritual, as in touching or hugging, one signal agreed upon at the beginning of the ritual is that if a woman would rather not, she just shakes her head, "no." The participants respect her wishes. For women in recovery, it is good policy to make rituals alcohol and drug free. Use water, fruit juices or nonalcoholic beverages in the chalices that are passed around, and state what's in the cup. Women who have colds or herpes lesions are asked not to drink. Drugs are not only an addiction issue for some women but are also illegal. They have no place in public rituals, where they could not only endanger someone's recovery, but get someone arrested. What women do at home is their own choice, but in respect for others and the Goddess, they come to rituals clean and sober. Some women have environmental allergies that make incense smoke in a ritual a threat to their well-being. There are other ways to do an opening purification, if it is known that someone has this allergy or at large rituals where this might be the case.

One further issue in ritual access is where the event is held. An outdoor ritual may not be accessible for a woman in a wheelchair or on crutches who cannot walk long distances or handle rough ground. A ritual that is held in the dark outdoors is not accessible for women with night-vision problems. One non-women's wiccan festival holds its main ritual outdoors at night at the top of a steep hill; many are excluded from it because they can't climb it or push a wheelchair up it. When planning outdoor rituals take the site into consideration for whether it will exclude any women. Indoors, stairs and narrow doorways may be difficult for chair-users and others, and incense can be more troublesome than it would be outside. Access is most often a matter of common sense and consideration for others. When in doubt about someone's needs, ask her. Women pride themselves for their awareness and work at improving it.

These are the beginnings of doing ritual in a Women's Spirituality/Goddess context. A purpose of ritual is to develop women's Goddess-within consequence in a space of complete safety and sacred beauty. That beauty is dedicated to the Goddess who is within all women and therefore to the women themselves. By sharing the decisions and planning, leading, and participating in ritual, women learn cooperation and community. By working in rituals alone and/or together women discover and develop their leadership and skills, and learn respect for each other and for the Goddess within themselves. By claiming their Goddess-within, women reclaim the fact that they have consequence, that what they do affects and determines their own lives and the lives of others, even to the point of changing the world.

Goddess spirituality is a way of embodying the values and meaning of feminism into the habits of Be-ing (rituals) that change and transform women's lives. Rituals are a way of validating women and creating ways of developing women's personal power. This power is not the patriarchal power to bully others, but instead is the inner power to self-determine and self-validate. Ritual done alone or with other women teaches the habits of Goddess-within, of learning in a safe and sacred space the skills to carry out into the daily world to make that world safer and more sacred. Women's Be-ing is sacred, is divinity/Goddess, and all women are Goddess. When women learn self-image and validation for self and others in the microcosm of the cast circle, they create a habit of Be-ing that is changing women and changing the course of the planet.

Notes

1. Buffie Johnson, *Lady of the Beasts: Ancient Images of the Goddess and Her Sacred Animals* (San Francisco: Harper and Row, 1988), p. 2.

2. Merlin Stone, *When God Was A Woman* (New York: Harcourt, Brace, Jovanovich, 1976), p. 20.

3. Patrice Wynne, "Practical Wisdom: An Interview with Luisah Teish," in *The Womanspirit Sourcebook* (San Francisco: Harper and Row, 1988), p. 40.

4. I thank Norma Joyce of Women In Constant Creative Action for making me aware of this distinction. See her article, "Ritual Planning and Making" in Diane Stein, Ed., *The Goddess Celebrates: Women and Ritual,* an anthology in progress (Freedom, CA, The Crossing Press 1991).

5. National Women's Music Festival, POB 5217, Bloomington, IN 47407; Michigan Women's Music Festival, POB 22, Walhalla, MI 49458, *Of A Like Mind,* POB 6021, Madison, WI 53716, and Womongathering, Rt. 3, Box 185, Franklinville, NJ 08322.

Chapter Two

———————◯———————

Altars and Beginnings

Most women start doing ritual by creating an altar. An altar is first a thing of beauty, containing objects of personal meaning to the woman who designs it. In its emphasis on art and natural objects it is essentially a symbol of Goddess, of Goddess-within, and of beauty in the world. In its more developed symbolism, the altar becoms a microcosm of the universe, which is Goddess, the center symbol within a symbol of the cast circle/sacred space, and the universe created in the ritual. An altar can be as simple as a seashell and a candle, or it can be highly elaborate, depending on what the woman who makes it wants.

Most women's first altars are spontaneous. On one corner of her dresser a woman keeps a bowl or basket with some favorite things in it. There might be a crystal, some seashells, a ring or necklace she likes, and a bird's nest she found at a picnic. She arranges them artistically in their container or on the dresser top, and finds that when she needs comforting or quiet, she comes to handle the objects or just to be in the room with them. The crystal is her symbol for earth, the shells for water, the silver ring for fire (metal), and the bird's nest for air. She may not notice the correspondences.

Another first altar is the single candle she places on her dinner table, or lights at night for meditation. The candle is a symbol of fire, the fire of life or the life force, and is a symbol of Goddess and Goddess-within. It is chosen for the beauty of its light, its ability to calm the mind and heart. (Many women beginning in spirituality learn to meditate, and a candle is a meditation aid.) She adds other objects to it to make her first altar. An altar is a miniature sacred space, a place to come for calm, beauty and peace. Nothing does these things better than a lit candle in a darkened, quiet room.

As the woman gains interest in the Goddess craft, her altar grows and changes. She adds her tarot deck to it, the gemstones and crystals she works with, natural objects she finds outdoors that feel good or reflect the season (like red leaves in autumn or a rose in summer). She adds a figurine of a woman/Goddess she makes of clay or buys at a flea market or a women's festival. She adds an incense burner, the handmade magick wand or stick she uses to cast her circles with, the collar of her dog that died, a photograph of her grandmother. Gradually becoming aware of the meaning of each object, she later chooses things with deliberate symbolism, but always chooses things that are personally powerful to her. Her one meditation candle becomes three perhaps — red, black and white — and she places her objects artistically on a brightly colored scarf. From one corner of her dresser the altar gradually becomes the whole dresser top or gets a table of its own. It becomes the focus of the room, of her apartment or house, the first thing seen on entering or waking, and its energy of sacredness envelops all who walk into the space.

A Woman's Spirituality altar is a center of personal power. It's a reflection of the woman who creates it, what she values, what interests her, what she is attracted to and likes. It's a reflection of Goddess in symbolism and objects, and brings that reflection of Goddess/universe into the earthplane space it rests upon. There are as many different altars as there are women who work ritual in the Goddess craft. There are as many different altars as there are Goddesses-within.

Says Luisah Teish:

> Your altar is your personal signature. Here's a place where you need not be scared that you're gonna do it wrong. An altar can be made of anything that appeals to you. There are universals— like you want to mark the four directions, you want to make sure you have the elements of earth, air, fire and water on the altar. Generally, when I build altars for specific rituals, I clean the space, smudge and spray. I invoke the directions. I place a glass of water and a candle on the altar. Then, I call the spirits of the space and I say, 'What do you want here?' Then I just do what they say.

> Now what tickles me very much is people who say, 'I'm not the slightest bit spiritual. I don't know how to build altars.' And you walk in their living room and they have a lamp, a candle, some flowers sitting on a doily, a picture of grandma, the image of the ancestors. You see what I'm saying. All they need is a glass of water and a stick of incense and they've got an altar. People do subconscious altar building all the time. We call it interior decorating.[1]

Altars can grow from a small space to a large one spontaneously. From Teish again:

> Once the ancestors decided I no longer needed a dining room and so the whole dining room turned into this incredible altar space. I had fabric canopied on the ceiling. I got seaweed from the ocean and made a serpent across the walls. There were shells and sand, driftwood and lickable rocks, dried plants and living plants and pictures of gods and goddesses everywhere. Folks would go in that room and be there for the longest while just touching and feeling and going on.[2]

My own altar is a five-foot-long dresser top, loaded with crystals, gemstones, ritual tools and Goddess images. It has a blue and silver brocade for an altar cloth. There are ceramic bowls of shells and stones, strings of beads, a vase of feathers, an athame that was once a red-handled dog-grooming tool and my Motherpeace tarot deck. There's a large mother crystal in the center and a vase of magickal crystal wands toward the side. It began as Luisah Teish described, with a lamp and a bowl of seashells. Then it just grew. It's the center of my bedroom and my home, and a psychic window for healing dedicated to my Goddesses Yemaya and Oshun. Each woman creates her own altar in her own size and way.

An altar is permanent or temporary, a portable temple. A woman making it in her bedroom or living room may leave it there indefinitely, changing it only infrequently to dust. One woman dismantles, cleans and remakes her altar every new moon, another every Sabbat. Another who uses a small altar primarily for meditation creates it new every evening. Others let their altars remain until it just feels like time to change them.

Altars in ritual are often set up for a specific occasion and dismantled at the end of the evening. A woman doing rituals alone may create a Sabbat altar for the evening, as part of, or along with, her permanent altar, and take it down when she's finished. Groups doing ritual can create an altar together, each woman bringing things to it and removing her objects when she leaves. Sometimes the high priestess sets up the altar, making sure that it contains the objects and tools she needs for her ritual, then inviting others to add things. This creates a beautiful altar, with personal meaning to everyone participating in the ritual. Sometimes in group rituals, the altar is strictly spontaneous. This can be impressive at a large festival, with a huge and varied altar a dozen feet long.

Despite the emphasis on creativity, a ritual altar contains objects put there for specific reasons, and an altar designed that way has definite and deliberate symbolism. The tools needed to perform the ritual are also included on it, chosen carefully for their effects on the mood, focus and theme of the Sabbat or evening. An altar created thoughtfully enhances the ritual's meaning for all the participants. It heightens the sacredness and power of the magick and increases its transformative effects. An altar is the main focus of group rituals, and created with that in mind, its beauty becomes the center symbol of the ritual's purpose.

The most basic symbolism of a deliberate altar is the four elements and spirit. (This can be stated also as the 'five directions,' except that various other numbers of directions are invoked in women's rituals, depending on the tradition used.) The four elements are earth, air, fire, and water, and in magick all that exists is composed of one or another of them. In directions, earth corresponds to the north, air to the east, fire to the south, and water to the west. Spirit is the life force that animates all that is living; it is otherwise defined as Goddess or Goddess-within. In directions, spirit is the center of the circle, and the four elements and spirit are the four corners and center of the earth.

The elements and spirit are also the five points of the wiccan star/pentacle, and the five directions or elements can be imagined as the pentacle's points. Spirit is then at the top and the four elements are the other four arms of the figure. Nonfeminist wicce places the altar traditionally at the north direction of the circle. A suggestion for women's rituals is to place the altar at spirit, at the top of the circle, imagining the circle as a pentacle or wheel. A Wheel of Life is created this way, and actual physical directions become optional. The altar can also be placed in the center of the circle.

The idea of the altar as the pentacle is a very old one in traditional wicce, with very female roots. In the traditional Goddess invocation below, the high priestess's body becomes both the altar and the points of the pentacle. She is described lying face upward inside the circle, head in front of the altar (at spirit), arms and legs outstretched to the other four points. Her yoni/gateway of life is the circle's center.

> Assist me to erect the ancient altar, at which in days past all worshipped;
> The great altar of all things.
> For in old time, Woman was the altar.
> Thus was the altar made and placed,
> And the sacred place was the point within the center of the Circle.
> As we have of old been taught that the point within the

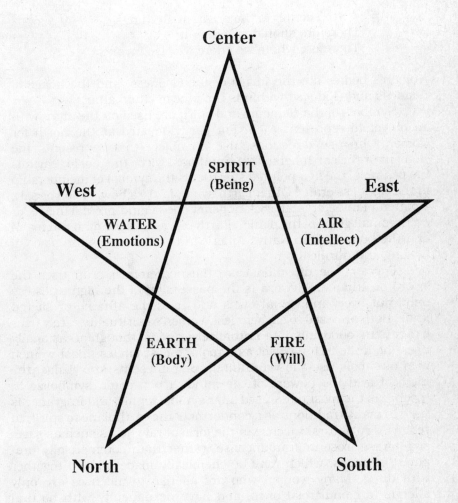

Center

SPIRIT
(Being)

West   East

WATER   AIR
(Emotions)   (Intellect)

EARTH   FIRE
(Body)   (Will)

North   South

The Pentacle
The Circle
The Altar

center is the origin of all things,
Therefore should we adore it;
Therefore whom we adore we also invoke.[3]

Women's bodies are the image of the Goddess, and the image of Goddess and Goddess-within is the wiccan ritual altar.

Symbols of the elements and spirit are used on the altar, with an object to represent each. For earth, located at the north for women who use directions, use an object that represents the element or the earth herself. In traditional wicce the tool for earth is the pentacle, the five-pointed star that is the symbol of membership in the Goddess craft.[4] Other earth symbols are a bowl of soil or salt, a potted plant, a crystal, rock or gemstone, a land-animal image, or even a small globe of the planet. Earth represents the material realm and the body, and in Native American traditions it is the place of healing and purification.

For air, the direction east, the nonfeminist craft uses the sword or athame. A sword is the possession of the high priestess only, but every individual owns and uses the athame or sacred knife. Both are used to cast circles. Women's spirituality rarely uses either item, choosing not to ritualize weapons, though occasionally uses the knife in its aspect as a tool. To cast circles, most women who use tools use the wand (fire). Air represents knowledge, the intellect and the powers of the mind; a pen could symbolize it. Incense is the most often used altar symbol for air, and fragrance is used in many traditions as a connector of the earthplane to spiritual realms. Try natural incense in the form of raw herbs such as sage, sweetgrass, rose or frankincense, rather than commercially prepared incenses, which may be chemically made or held together with dung. Many women who are allergic to incenses are only allergic to commercial ones, and have no difficulty with natural herbs burned on charcoal. Other symbols of air are feathers, winged circle or winged heart images, and images of birds. Try casting circles with a feather; it's much nicer than a sword.

The element of fire is most often represented by a candle to symbolize the life force/Goddess/Goddess-within. Candles come in a wonderful variety of styles and colors, and each color has meaning, but in the beginning use white or natural-colored beeswax tapers. Traditional nonfeminist craft uses the rod or wand as its symbol for fire. Women have used wands less in the past, but recently have begun hand-creating crystal wands of copper, silver, or wood as ritual and healing tools. A smooth-feeling stick of willow or oak also makes a good wand, as does a long-stemmed flower, but when a wand is made of wood or plant matter it is no longer fire but an earth symbol. Wands channel energy and are positive representations of fire, but candles are still central on the altar, and can be used alternately for spirit. Most objects of metal are representative of fire, and Starhawk lists the incense burner/censor as a fire symbol. The direction for fire is the south. Fire represents energy, women's power, sexuality and the will.

For water, both the traditional and women's symbol is usually the chalice or cup, which is also a symbol of the nourishing breast. The element represents the emotions, intuition, healing, fertility, psychic ability, loving, and flowing. Seashells or sea objects (starfish, sand dollars, seaweed, pearls, fishing balls) are also used as water symbols. Try the Priestess of Cups card from the Motherpeace tarot deck, a picture or image of a mermaid (the Goddess Tiamat or Yemaya), a snake or serpent image, or an aquamarine crystal. Most dragons are water but the flame-breathing ones are the fire element. The direction is the west, and all life originated in the sea.

Spirit is the head of the pentacle and altar, but can be placed at the altar's center. Spirit is Be-ing, the life force, divinity and reincarnation. In traditional craft its tool is the cauldron, representing emergence from the womb and transformation. The Hopi people call this place of emergence the *sipapu* or *sipapuni*, basically the vagina/birth passage. Symbols for spirit are womb symbols and include a bowl or cauldron, an eternal-light type of candle flame, a mirror, yoni image, large mother crystal, crystal cluster or crystal ball, an amethyst cluster or geode, any Goddess image, or even an origami butterfly or metal scales, as these are symbols of the soul. If a cauldron is used, it may contain salt water, crystals, a burning candle, or burning incense — or it may be empty. Goddess images are of any aspect the woman or women like. Any female image is a Goddess, and a photograph can be used, particularly the photo of a foremother or ancestor. Spirit is the 'you and me' of the universe.

A consciously created altar contains an object for each element and usually one for spirit. These can be very simple or very elaborate, whatever is wanted. They don't have to cost much money. Some examples might be using a candle for fire, seashell for water, feather for air, crystal for earth and grandmother's photograph for spirit. They can be small objects or large ones, depending on what's available and the size of the altar. Place them so the elements match their directions, with spirit in the center, or all five in a circle. They don't have to be in an exact arrangement. If a variety of items is included, arrange them artistically. Place them on a dresser cover, placemat, scarf, piece of woven cloth or lace to delimit the boundaries of the pentacle. These alone, the five symbols on the altar cloth, become an altar.

Putting other objects on altars is a matter of choice. Anything with personal meaning or coming from nature can be there, anything a woman wants there. Suggestions include: three candles for the three aspects of the moon/Goddess, a wishing box for written affirmations, a tarot deck or runeset if they are personal tools, flowers in spring and summer and colored leaves in fall, tinsel snowflakes and glass icicles in winter. Use a round mirror for the full moon, or a silver moon crescent necklace, or gemstones of all types. Burn candles in colors to match the seasons and Sabbats or to reflect on personal needs and wants.

Basic altar candles are white or natural wax, but colors are used to reflect the seasons. Yule (Winter Solstice, December 20-23) candles are red for rebirth; Candlemas (February 2) candles are white or red and white; Spring Equinox (March 20-23) candles are pastel colors for the softness of new growth; Beltane (May 1) candles and Summer Solstice (June 20-23) candles are red for self-love, love and passion; Lammas (August 1) candles reflect the green of first fruits; Fall Equinox (September 20-23) candles are the fall colors of oranges, yellows, reds and browns; and Hallows (October 31) candles are white, black and red for birth, death and rebirth. For individual needs, try red or orange candles for sexuality and arousing, warmth and stimulation. Use yellow for mental growth and the intellect, and for asserting the will and energy. Try green or blue for healing and rose for self-love and to draw love or friendship. Use indigo or violet for spiritual opening, psychic development, meditation and connection with the Goddess. Black candles are for grounding with earth energy, calming, and transformations. White candles, like black ones, contain all the colors of the spectrum; use white for general spirituality and any altar work, for spiritual growth and purification.

Goddess images for altars come in all types, from the simple clay Venus of Willendorfs to intricate jade Kwan Yins. Try making them at home of modeling clay, watch for them in flea markets and at women's festival crafts booths, find them in museum gift shops. Wonderful images of the Yoruba Goddesses can be bought for very little cost in botanicas and voudoun shops, and Egyptian images can be found in museums. Try Asian groceries or Chinatown variety stores for Asian Goddess images, and even Christian religious stores for images of Mary — who really was and is a Goddess. Any female image is a Goddess image — why not try something glass from the five-and-ten or the women painted on antique valentines and postcards? Use a photograph of a woman of herstory or an ancestor, or even an admired neighbor woman. Choose images in all the ages, Maiden, Mother and Crone, and images of all ethnic types, body sizes and races. All of these are the Goddess, including the image in a mirror and a photo of oneself.

Once an altar is designed, it is dedicated, usually to the Goddess or a specific Goddess name, and with an intent. Dedicate altars to Yemaya for healing, Athena for learning, Kwan Yin for spiritual growth, Spider Woman for psychic development, Oshun for bringing love into one's life (don't specify directly *whose* love, unless both parties agree to it). Or dedicate the altar to the intent and focus of the Sabbat or the moon phase of that ritual. Permanent altars are usually dedicated, temporary ones for a single ritual become part of the ritual and are less likely to be dedicated in themselves. Watch the magick come alive in an altar as, and after, it is dedicated for a purpose. Use the occasion of dedicating a new altar to dedicate or re-dedicate oneself, if the time feels right for doing that. In choosing the Goddess names to use, pick those that are personally meaningful, aspects that feel close and protecting. An altar dedication ritual follows, and a self-dedication/initiation is the focus of the Candlemas ritual later in this book.

Altar Dedication Ritual

Before doing this ritual, read the rest of this chapter and the next on ritual structure. For less experienced women, all the needed information is there. For women who are familiar with ritual, the steps will probably be familiar. A full explanation of the Self-blessing is also given in the next chapter. To dedicate oneself along with the altar, do the Self-blessing and afterwards extend it by saying, "I dedicate myself to the Goddess (chosen name or aspect), as a priestess of the women's craft and as a (healer, tarot reader, psychic, ritualist, witch, etc.). Design the dedication, and all of the ritual, to individual needs. When choosing to do a self-dedication, realize that it is a serious commitment. Do it only when the time is right, do it by free choice, and know that major inner transformations are about to begin.

When doing the Altar Dedication, follow the steps in order but feel free to change any part of the ritual to make it more personal and meaningful. Choose Goddess names that are your own, descriptions for your own work, and wording that has individual consequence. Read over Chapter 3 of this book, then the ritual outline, gather together the things needed, and begin. Come to the ritual after a purifying bath or shower, dressed in loose clothing or skyclad (nude), and do it when there aren't likely to be interruptions. Take the phone off the hook. Never do magick on a full stomach; the last thing at night is usually a good time. (More on these directions later.) The ritual is given in outline form for easy following; keep the outline near as a guide for performing the ritual. As in any carefully planned ritual, the Altar Dedication given here is an experience of magick and beauty.

Items needed to perform this ritual include the altar, containing objects for the elements and spirit. For earth use a crystal; for air use incense; for fire use one, three or five candles in white or a color; and for water use a bowl of water or salt water. For spirit use a larger candle, cauldron, gemstone cluster or Goddess image. (Items can be substituted.) Smoke-allergic women can use a feather for air and purify by stroking their auras with it. Place personal ritual tools on the altar, particularly the magick wand, or optionally a long-stemmed flower. Use a Goddess image, seashells, crystals, flowers and/or whatever else you wish for altar objects and tools.

Need

Crystal, potted plant or bowl of soil (earth).

Incense — Stick or loose herbs, try frankincense for protection, amber for clarity, rose for love, or sage for immortality and purification (air). Or use a feather.

Candles — White or all the same color — one, three or five tapers in holders (fire).

Bowl of water or salt water. For the Self-blessing use water, a natural fragrant oil or menstrual blood (water).

Goddess image or larger central candle, or crystal or amethyst cluster (spirit).

Ritual wand — Or use a long-stemmed flower, leafy thin branch or athame.

Altar and altar objects, personally chosen and arranged.

Matches to light candles and incense.

Charcoal block for use with loose herb incense.

This ritual can be used as the first step in a house blessing, as an altar dedication only, or as an altar and self-dedication together. Intended to dedicate the permanent, personal altar, it can also be used to dedicate the 'big altar' at a large group ritual.

Outline

Light candles.

Purify — With incense smoke, self and room, smudge altar.

Cast Circle/Invoke a Goddess for each element and spirit:

> Earth — Flora, Roman Goddess of beauty.
>
> Air — Sappho, Greek foremother of inspiration.
>
> Fire — Amaterasu, Japanese Goddess of women's power.
>
> Water — Yemaya, Yoruba Great Mother, Goddess of healing.
>
> Spirit — Spider Woman, Hopi/Navaho Mother of immortality.

Priestess first dedicates her ritual wand, if she uses one (or her flower, athame or other circle casting tool), then uses it to dedicate her other altar objects. She holds it up, and says:

"I dedicate this wand to the Goddess (Goddess name, optional), to help me in my work."

Touch the wand to salt water (water), then to the crystal (earth), through the incense smoke (air), and near — not in — the candle flame (fire). Last, touch it to the spirit candle or Goddess image (spirit). Then say:

"I dedicate this altar to the Goddess and the five elements, and dedicate it to helping me in my work of (*healing, meditation, divination, inner growth, etc.*).

Place the wand on the altar and do a meditation on what the altar means and how to use it.

Do the Self-blessing (see next chapter for description).

"I dedicate this altar as a tool for Goddess, magick, beauty and growth."

If dedicating herself, she adds:

"I dedicate myself to the Goddess (Goddess name or aspect optional) as a priestess of the woman's craft and as a (*healer, tarot reader, ritualist, witch, etc.*).

Take a moment's quiet to feel the energy. Direct the energy mentally to surrounding the altar and self with a bubble/cone of charged light (try blue, gold, or rose).

Ground — Place palms to the earth, let the excess flow out.

Open Circle — Thank each Goddess/element, inviting them to remain daily for power, protection and growth.

Extinguish candles — Blow them out or use a snuffer or wet fingers.

Once the altar is made and dedicated, the question of how to approach ritual, how to come prepared for it, is central to the results. To come to the ritual unprepared is to negate all the work and effects of the magick. To come to the ritual ready for it is to increase its power and transformative ability on the participant(s). This doesn't only mean having a ritual planned carefully and the objects to perform it near to hand, though these are the first steps. It also means that each woman entering the ritual comes to it ready to do magick, ready to experience her own consequence and God-dess-within. To do that means letting go of the out-of-circle daily world and entering the sacred space cleared mentally and physi-cally of negativity and outside distractions.

There are several things to do in this. First, don't do ritual on a full stomach. The purpose of ritual is to let go of the earthplane for awhile to create an astral/idealized universe of women's conse-quence. Digestion is an earthbound body process and while doing it, psychic work, circle work in the astral, becomes much harder or impossible. So work on an empty stomach, and save the potlucks for after the ritual ends. When working at ritual alone, a suggested time for doing them is the last thing at night before going to sleep.

Another issue in being prepared to enter the circle is that of being 'ritually cleared,' 'ritually clean' or 'ritually purified.' This can mean different things to different women. Personally, taking a shower or bath before doing ritual is a must. The running water of a shower is a way to wash off the cares and this-world concerns of the day. Visualize/imagine them running down the drain and use the shower or bath to feel clean, new, like Diana emerging from her sacred pool a virgin again. By making the shower into a separation and letting go of the real world, it becomes easier to enter the ritual ready for it. All the daily stuff is gone for awhile, long enough for the magick to be felt in the circle.

Meditation is another way to prepare for ritual, for entering sacred space. Use it as a bridge between the daily hustle and the calm of the cast circle. Before leaving home for the ritual, or before beginning a ritual at home, sit quietly for a few moments in front of a lit candle. Do it in a place without interruptions, a darkened room with the phone off the hook, and shoes off. Sit in the glow and breathe in its calm and beauty. Breathe out anything that's troub-ling, any distraction. Let go of the drain that needs fixing, the bills piling up, homework to do, job problems and worries. Let go of all the stresses with each out-breath, drawing in ritual calm and candle light with each breathing-in. Do it for a few minutes before leaving for the ritual or before starting.

Meditation has always been a primary technique in any spirituality system worldwide. It is a primary technique in Women's Spirituality and in women's rituals. Meditation is a tool for leaving the everyday behind and entering between the worlds, the place of women's consequence. It is a primary and essential tool for any psychic development work, of which ritual is part, for healing both present and past, and for any form of divination. It is an essential tool, recognized or not, in any form of women's creativity. Many or most women begin in spirituality by learning to meditate. It's the first tool to learn, and it is not necessarily the easiest.

There are two major types of meditation. One is the Eastern type in which the mind is made totally clear of all thoughts and images. This takes much experience to learn, and often many years of practicing to achieve it. The woman empties her mind and pushes aside any thoughts that come in. A totally clear, totally blank mind is said to be the opening pathway for nirvana, bliss or enlightenment. For the woman beginning it, it seems almost impossible to do, even for short periods of time.

The other type of meditation, based on visualization (creating images), is the type most used in the Goddess craft. In this form, women let go of their everyday concerns and enter ritual space, psychic reality, or the place between the worlds. They guide the thoughts and images that come to them, using them to create a reality they choose with care. No negative thoughts or images are allowed; they are transformed into positives. The women use their powers of will and mind to create the universe they want to have happen. 'Be careful what you ask for' means this form of thought is powerful enough to manifest exactly what is visualized. Part of this method is used in guided visualizations or guided meditations, where the women are taken on a journey. This can be from a voice on tape, a woman leading the meditation for the group, or self-written in each woman's mind as she goes along. In the journey the women leave the real world for a beautiful forest or seashore, a place between the worlds, as the cast circle is in ritual. There each meets someone — the Goddess, a spirit guide, ancestor, wise crone or her inner self. The Be-ing offers each woman a message, an image, a solution to a problem, or a gift. The women return to the earthplane refreshed, with new insights about their lives, and in a calm, positive state of mind. Each has created a new world for herself, a personal reality.

Another form of meditation is psychic healing, in which the woman sees psychically someone who needs to be healed, and in the meditation changes her dis-ease to well-being. She pictures/visualizes/imagines the woman as totally well before leaving her. In divination with a crystal ball, the woman enters the meditative space, using the ball as a focusing tool. In meditation she sees images stimulated by the ball that give her the information she seeks. A pool of water, dark mirror, or bowl of water with crystals in it is also a focus for crystal-ball gazing or scrying. The meditative state is the basis for all psychic work, including telepathy and empathy, and from this place of calm groundedness all forms of women's creativity arise. Women who do not meditate describe a creative state or place that in spirituality is called meditation.

Meditation is also a primary part of ritual, as it is the key to entering the astral magickal world, the realm between the worlds. Since the cast circle with its altar for focus is a way for women to create and live in a world as they want it to be, meditation is the connection by which women enter that Goddess-within place. The images of meditation are the images that the subconscious/Goddess-within understands and uses to create new realities. Words work well on the earthplane, but are not effective in ritual, where symbols and images are the ritual language of women's consequence and transformation. Meditation is the use of that language, those images involving all the senses, to design a realm of women's psychic consequence and reality.

In its use in ritual, meditation is done to take the group or individual on a journey into the conscious focus of the ceremony. If it is a ritual of childhood, as in Spring Equinox for example, the meditation might be a journey to each woman's childhood or child-within. If it is a Croning ritual or a Hallows ritual the meditation might journey to the Wise Crone to learn her wisdom and advice. If it is a birth and rebirth ritual, the meditation is a guided journey from birth to death and into rebirth. The women travel to the place of the visualization, the place between the worlds, which is also the place and purpose of the ritual. Women return from such journeys quietly transformed. Used as preparation for beginning a ritual, meditation is a way of letting go of the earthplane and entering the ritual state, a beginning of the ritual space or cast circle. Such letting go and preparation is one way of entering the circle ritually ready or 'ritually purified.'

An aspect of the 'ritual purity' issue that cannot be ignored is the issue of drugs. This issue has caused the destruction of more than one coven, including my own first one. Some women are into it and others are not, and some even feel that a little "grass" before a ritual helps them to connect with Goddess. For them it's a way of entering the circle ritually purified or it's something to use in the ritual. Other women are in recovery or otherwise horrified by the idea of drugs, in circle or out, but definitely have no wish for them in a ritual. Where the two viewpoints exist in one coven there can be major conflict, and major pain for all involved.

Peyote is a drug used for religious purposes in some Native American traditions. It is *only* used in ritual, and only by people of that tradition who are properly prepared and ritually purified beforehand. Women who bring marijuana, alcohol or other drugs to rituals feel that their use is similar. On the other side, women who come to a ritual under the influence are no asset to the ritual or the group; they are a disruption and a detriment, and their energy in the circle is anything but positive. Drugs or alcohol within the ritual feel threatening for women who do not approve of them, and for women in recovery who are fighting to overcome them. Drugs are also illegal and are threatening in that way. What to do about the conflict?

This is a question for covens to resolve individually, and I can only give you my own solution, which is simply to respect others. No woman is ready for ritual work if she comes to the circle acting high or drunk. No woman battling addiction should be faced with the substance she is battling in what is supposed to be safe and sacred space. The safe space issue is one to take seriously; it means that everyone who comes feels welcomed, honored, safe and comfortable. It means that drugs and alcohol have no place in women's rituals unless the entire group gives free consent to them beforehand and unanimously.

What women do outside the circle is their own responsibility and choice. If a woman chooses to use drugs before coming to the ritual, and does not enter the circle under the influence, fine. If she uses drugs before a ritual and is not capable of taking responsible part in it because of them, she has acted in a disrespectful manner to her sisters and in violation of safe space. In the ritual itself, because of recovery and legality issues, the same is true, for both drugs and alcohol. A woman who works individually becomes aware that these substances hinder, rather than help her rituals' effects. This is only one opinion, but I feel very strongly about it. *Drugs and alcohol have no place in women's rituals.*

What to wear, or not wear, in doing ritual is also part of the preparation. Leaving behind daily clothing is another way of leaving behind the earthplane and of becoming ritually pure. In "The Charge of the Goddess," actually the only written "prayer" of the Goddess movement, the line goes:

> You shall meet in freedom, and as a sign of trust you
> shall be naked in your rites.[5]

Yet, other than at women's music festivals where shirtless is the accepted style, few women participate in skyclad group rituals. Those who do are usually members of a coven in long standing where time to develop trust has made it safe and comfortable. Many women also live in colder climates that make skyclad work, even indoors, usually too uncomfortable to consider. And in working outdoors, both privacy and climate are major issues. Of the women who do skyclad rituals, most do them at home alone or with a lover.

So what do women wear to rituals, if they wear anything at all? Some women wear the long, loose robes traditional in nonfeminist wicce and usually make them themselves. Others find festive ritual clothing in a variety of places, from women's music festival craftswomen to thrift shops. Some have one dress or blouse or outfit that is special for them, that they wear to every ritual. Others wear what their moods dictate for each occasion, sometimes wearing clothes and other times working skyclad. Any of these is a way of preparing for ritual, separating from the everyday earthplane.

As far as do's and don'ts, when clothes are worn they should be comfortable, loose-fitting and easy to move around in. Natural fibers hold the ritual's energy around the body, where synthetics keep it away, and the energy accumulates from ritual to ritual. The stereotype of witches wearing black is seldom true in Women's Spirituality, though some traditional covens wear black robes, black symbolizing magickal potential. Most women choose colors and styles that appeal to them, and have one special outfit for use in all their rituals. In the circle, it makes connection with the earth and the sensing of energy easier if the participants are barefoot. In general, women wear what they want to in rituals or wear nothing at all.

When a group chooses to go skyclad, for a particular ritual or for all their rituals, it is usually decided by consensus. In large festival rituals, it can be spontaneous, and is always up to the individual. In Women's Spirituality, women's bodies are valued in all their varieties, races, ages, abilities/disabilities and sizes, and the trust required to do ritual skyclad should not be so hard to develop. It is generally considered a mark of respect to the Mother to do ritual barebreasted; it is also a validation and honoring of the participants' own bodies to work skyclad. Women are images of the Goddess and hold her within their bodies and their Be-ings.

The one symbolic item of apparel required in the circle is a necklace or long tied belt, called "the cords." Both of these represent the circle, whose endlessness also represents the Wheel of Life, the Wheel of the Year, the lunar cycle, and the Goddess. Only some

Women's Spirituality covens use the cords, which are emphasized more in traditional craft. Red is the cords' traditional color, but any color works. All traditional and Women's Spirituality witches, however, use the necklace as a symbol of the craft in circles. They often wear a pendant, usually in silver (the Goddess' metal) of a pentagram, full moon or moon crescent, or Goddess image. The necklace can be a simple string with a seashell, holey stone, acorn or other natural object on it. Often the necklace symbol is a crystal, and sometimes a string of African or gemstone beads. The necklace should be something meaningful to the wearer, and is her personal choice. By wearing a necklace or cords in the circle, the woman identifies herself with the Goddess and the circle of life, and recognizes her unity with other women so-minded.

Visualization is the language of women's rituals, used in meditation and in ritual symbolism. To visualize is to imagine, to create in the mind with pictures or symbols, and less importantly with words. In meditation, women go on imagined journeys, find themselves in woods and on seashores when they are physically sitting in someone's living room. Yet the travel is real, and it is visualization that makes it real. In the circle, much of what happens in a ritual happens by visualization. The example of meditation in ritual has been given, and the next idea that comes to mind is the cone of power.

In most rituals, women raise energy. They do this by a variety of means and methods from humming together to chanting and singing to simply imagining the energy happening and rising. In a classic way of raising power, the women imagine a spiral, cone or bubble of light in any color forming and rising around and above them. The light or power is focused on manifesting the goal of the ritual — making Full Moon wishes come true, effecting a healing for a woman or the earth, bringing crone wisdom to a woman at her Croning, bringing womanhood to a girl at menarche. The energy of the cone of power is invisible, but is there and strongly real, and by visualization it is given form and directed where the women choose it to go.

Another example of visualization is in casting the circle. The ritual circle/sacred space is created/cast by a symbolic movement of the high priestess with her athame or magick wand. Yet the circle once cast becomes as formed as the walls of a room. By visualization, the circle becomes a real entity with life force Be-ing. Visualization is important in meditation and in most of the actions that occur in ritual. It makes the idealized/as-it-should-be universe that women create in the circle happen.

Visualization also takes astral/psychic energy and brings it to reality on the earthplane, and this is its major importance in women's rituals. When a woman enters the cast circle and draws the moon into herself at the Full Moon, she becomes the Goddess incarnate in the circle. She then draws down the moon into all of the women in the ritual with her. The energy and power of this is more than symbolic, it is very real on the astral magickal between-the-worlds plane. The women's visualizing makes that energy real, makes it manifest in real women, carries it from between-the-worlds to now. And the woman who has drawn the moon into herself in the circle, who becomes the Goddess ritually for however short a time, takes that feeling of power and consequence with her when the ritual is over. This is a major visualization; it develops women's consequence and Goddess-within.

Because of this power, the images created/visualized in the circle are always positive, present-tense ones, with care in what is chosen and asked for. In healing, for example, always visualize the woman be-ing healed in perfect health and with a smile on her face at the end of the healing ritual; don't dwell on her dis-ease. In wishes at the Full Moon, for another example, imagine things being true that are fully positive, what you really want. Don't go half way, and don't ask for *shoulds* — literally ask for the moon. Visualizations are also made in the present tense, as things happening right now. To imagine something coming later puts it off indefinitely.

Thought-forms are powerful things, and that is what visualizing creates. A thought is an energy entity with a life of its own, and an ability and force to manifest and become. When women create these images/thought-forms/visualizations in ritual, they do so in ways that manifest the most positive Goddess-within, power-within consequences possible. What this basically means is that one asks for only good things, and ask with regard to the implications of having them. When requests are put into words to match the visualized images they are called affirmations. A typical affirmation along with its pictured or symbolic image is "I am a powerful woman": the woman imagines herself in ritual, drawing down the moon.

One caution here. Though the word *visualization* includes the word *visual*, it is much more than that. While many women, perhaps most, visualize in pictures, many others do not. A visualization can be in sounds, fragrances, taste or touch, feelings or symbols. For example, a woman who is blind thought she couldn't visualize because she has no vision. After going through a guided meditation/visualization on "peace," she realized that peace for her means the scent of lilacs, the sound of a cello and the touch of her cat's fur. A visualization is not confined to visual images, but is all-sensory. A symbolic visualization example for "peace" might be a seashell or a dove, both Goddess images anciently (and presently) used for the concept.

Another ritual concern is the directions/elements. While most women connect the elements with their directions, some do not. While most women in Women's Spirituality use five elements or directions — earth, air, fire, water and spirit (north, east, south, west and center) — others use only four: earth, air, fire and water. Still others do it in other ways. In casting my own circles, I use seven directions, saluting the earth and universe before invoking Goddess names for the other five. Some Native American traditions invoke eight directions. Any of these choices is valid and there are other possibilities.

The separation of the elements from their physical locations/directions was shown me by Shekinah Mountainwater, as a personal aid in casting circles. As a dyslexic with spatial disabilities, finding the compass points in many new places and houses was a major confusion and stress for me. Calling the elements without having to worry about their directional correspondences is a great relief. To do this, invoke earth, air, fire, water and spirit rather than north, east, south, west and center. Again, both ways are valid and work beautifully in ritual.

In calling on Goddess names for invoking the elements, choosing a favorite Goddess, or to personify the energy and focus of a ritual, remember to use Goddesses from all cultures and traditions. Women's Spirituality is a multi-cultural movement, comprised of women from a rainbow of traditions, races and backgrounds. This is as it should be, the honoring of all women and heritages, and by using the Goddess' many names multi-culturally this inclusion of everyone is emphasized and enhanced. Multi-cultural Goddesses make it an affirmation that women want to work in a rainbow environment even if their particular circle lacks cultural diversity in its women. The unity of all women is a major concern of the Goddess and women's movements. Everyone is included, everyone is equally a part. By invoking into the cast circle names of Goddesses who are white, black, yellow and brown, European, African, Asian, Indian, Native American and more, women most truly represent who the Goddess is. By visualizing her in all the varieties that women are — all races and ages, fat and thin and variously abled — all women and the Goddess are best served, and consequence for all women is enhanced.

There are times when it is positive to do ritual and there are times when it is also positive *not* to. Do ritual only when it feels right to do so, when the woman or women involved choose it. Some occasions are the waxing, full, or waning moons, the eight yearly solar Sabbats, and personal rites of passage — birth, menarche, relationship bonding, menopause and memorial. Do rituals in time of emotional need or times of just wanting to. Self-blessings, healings and a variety of candle rituals (please do only positive ones) are among the ways of doing ritual. Do ritual to manifest into the earthplane things desired — jobs, money, the best apartment or relationship. Remember to "Be careful what you ask for" — you may get it.

There are also times when it is more positive to *not* do a ritual, and these times have nothing to do with the calendar or moon phase. Avoid doing ritual when angry or emotionally upset. Energy is magnified in ritual work and magnifying negative energy or upset feelings is no good for anyone. Avoid doing ritual when in a non-private place. Interruptions are highly disturbing and can be harmful, from an energy standpoint if nothing else. If the group cannot agree on a ritual plan and consensus is impossible, it is not time to do a ritual for that occasion. To go ahead against the group flow is to invite negativity, with possibly serious group dynamic repercussions. If there is no focus or purpose to a ritual, it is not a ritual and the plans need rethinking. The occasion may call for a celebration instead. Another time to avoid doing ritual is when drunk or stoned.

When To Do Ritual

Waxing, Full or Waning Moons
The Eight Great Sabbats of the Year
Rites of Passage
Times of Need
Times of "Want To"
Healing
Self-Blessing
When It Feels Right

When Not To Do Ritual

When Angry or Upset
When Not in Private Space
When Group Can't Agree on Plan
When There is No Focus for a Ritual
When Drunk, Drugged or Emotionally Unstable

When It May Violate the Free Will of Any
When It Doesn't Feel Right

Never do a ritual if it violates the free will of any member of the group or of anyone else, present or not. This is basic wiccan ethics. Women have a right to unhindered free choice and their own decisions; their mistakes are their own responsibility and karma, no one else's. Interference with the freedom of anyone in ritual, candle spell, thought, or deed directly violates the first wiccan law: 'Harm none.' At times there is a real temptation to do this "for her own good." The woman who when asked if she wants a healing and refuses it is a classic example. To do the healing anyway "because she needs it" violates her free will, and the karma rests on the woman who goes ahead with it. Another example is in love affairs; never do love spells to bring two people together unless both directly choose it. If only one is asking for the relationship, and the other's wants are unknown, ask instead for the best possible relationship for her, rather than for a relationship with the specific individual. If the relationship is meant to be, it will happen.

While some priestesses disagree with this, I feel it is also a violation of the 'Harm none' and free-will ethic to do hexing. A hex is a witch's curse designed to bring down retribution on a wrong-doer or at least the return of negative energy to one who has sent it out. The classic example used to justify hexing is rapists, with the argument that they are men who harm women and beyond the bounds of all mercy. Another argument is that by returning their energy to them they are getting what they deserve. This is a major controversy in the Goddess craft, with lots of good women very set on different sides. As with the drug and alcohol issue, I can only give you my own opinion.

The wiccan ethical rule is 'Harm none' with the further warning that 'What you send out returns to you three- (or ten-) fold.' By this law, a hex returns to the sender, magnified. Karma takes care of the rapist, and to take it on oneself is an interference with the Goddess' justice. Instead of hexing a particular rapist, it seems more productive to take care of the woman he raped and to prosecute him through the legal system. She has more need of her sisters at this time than of any productive results that could come from the hexing. Why not do a ritual to banish *rape*, instead. This might protect and help many more women than the hexing, and leave women's karmas clear. Interfering with someone's karma makes it yours — is a rapist worth it?

When in doubt about ethics, stop the action or make the

following affirmation as part of the ritual. This is one derived from the work of Marion Weinstein's book *Positive Magic:*

> I ask for these things,
> Their equivalents or better,
> According to free will,
> Harming or manipulating none,
> And for the good of all.
>
> So mote it be.[6]

Use this when the action seems okay, but may not be. When the action is clearly manipulative, just don't do it. Since what is sent out returns three- (or ten-) fold, it makes good sense to avoid manipulative actions that could return again. Even when an action seems to be the right thing to do, as in the healing, be very careful not to violate personal choice.

This has been a chapter on basic advice for starting ritual work. The next chapter deals in specifically detailed ways, with the structure of doing ritual.

Notes

1. Patrice Wynne, "Practical Wisdom: An Interview with Luisah Teish," in *The Womanspirit Sourcebook* (San Francisco: Harper and Row, 1988), p. 41.

2. *Ibid.,* pp. 41-42.

3. Janet and Stewart Farrar, *Eight Sabbats for Witches* (London: Robert Hale Ltd., 1981), p. 51.

4. For more detailed correspondences, see Starhawk, *The Spiral Dance: The Rebirth of the Ancient Religion of the Great Goddess* (San Francisco: Harper and Row, 1979), p. 201 ff.

5. Traditional, probably written by Doreen Valiente and revised many times. See Diane Stein, *The Women's Spirituality Book* (St. Paul: Llewellyn Publications, 1987), pp. 59 and 81. The full 'Charge' is printed in Chapter III.

6. Marion Weinstein, *Positive Magic* (Custer, WA: Phoenix Publishing Co., 1981), Chapter VIII. Highly recommended.

Chapter Three

———————◯———————

Ritual Structure

While there are as many types of rituals as there are women to create them, there is also a definite structure that underlies them all. When women know the basic pattern of designing ritual, it demystifies the process and brings it into reach for anyone who wants to do it. In the Goddess craft, everyone is a priestess and can be a high priestess if and when she chooses. This is very different from the standard religions that reserve such information and action to a designated few male/ordained people. Anyone can do ritual, but to do ritual properly requires how-to information. This chapter presents the information, the pattern and structure, to use in creating any type of Women's Spirituality ritual. It is easier than it seems.

Anyone can talk to the Goddess. She exists all around us, in every living thing and every creation. She exists within. Women are a part of the Goddess and contain the Goddess within themselves. The earth is the Goddess, as is everything on the earth. She is the eternal mother. If a woman wants to speak to the Goddess, she just sits down and talks to her. If a woman wants to see the Goddess, she looks in her mirror or into her lover's eyes.

Ritual is a way of speaking to the Goddess. In it women invoke both the inner and the universal deity into the circle or group. Ritual is a way of reaching the Be-ing of the Goddess, of the earth mother, and of women's Goddess-within. It is a way of causing thoughtfully chosen changes in the earthplane and in women's individual lives. By reaching and invoking the Goddess into the circle or ritual, into the women of the circle, ritual shows women who they are — that they are Goddess — and reclaims consequence and divinity in them. Once a woman has drawn down the moon into her self in a ritual, been high priestess for a Sabbat, experienced a rite of passage, or journeyed in meditation to her own Goddess

Be-ing, every possibility on the earthplane and the astral is opened to her. In traditional wicce, only the coven high priest draws down the moon, and only on full moons, but this is not so in women's craft. The experience of ritual, of reaching divinity and designing the universe, changes and transforms, showing women their consequence and power in the circle and without.

To assure that the magick happens, and that it is available to any woman who chooses it, there is a fairly standard and simple ritual outline to follow. It offers a guide to doing rituals that connects women to their Goddess-within consequence and invokes the power of the immanent Goddess. Though the outline is a standard pattern, the ways of following it in each step are multi-varied. The outline does not hamper creativity, but offers a structure that frees it.

In the ritual structure there are many options for completing each step. In choosing options, be first aware of the purpose of the ritual and its focus. Keep the actions and tone of each step in accord with them. In a quiet Fall Equinox ritual where the focus is healing, for example, it is not appropriate to use dancing or a Beltane maypole. In a drumming ritual and spiral dance, it would be equally ineffective and inappropriate to use a quiet meditation that would be lost in the rhythm and the music. When you set a purpose and choose a tone, the way to use the different options becomes clearer. Keep the style consistent and the focus in mind, and each step of the structure falls into place.

When doing ritual for the first time, or until it becomes easy/ habit with experience, keep the workings simple. A simple ritual is as powerful as a more complicated one, and sometimes more so. Even when experienced at doing ritual, use simplicity as a tool for magick. The subconscious/Goddess-within responds more easily to straightforward things. She wants to be entertained and shown, made to feel and experience, but can also easily be confused. With this idea in mind, use sensory impressions and actions over words whenever possible.

The ritual begins when all of the women have arrived. Don't wait too long, or discussion and socializing can turn the evening into a celebration, putting off the ritual until no one wants to do it. Women need to learn to be on time, out of respect for themselves, their word, the ritual, and the other women. If someone is consistently late, she may learn respect by being refused entry to rituals that have started without her. Once the circle is cast, no one comes in. Leave the potlucks, give-away blankets, and socializing till the ritual is over.

The entire ritual evening is focused on the reason and purpose of the ritual. Women come dressed for the ritual, if they are not to work skyclad, and decorate the altar and ritual room to reflect the reason for the ceremony. If the occasion is Summer Solstice, for example, the room is decorated for summer with flowers and colors of the season. Red is a good theme color for this Sabbat. To bring the pastels of Spring Equinox or the evergreens of Yule to Summer Solstice would put the whole focus out of place. To design the altar and surroundings appropriately for this Sabbat enhances the entire evening.

The altar is decorated by the woman who hosts the ritual, by the high priestess of the evening, or by the whole group together. The women bringing tools and decorations for the ritual add them to the altar, and everyone adds her own items, things meaningful to her for the Sabbat. The altar decorations also emphasize the purpose of the ritual, which has been decided and agreed upon at the ritual planning sessions. The ritual outline and structure begin when the ritual is planned.

Ritual Structure

1. Purification
2. Casting the Circle
3. Invoking the Directions/Elements
4. Drawing Down the Moon (Full Moons)
5. The Charge of the Goddess (Sabbats and Full Moons)
6. Invocation/Purpose of Ritual
7. Meditation (Most Rituals)
8. Body of Ritual
9. Self-Blessing
10. Raising the Cone of Power (Most Rituals)
11. Grounding
12. Opening the Circle/Thanking the Elements
13. Endings/Group Hugs/Sharing Food

Rituals are held in surroundings that are safe, peaceful and beautiful, and in preparing the space this is the mood to create. Outdoors, pick a place that is private, where strangers won't walk by. Clear the area of trash and set the altar at some especially beautiful spot. In front of a large tree, between two trees, on a large flat rock, or where the land feels particularly good are places to center the ritual. If there is a stream nearby, place the altar on her banks, or where the sound of water can be heard throughout. Make an offering of something organic, an apple perhaps, to the flowing stream. This is a way of invoking the water Goddess.

Indoors, do rituals in rooms that feel good, protected, and safe. Bedrooms are nice for this, particularly bedrooms that contain a permanent altar and so have been influenced by ritual energy all along. Close the drapes against the light and the outside, and the room feels like sacred space even before the circle is cast. Take phones off the hook. If there are pets, and the group agrees, allow them into the room and ritual as long as they behave. If they are disruptive, close them in another room or put them outside for a time. The same for children; if they are able to participate or are quiet, let them be there. They are witches and priestesses in training. When the ritual begins, light the candles and turn off the electric lights. The room is transformed into a temple.

The women enter the ritual space when the altar is prepared, the high priestess is ready, and everyone has arrived. Until then, they assemble in another room, living room or kitchen indoors, or in summer outside on the porch, except to make the altar. When entering the ritual space, the women leave socializing outside the room and enter ready to cast the circle and do sacred work. In the nonfeminist craft, the circle is often cast before the participants enter; in Women's Spirituality the circle is usually cast when everyone is present within it. The women are quiet and waiting.

My personal signal for beginning a ritual is to **light the candles** on the altar. Electric lights are turned off and the candles are the only source of light in the room. Candlelight is the first and most powerful signal to the subconscious mind/the Goddess-within that something out of the ordinary and into the sacred is about to happen. A room lit by candlelight is the beginning symbol for doing ritual, and it is a powerful and beautiful one.

Purification is the next step, letting go of the earthplane and everyday concerns before entering between the worlds. Light a stick of incense from a candle flame, being sure to use natural incense without chemicals. If loose incense burned on charcoal block is used, the block needs to be lit a few minutes before starting, as it takes some time to heat up. If using a smudge stick there needs to be somewhere safe to put it or to put it out after the purification, as it will keep on burning. Try a clay flowerpot saucer filled with water to put it out, or filled with sand to rest the burning stick on. Watch for sparks when using smudge sticks, too.

The high priestess holds the incense stick or censer/burner close to her to breathe the smoke, and passes the smoke over and around her body. She smudges (smokes) the fragrance over all of her chakras, her body, front and back, including her head, hands and feet. Then she either passes the incense clockwise to the next woman or carries it to each woman in the ritual herself, passing the smoke over and around each woman's body. As the purification continues, each woman is smudged or smudges herself with the incense smoke. The women are silent, using the smoke and the process to let go of outside concerns and worries, to enter fully into the ritual. They breathe in the incense, and breathe out calm. Purification means letting go of the earthplane in readiness for entering between the worlds, the place of connection with Goddess.

For women who are allergic to incense, or simply for variety, there are other ways to do purification. One is to pass around a chalice or bowl of salt water and do the purification by sprinkling drops of it on the women's bodies. Salt is a natural purifier and disinfectant, and works fine at ritual purification. Used with the same intent as smudging — letting go of the earthplane — sprinkling or spraying water does the job. Direct the water drops at the women's heart chakras: just a few drops, not a dousing.

Another way of doing purification is stroking or combing the women's auras. This can be done by working in pairs to comb each other's energy fields (not physically touching each other). The partners can use their hands, brooms, or feathers in fall, the dried leaves at the end of an ear of corn. Even a flower can be used to stroke the aura/energy field and cleanse it. Be imaginative. When using a flower, corn shuck or other tool, do not use it again in the ritual until it has been cleared of any negative energy it may have picked up. Try just shaking the energy off of it, into the earth or an imaginary fire.

Another way to purify is for the women to hold hands together and do some deep breathing, visualizing the earthplane leaving them and the purpose or sacredness of the ritual filling them instead. The high priestess can do the purifications, the women do them for each other, or each can do it individually.

Casting the Circle is next, done by the high priestess with her athame or ritual wand, a long-stemmed flower or a leafy branch, or at tryst rituals with the trysting broom. In rituals where the priestessing job is shared, one woman might do the purification and a different woman cast the circle. To cast the circle means to create sacred space, to set the room off from earthplane reality and enter between-the-worlds. Once the circle is cast the ritual is closed. No one enters the room from this point, and no one leaves. If it is absolutely necessary to leave the circle, a visualized "door" is made in the circumference, traced with the casting wand or tool, and traced closed again when the woman exits. People moving in and out of the circle is the quickest way to destroy the mood and effectiveness of the ritual. Have all the tools in the room before the circle is cast, and ask the women to remain within the circle. Animals and small children are the only Be-ings who can enter and leave the circle at will without disturbing the energy. As natural and innocent forms of life, they are the circle of life in themselves.

The circle is cast by visualization and by a physical gesture made with the wand or casting tool. In most women's circles, the high priestess actually traces the circumference of the circle with her wand, moving around the room outside the circle of women. In traditional wicce the sword or athame are used. Another way to do it is symbolically, by standing in one place and sweeping the wand at arm's length around the circle without actually tracing it. Move in the clockwise direction, from left to right, as the direction of invoking. (In the southern hemisphere it is the opposite.) Here is the place where a highly decorated and imaginative ritual wand adds much to the visualization and the effect of creating a sacred boundary. Do the casting dramatically.

Remember that the circle is three dimensional, it is not simply a line on the floor but a spiral surrounding all of the room, above and below, the altar and the women of the ritual. To cast a circle is to create a place of protection, a totally safe space in which the women can be who they really are, and feel fully validated and loved. Once the circle is cast, all differences, fears and lack of trust are banished, if they haven't been already in the purification. All day-to-day cares are left outside, exchanged for the sacredness of the circle. The circle is the safe and confidential space created to welcome the women and the Goddess, and the Goddess is invited/invoked into the circle next. To be within the cast circle is to be in the presence of the Goddess, to be between the worlds of earth and universe.

The elements and spirit are present on the altar and are now invited into the ritual. **Invoking the elements** means to invite (not demand) the presence in the ritual of earth, air, fire, water and spirit, as represented by Goddess aspects and Goddess names. It is also an opportunity to invite into the ritual any qualities or other Be-ings that would add to the focus of the evening. Invite with each Goddess/element a quality, such as beauty for earth, inspiration or poetry for air, women's power or passion for fire ("Be careful what you ask for!"), healing and love for water, and immortality for spirit.

In choosing Goddess names and personas for the directions/

elements, it is good to choose a list of Goddesses that include a variety of cultures. Use the Yoruba pantheon for African Goddesses, and choose Goddesses from every continent and race, not forgetting Native American and Asian traditions. When reading about the craft, keep a list of such Goddess names and have them handy when planning rituals. The work of learning what Goddesses to use is pleasant, and doing it adds great richness to any ritual. The women's movement and Goddess movement are committed to ending racism, and awareness of women's heritage and Goddess names worldwide is a step in that direction. The validation is important in the women's craft for everyone.

Some books listing Goddesses from many cultures are: Lawrence Durden-Robertson, *Juno Covella* and *The Goddesses of Chaldea, Syria and Egypt* (Erie: Cesara Publications, 1982 and 1975) / Migene Gonzalez-Wippler, *Santeria: African Magic in Latin America* (Bronx, NY: Original Publications, 1981) / Patricia Monaghan, *The Book of Goddesses and Heroines* (New York: E.P. Dutton, 1981, reprinted by Llewellyn Publications, 1989) / Diane Stein, *The Goddess Book of Days* (St. Paul: Llewellyn Publications, 1988) / Merlin Stone, *Ancient Mirrors of Womanhood* (Boston: Beacon Press, 1979) / Luisah Teish, *Jambalaya, The Natural Woman's Book* (San Francisco: Harper and Row, 1985).

Some examples of how to do this are to use for water a choice of such Goddesses as Yemaya (Africa), Mari (Middle East), Tiamat (Semitic), Kwan Yin (China), Isis (Egypt), Sarasvati (India), Kwannon (Japan), or Atargatis (Semitic). For fire, try Oya (Africa), Pele (Polynesia), Hestia (Greece), Amaterasu (Japan), Vesta (Rome), Igaehindvo (Native American), Sun Woman (Native American). Goddesses for air might include Sappho, a foremother who is rapidly becoming a women's deity, Lilith (Hebrew), Artemis (Greece), Diana (Rome), Arianrhod (Wales), Aido Hwedo (Haiti), Cheng-O (China), Athena (Greece), Cybele (Middle East), Aradia (Italy) or Shekinah (Hebrew).

Earth Goddesses include Demeter (Greece), Ceres (Rome), Copper Woman (Native America), Old Woman (Slovak), Hecate (Greece and Egypt), Ishtar (Middle East), Rhiannon (Wales), Habondia (Italy) or Oshun (Africa). For spirit use the many names of the Great Mother: Spider Woman (Native American), Gaia (Greece), Copper Woman (Native American), Hera (Greece), Sedna (Inuit), White Buffalo Calf Woman (Native American), Mawu (Africa), Obatalla (Africa), Ceridwyn (Wales), Isis (Egypt) or Hecate (Greece). Spirit represents immortality. For each of the five elements choose Goddess attributes to enhance the meaning of the ritual. Many cultures have a Mother Goddess, Love Goddess, Goddess of the Underworld, Moon Goddess, etc.

The procedure for invoking the elements is as follows. Once the circle is cast, the high priestess points her wand or athame first to salute the sky and the earth, and then invokes each direction with spirit last. She says:

> Flora, Goddess of the Earth, be with us tonight and lend your beauty to this ritual. I invite you to be with us.
>
> Sappho, Goddess of air, be here tonight and lend us your inspiration and your poetry. I invite you to this circle.
>
> Great Mother Amaterasu, Goddess of fire, be with us tonight and lend us your passion, your fire of women's power. I invite you to be with us.
>
> Yemaya, Mother of waters, be with us in this ritual. Lend us your peace, healing and gentle emotions. Lend us your love in this circle.
>
> Spider Women, Great Mother of all, be with us in this ritual. Lend us your knowledge of immortality, of the unending Wheel. Be here now.
>
> The circle is cast, we are between the worlds. The Goddess welcomes her women. Blessed Be.

Different women can invoke the different elements, and can also light a candle at each direction or on the corners of the altar as each Goddess is invoked. The invocations for each element can be poems, musical pieces or songs, and be acted or danced. They each name a Goddess, connecting her with her element and the element's attributes and correspondences.[1] The invocations can be very simple or highly elaborate; they can be highly dramatic or very quiet. The simple statements given here are only a beginning of the possibilities. This is a place for creativity and much beauty. The statement at the end, "The circle is cast, we are between the worlds. The Goddess welcomes her women. Blessed Be," is the formal and traditional opening of the ritual, usually said by the high priestess of the evening.

Also use invoking the elements as an opportunity to invite into the circle others that the women want to be there. Go around the circle after saying "Blessed Be" and have each woman invite a fore-mother, herstorical figure, or living relative or friend not present. On Hallows, the night of blessing the dead and the living, invite to the circle the spirits of ancestors or friends who have passed over. Invite to the circle qualities positive for the ritual — peace, love, friendship, laughter, etc. Each woman can choose an attribute to invoke, but invoke the elements and spirit first and separately. Another way of doing this is to invite the participants themselves into the circle by singing each woman's name. The group sings it back to her three times, then goes on to sing the next woman.

On Full Moons only, the high priestess draws down the moon, and on Full Moons and the eight Sabbats she reads "The Charge of the Goddess." On other occasions she might read or speak an invocation or poem, or use music to set the mood and focus of the ritual, but the "Charge" and Drawing Down the Moon are reserved for their specific rituals only. In **Drawing Down the Moon**, the high priestess draws the power of the Full Moon/Goddess from the universe down to the earthplane, specifically drawing it into herself to become the Full Moon/Goddess. In Women's Spirituality wicce, as different from traditional craft, she then transfers that power into the other women of the ritual. The gesture is symbolic, dramatic and a visualization.

With her magick wand or athame in hand, the high priestess faces the moon outdoors, or the candle flames on the altar as the Moon Goddess' representative light inside. She stands with feet wide apart and hands at her sides, then raises her arms slowly out to shoulder height and upward to form a chalice shape with her body, palms facing inward. The gesture is one of salute and of ritually opening to receive the Goddess' energy and power. She uses the wand to point to the moon or candle flame, tracing an invoking (drawn clockwise) pentacle over the image of the moon or the candle. Then she brings the tool down to touch her heart with its point, and says:

I invoke the power of the Moon Goddess within me, Selene, Yemaya, Hathor, Kwan Yin.

I invoke the Moon Goddess' power, the power of women, Enter and live in all the women of this circle.

Blessed be.

Then she reads, recites, or sings "The Charge of the Goddess."

The Charge of the Goddess

Here are the words of the Great Goddess, the Great Mother of the Universe — Gaia, Yemaya, Spider woman, Ishtar, Mary, Isis, Kwan Yin — known by a thousand names across geography and time:

> Whenever you need anything, once a month and best when the moon is full, and eight times more in the year, you shall meet in some safe place to celebrate my spirit, who am queen of all women. You shall meet in freedom, and as a sign of trust you shall be naked in your rites. Sing, feast, dance, make music and love, all in my presence, for mine is the ecstasy of the spirit and joy on earth. My only law is love unto all. Mine is the secret that opens on the door of birth, and mine is the mystery of life that is the Cauldron of Hecate, the womb of immortality. I give knowledge of the all-creative spirit, and beyond death I give peace and reunion with those gone before. Nor do I ask any sacrifice, for I am the mother of all things and my love is the breast milk that nourishes the earth.
>
> I who am the beauty of the green earth and the white moon among the stars and the mysteries of the waters, I call upon your soul to arise and come unto me. For I am the soul of nature that gives life to the universe. From me all things proceed and unto me they must return. Let my worship be in the heart that rejoices, for behold — all acts of love and pleasure are my rituals. Let there be beauty and strength, power and compassion, honor and humility, mirth and reverence within you. And you who seek to know me, know that your seeking and yearning will avail you not unless you know the mystery: for if that which you seek, you find not within yourself, you will never find it without. For behold, I have been with you from the beginning, and I am that which is attained at the end of desire. (Traditional. Adapted from Starhawk, *The Spiral Dance*, San Francisco, Harper and Row, 1979), pp. 76-77.)

"The Charge of the Goddess" is the only written passage or "prayer" that is a universal standard in the Goddess religion. It was probably written by Doreen Valiente, possibly taken from traditional sources that came before her, for Gerald Gardner's early covens in the 1950s. Her writing includes archaic language and verse that is awkward for women today, and it has been revised many times. The version most used in Women's Spirituality is that of Starhawk, from her 1979 book *The Spiral Dance.* The "Charge" given in this book is close to hers, but has been slightly changed by me, particularly in the first half. Set to music, the "Charge" is even more powerful. Listen to Shekinah Mountainwater's audio tape, *Songs and Chants of the Goddess, Vol. I.*[2] The "Charge" is a piece of poetry almost breathtaking in its beauty. It is worthy of the Goddess and of the women who read or recite it at every Sabbat and Full Moon ritual.

The "Charge" is also the most concise and precise explanation of what the craft is about, what it believes in, how it operates. It sets out the standards of women's freedom, joy, reverence for others and oneself, reverence for sexuality and pleasure, and reverence for the earth. It talks of love, abundance and giving, and of life, death and rebirth. The next-to-the-last lines are the most profound:

> If that which you seek, you find not within yourself, you will never find it without.

The women's craft, Women's Spirituality movement, takes these lines very seriously, focusing the movement on the empowerment (which is self-empowerment) of women. "The Charge of the Goddess" is a major part of Goddess spirituality, and when used in rituals is an important tool for empowering women. The power, wonder and beauty of this piece of literature has to be experienced.

For rituals where the "Charge" is not read, use other invoking poems, passages, etc. Whether the "Charge" is read or not in a ritual, there is also a *ritual invocation*, often very short, that describes the reason for the ritual and its focus. The high priestess makes this invocation, which can be a few sentences simply telling the women what the focus is, or a poem, song, or written piece. For a Yule ritual, it might sound something like this:

> Tonight we are here to celebrate Yule, the rebirth of the Goddess. All is still on this longest night of the year, and all is cold. But the promise of spring is intrinsic in the deepest winter, and we come together tonight to turn the Wheel.

The invocation can lead into a *ritual meditation*, if there is to be one. At the end of the invocation, the high priestess says:

> So follow me in this meditation, to the land of the Crone

and the newborn.

She takes the women on a guided journey to the Crone, whose time of power is now ending, replaced by beginnings and rebirth. The meditation might be a journey of pregnancy and giving birth to oneself, or of birth, growth through life, aging, death and being reborn. The theme for Yule is renewal that manifests as the Wheel turns and the seasons change into spring. Another theme for Yule is resting in the positive darkness, waiting for new growth. The ritual meditation can take these themes and lead the women on a journey to them, to make them felt, and to show women by experience what they mean.

Not every ritual involves a meditation, but most of the Sabbats do. In my experience, they are a powerful and positive way to take women within to the place where they reclaim their consequence. There are as many ways to do meditation, as many journeys to take, as there are women. The first step in leading meditation is to direct the women to be fully relaxed, sitting or lying down. The ritual process to this point will have made that relaxation already, predisposing the group to highly effective journeys into themselves.

In leading a meditation, know before the ritual where it is to go, but keep the script loose and open. Very often in meditations in ritual the plans change as they develop, and it is good to go with the flow. The woman who leads the meditation probably cannot participate in it herself, though with some ritual expertise this also becomes possible. Meditations can be prerecorded so the leader/ high priestess can participate, but this is less powerful than a meditation done live. There is also a growing number of professionally taped meditations that can be used in rituals. Again, the meditation is best tailored to the ritual's focus when it is written and delivered by a woman in the circle.

Women leading meditations learn to keep their voices steady and low, and speak slowly and calmly. First have the women relax, possibly taking them through a full body relaxation sequence. (Relax your toes, relax your feet. Now relax your lower legs, etc.) Once into the ritual, this is less necessary. In the meditation's guided journey, take the women logically from where they are sitting to an idealized world, by way of a pathway through the woods, a descent into a labyrinth or some other form of leaving the "now." When telling the women to do something or see something in the meditation, they give them time to experience it. Timing is important here — too little space hurries things and too much becomes boring. The action is kept moving as steadily as it needs to move, but no faster than that.

When the women have experienced what the meditation is designed for, the high priestess leads them back to the circle. She does this in logical steps, as she did in leading them into the meditation world. They find the path and walk back from the woods, ascend the stairs from the labyrinth to the meadow, follow the seashore home. The last phase might be opening a doorway that leads back into the room of the ritual. The last direction is to "Open your eyes when you are ready and come back to now." Give the women a few minutes to return to the circle. Watch their faces and begin the next part of the ritual only when everyone is ready. Don't wait too long after that or risk losing the ritual's momentum.

Good sources for meditations to use in rituals are: Margo Adair, *Working Inside Out: Tools for Change* (Berkeley: Wingbow Press, 1984) / Diane Mariechild, *Mother Wit: A Feminist Guide to Psychic Development* (Trumansburg, NY: The Crossing Press, 1981) /Starhawk, *The Spiral Dance: A Rebirth of the Religion of the Great Goddess* (San Francisco: Harper and Row Publishers, 1979).

The next part of the ritual is the purpose, or **body of the ritual.** By this time the women are very much in a between-the-worlds place, separated from the earthplane and secure in the psychic/astral realms of the cast circle. This is the time to put into effect the reason for the ritual, what has involved so much planning in the planning sessions. The body of the ritual has three requirements: that it involve all the women of the circle; that it contain elements of healing, change or transformation; and that it be a validation of each participant as Goddess. This is not as hard to do as it sounds.

A Summer Solstice ritual that is a favorite of mine involves a body of water, which can be a child's swimming pool indoors.[3] The women are directed to bring to the ritual a red candle and a bunch of garden flowers. In the body of this ritual, each woman comes in turn to the altar and lights her candle, then takes her flowers from the altar to the water. At the water, she washes her hands, washing away all the things she would like banished from her life. She may state these things aloud or silently. Then, as she places each flower one by one into the water, she makes a wish. She might have several wishes. She asks for what she wants to manifest in her life, positive things to replace what she has banished. She makes her wishes in present-tense, "I have" statements, says "Thank you" to the Goddess and returns to her place in the circle.

This ritual contains the three criteria. Every woman takes her turn at the water (in a very large group send several women at once or even all at once). There are elements of healing, change, and transformation in the release of negatives and the affirmations of things to invoke into each woman's life. There is a great healing in letting go of old stuff, and great empowerment in "I have" statements of positive change. By making the wishes in a way that says they are already true, the women feel the ability to make their wishes happen and to make their lives into what they want them to be. That feeling is Goddess-within and is women's consequence in the world. The women of the circle watch and accept each other's banishings and wishes, with support and caring and total respect. Though the action of this body of the ritual is very simple, it is very powerful for the women who participate in it.

All of the rituals in this book contain a body of the ritual that is designed to effect healing and women's empowerment, an internalizing of Goddess. Analyze them for what they do and how they do it, and carry on the tradition by using the process in every women's ritual. These rituals are crafted for women's healing from the patriarchy, for women's Goddess-within consequence. Their emphasis on this is my contribution to Women's Spirituality rituals, something others may do but less explicitly. There is something of a learning process, a development of intuition, in knowing how to do this in a ritual. With experience and trust in oneself it comes, and is the thing that makes women's rituals so quietly powerful. Learning to understand it and do it is worth the effort. It's the magick that makes women's rituals effective, and changes women's lives in the circle.

Remember the three criteria:

1. That it involve all the women.
2. That it contain elements of healing, change or transformation.
3. That it be a validation of each woman as Goddess.

The ***Self-blessing*** also passes the three criteria but it usually follows the body of a group ritual, rather than being the ritual's sole purpose. It is a universal process in Women's Spirituality, with origins unknown. The earliest women's use of it, to my knowledge, was by Z. Budapest in her *Holy Book of Women's Mysteries, Vol. I,* but it has been adopted as one of the standard practices of the Goddess craft. Traditional nonfeminist wicce also uses the Self-blessing, in one version or another, universally.

The Self-blessing is used always in dedication or initiation rituals, and often at the New Moon. It is a process of validating oneself as Goddess by validating and honoring one's own female body. The body is the temple of the soul and the Goddess's altar; it is the place of Be-ing of the Goddess. The amount of consequence and self-empowerment gained by doing a Self-blessing is impossible to describe; it has to be felt and experienced to be appreciated. Along with "The Charge of the Goddess," and though not specific for wording or poetry, the Self-blessing is perhaps the most important action/ritual of Women's Spirituality. Its purpose is the purpose of the women's craft, of instilling Goddess-within, self-image or consequence upon women.

Use the Self-blessing frequently and in every type of ritual. It is powerful for groups and powerful alone. It can be used by itself as the body of a ritual, usually in solitary rituals, and it is powerful used as a part of group ritual structure. In rituals done alone, it is probably the most transforming altar work available. The effects of standing skyclad in front of an altar, candles lit, and doing the Self-blessing in a ritualized, sacred way, are immeasurable in their beauty and consequence for any woman who does it. This is a ritual to make into a habit, and a piece of ritual drama to include in as many ceremonies as possible. Anywhere that women need validation — which is everywhere — is a place to do the Self-blessing.

Do the ritual alone standing before an altar, or in a group with the women sitting in the circle. Tools needed are simple: a bowl of water, or more powerfully a fragrant natural oil or even menstrual blood. For women who have premenstrual syndrome or otherwise need physical validation for their women's bodies, the use of menstrual blood in this ritual process is immensely positive and healing. The Self-blessing is the ultimate healing ritual for women forced to live in a patriarchal world; it's a major reclaiming of women's bodies and Be-ing.

The ritual involves touching several parts of the body with the oil, water or menstrual blood. Most sources that describe the Self-blessing list the sense organs to do it with. The participants touch the oil or water with the fingers, then touch their fingers to the forehead, eyes, nose, mouth, breasts, genitals and feet (or genitals, hands and feet).[4] The version that follows differs slightly and is my own, and it touches and opens the chakras rather than the senses/ openings of the body.

The chakras are seven energy centers on the astral body/ etheric double, part of women's nonphysical energy anatomy. The locations for these are as follows, and are the places to touch with the oil or water in the Self-blessing ritual. Beginning from the top, touch the crown of the head (crown center), the forehead between the physical eyes (third eye), the hollow of the throat (throat chakra), the space between the breasts (heart center), the center of the abdomen about two inches above the navel (solar plexus), the center of the abdomen about two inches below the navel (belly chakra), and the vagina (root center). The last two places are the palms of both hands and the soles of both feet, less major chakras but important ones.

In a group ritual after the body of the ritual or alone at the altar with candles lit, do the Self-blessing, powerful and positive in its simplicity. In group rituals, the high priestess passes around a bowl or bottle of oil, or a selection of natural oil fragrances. The oil can be plain vegetable oil, but it adds to the ritual to use oils with meaning. Oils can include fragrances for love (rose), protection (pine), women's power (van van or High Joan the Conquerer), Blessing oil, Healing oil, Goddess oil, oil for the Seven African Powers, etc. All of these are available at botanicas or magick shops and can be made at home.[5] Use oils made without chemicals wherever possible. The bowl could also contain water, water and wine, or menstrual blood (if the women of the circle are comfortable with that). The women take a drop of the oil(s) on their index fingers and the Self-blessing begins when all the women have the oils they choose. This can take a few minutes.

The high priestess or the woman leading the Self-blessing touches the crown of her head with the oil and says:

"Bless me Mother, for I am your child." The women repeat after her, touching their own crowns with the oil or water.

The high priestess touches her third eye with the oil on her index finger and says:

"Bless my sight to see your path and mine." (The women repeat.)

"Bless my throat that I may speak truth and speak of you." (The women repeat after her, touching their throat chakras.)

"Bless my heart that it be open to you and to all women." (The women repeat, touching their hearts.)

"Bless my solar plexus that I have energy to live my life." (Repeat, touching center abdomen above the navel.)

"Bless my belly chakra, for all acts of love and pleasure are your rituals." (They touch their center abdomens, below the navel.)

"Bless my vagina, the gateway of birth and death."

"Bless my feet that they may walk in your paths and my own." (Touching both feet.)

"Bless my hands that do your work and mine." (Repeat, touching both hands.)

Touching crown again:

"Bless me Mother, for I am your child and I am a part of you."
(The women repeat after her.)

At this point in the Self-blessing I like to pass around an object wrapped in red silk that is waiting on the altar, telling the women:

"Behold the mystery, here is a picture of the Goddess." The cloth contains a small, round mirror and never fails to evoke laughter and gasps from women who should be familiar with it by now. The idea comes from Starhawk. The women who have followed and completed the Self-blessing feel a tremendous surge of energy and well-being. This is something to go to anytime it is needed; it's a simple ritual to do alone at home. The feeling of empowerment from the Self-blessing leads naturally into the raising of the cone of power.

Raising the cone of power is the energy climax of the ritual and it is done in almost every group ritual in some way. Solitary rituals also use it, but to a much lesser extent, though there is no reason not to do it alone. By this time in the ritual a great deal has happened on the psychic/subconscious/Goddess-within levels for the women in the ritual. The body of the ritual alone, the meditation alone, and certainly the Self-blessing, have brought about profound inner feelings and possibly inner changes in the women who have taken part in the evening. The cone of power is raised to concentrate that energy and to direct it, as energy without direction either degenerates to nervous tension or dissipates without an outcome. In raising the cone of power, that psychic energy is collected, formed, concentrated and sent. Its direction is to further the purpose of the ritual, the inner transformations, within each participating woman.

The cone is basically a visualization. It is a highly charged and powerful thought-form that has taken on life and Be-ing in the ritual. It is the group mind, the group power, the women's consequence and ability to change things in the world. It contains all the energy of the ritual and all of the focus, directed in an image toward making the purpose happen in the women's daily lives. The image is directed in a visualization by the high priestess into a cone, bubble or spiral, or even as fireworks or the waterfall from a fountain. It is sent out to the universe/Goddess, or sent out and brought back to the individuals, who receive it within themselves.

First the energy has to be raised and concentrated. This is done in a variety of ways, usually by using sound. The high priestess starts a group hum, or group toning, and encourages the women to continue it. As the tension/cone raises, the pitch and speed of the sound intensifies. It is a learned skill for the high priestess to keep the sound coming and rising in intensity and to know when the tension is at its highest pitch. She must raise the energy and stop it at its height, before it passes the height and begins to fail or fade. When the energy reaches its topmost pitch, the high priestess by a signal (usually her upraised arms in a throwing motion) stops it short. Then the women, arms also raised, visualize the cone, using an image the high priestess describes, going out into the universe. It carries with it the transformations that the women wish to create, the energy for change. The cone can also be visualized as going out and coming back, and when it comes back the energy goes into the women.

Other than a group hum or group toning, there are a variety of ways to raise power with sound. Chants and songs do it, and the high priestess needs a list of three or four songs so that as one fades she can begin the group with another. The women usually know what songs are planned. The songs begin with softer, quiet ones and then change to increase in speed and intensity as the cone builds. Howling at the moon is another way to use sound to raise power, something Z. Budapest has been doing in her workshops and rituals. Once the women get it going, it's really powerful. The use of drumming, rattles and other percussion instruments is another way to raise power. Many women are developing an interest in this, and some are less self-conscious with instruments than with using voice. Drums have the quality of a heartbeat and are hypnotic. Their rhythm opens the lower chakras and is very healing, and drums have a sound of deep, resonant women's womb power.

All of these methods can be noisy, and they could be a problem for a ritual indoors. Humming, chants or songs have the least volume. Where silence or at least quiet are important, raise the cone of power by a meditation or visualization. In a meditation create just a short image, not a long journey this time. There is no need for the body relaxation sequence or the preliminary path into the meditation world. Lead the women very simply to seeing their wishes or the purpose of the ritual happening for them, each in her own way. This is very similar to using the cone of power as a group visualization.

In visualizing the cone as a group, lead the women to a group image, rather than the individual happenings and applications of meditation on the energy. The high priestess directs the women to see the energy in some physical form. A good one for this is a fireworks rocket rising off into the universe, bursting into the gold, blue and green of a Fourth of July display, and the bursts of light returning to the earth. The women draw the colors and light of the energy into their heart chakras, where it manifests the transformations of the ritual. Another way to see the cone is as a fountain of water, light or energy rising and then falling. Draw that energy within.

See the cone of power as a bubble of light surrounding the women and the circle, and ask the women to breathe that light into themselves with each in-breath. See the light as the focus of the ritual coming true within each woman who accepts it into her Be-ing. Another way is to see the cone as a spiral, swirling with its tail on the altar and its wide end reaching into the universe. The spiral contains all the women's wishes and needs, and carries them to the universe/Goddess and back to the earth. Be creative — use sounds, colors, shapes.

Some women feel threatened by loud noise, heavy rhythm, drumming, singing or physical movement and activity in rituals. Women's emotions have been forcibly separated from their bodies and anything that is physical in nature can feel threatening to those who are out of touch with themselves. Women with intimacy issues, in incest or rape recovery, are especially vulnerable to feeling threatened this way. Be sure there is a safe space in the circle for women to opt out of this part of the action if they choose to. As time goes on and the coven works together and develops trust in each other, the action becomes less threatening and the women will feel more easy about participating. Women have been taught to deny their own power, and the claiming of it comes with difficulty for some. If a woman chooses to watch rather than take part in a portion of the ritual, or chooses to go to the safe space part of the circle, the others in the group are supportive of her and validate her choice.

Once the cone of power is raised and let go to do its work, the women need to ground the energy, and **grounding** is the next step and almost-end of the ritual. After the cone of power is released and/or received into the women, the music, humming, chants, or drums stop and there is silence in the circle. The women, usually following the high priestess who does it first, bend or sit down to place palms on the ground or floor. They hold their hands to the ground for a few minutes, sometimes bending to touch their foreheads to the earth also. Another name for this is "earthing the energy."

The purpose of this is to release any excess energy that remains. There is no danger of losing energy that is positive or needed, but the excess needs to be released or it gets uncomfortable. In one ritual I forgot to lead grounding for, I found myself bursting into tears about half an hour after it was over, for no apparent reason. Other women said they had trouble sleeping that night. An excess of unreleased energy manifests as nervous tension and grounding is a way of preventing overload. A great deal of energy passes through women's bodies and Be-ings in a ritual and cone of power raising. Grounding brings the energy back into balance. Nothing needed is ever lost.

Some rituals have the women sit on the earth for awhile to ground and others ground by offering food. A basket of moon cakes or crescent cookies, or a food that represents the season helps to ground ritual energy. Grounding is part of the reason for food sharing or a potluck at the end of rituals. It brings women back from between the worlds to the earthplane again, so they don't end the ritual feeling spacey. Grounding by placing palms to the earth does the same thing and should always be done. Visualize/feel any excess energy leaving through the palms and entering the earth. Direct that energy for earth healing.

The last ritual action is **opening the circle** and thanking/ releasing the Goddesses/directions that were invoked into it when the circle was cast. This is the formal ending of the ritual. Once grounding has occurred, the women are returning to earthplane reality and the energy of the cast circle is dissolving anyway. Before the energy dissipates, do it with aplomb and beauty for a satisfying finish. First the high priestess, or the women who have called them initially, thank each Goddess that was brought into the circle at the beginning. Nonfeminist craft calls this "dismissing the directions" but dismissal is hardly the word to use with Goddesses: thank them instead. In nonfeminist wicce, Goddesses are not usually invoked at the directions but into the fully cast circle, and are thanked; when elementals or devas are invoked they are dismissed.

Thank the elements in the opposite order from which the Goddesses were invoked. The high priestess or women calling the elements say something like this, again allowing for creativity:

> Spider Woman, mother of immortality, we thank you, bless you and release you, and ask that you be with us in our daily lives. Blessed be.

> Yemaya, mother of waters, we thank you, bless you and release you, and ask that your healing and love be with us daily in our lives. Blessed be.

> Amaterasu, Goddess of women's power, we thank you, bless you and release you, and ask that your fire remain

with us everyday. Blessed be.

Sappho, Goddess of air and inspiration, we thank you, bless you and release you, and ask that your poetry be with us always. Blessed be.

Flora, Goddess of earth, we thank you, bless you, and release you, and ask that your beauty go with us from this ritual to manifest in our daily lives. Blessed be.

As each Goddess is thanked, the candle for her direction on the altar (if these have been used) is blown out. Sometimes the center candle for Goddess/spirit is left to burn out itself.

The high priestess then takes her magick wand and uncasts/opens the circle with the same image she used to cast it, except moving in the opposite (counterclockwise, right to left) direction. She speaks the traditional ending for coven rituals:

The circle is open, but unbroken, May the peace of the Goddess go with you.

Merry meet and merry part and merry meet again. So mote it be.

The women of the circle recite this with her, and there is a musical version of it that is wonderful to sing. The ritual is now ended and the women get up if they've been sitting, and make the transition from the ritual space/cast circle back to daily life.

This can be the **ending** of the ritual, and often is, but I like to end all my rituals with either a group hug or with asking all of the women to hug everyone there before leaving. The second takes longer, which is the whole idea. In a group hug the women come in close together as a group and do one big hug and holding. After the intensity of the ritual, this feels fine and is also very grounding. When all of the women are asked to hug each other, the women remain in the room and begin to socialize, making a great transition into the potluck dinner or a social time to end the evening. The women tend to hang around in the ritual space for awhile (till someone mentions food). When they finish hugging, they gradually reclaim their personal things from the altar and begin to leave. Make sure remaining candles are blown out, or are in a safe place to burn.

Another good way to end a ritual is with a potluck dinner. Each woman brings a dish and at the end of the ritual the women gather together to eat, talk and share experiences of the ceremony. It's a good way to promote group bonding, to help the women become friends as well as ritual/coven partners. To keep the energy of the ritual high and flowing, have the dinner wait till the ritual is over. The shared work of preparing food and cleaning up, and the shared joys of eating together are a wonderful end to the evening. (Don't leave the high priestess with the dishes.) This is the time to turn the finished ritual into a group celebration. In traditional wicce, the sharing of "cakes and wine" (often cookies and fruit juice) is made part of the ending of the ritual.

A give-away blanket is another good way to end rituals. Each woman brings to the ritual an object she wants to pass on to someone else. These are usually discarded jewelry, a special sea-shell, a crystal — flea-market things, not things to run out and buy. Everyone who brings something gets to take something home, and the time spent at the blanket choosing and picking is another way of group bonding. Every item on the blanket has a story behind it and the women get together in the telling. Put the give-away blanket in another room, or put it in the center of the circle. Wait till the ritual is over to do the give-away. It's another good way to ground the high energy of the ritual.

One more idea is a skills-sharing, which can also be done as the body of the ritual. Each woman brings something to teach or to "show and tell." When it's her turn she has a few minutes to talk and to share her skill. Make the sharings short, limit the time to five or ten minutes; this is an activity for smaller groups. The kinds of things to offer at skills sharings are varied. The women can bring poems to read, an herb to describe the uses of, a healing technique, a drumming stroke or a new chant. They can demonstrate something or teach something to the group as a whole. It's an opportunity for each woman to be the center of attention in the ritual or outside of it, a time for each woman to shine.

This basically is how to do rituals, from beginning to end. With the outline steps in mind, it becomes easier to plan a ritual and easier to perform and be part of it. There are common expectations among the women as to what will happen and in what order, and a wide range of space for individual creativity. When planning rituals by the outline, remember to leave some leeway, for "anything can happen." In a ritual it often does, and the energy of the circle takes its own way — you've invoked the Goddess, after all. If the ritual takes off in its own pattern, be ready to let the ritual manifest as it needs to happen. Forcing it into the pre-designed pattern, however well-planned it was, may not be positive. The high priestess is ready to return the ritual onto the structured path. This ability to flow and ad-lib is another skill that takes a bit of experience, but that happens in time.

Remember too, that there is no requirement that everything in the ritual happen to perfection or exactly as it was designed. It should be made clear in the group that any ritual critiquing is done with love, and with support for the woman who has led it and the women who have planned and participated. If the circle gets cast in the wrong direction or the same Goddess is invoked for the elements twice, it's okay. The Goddess has a sense of humor, and patience with women who are learning, and so should her women. Have love, fun and reverence in the circle and the rest takes care of itself. Enter the ritual prepared, and with good intent, and leave the rest in the hands of the Mother. All will be well.

Doing ritual is easier than it seems, and with a bit of experience and a few attempts at using the structure/outline, it becomes a natural habit. Take it easy doing it, have fun doing it, and learn as it happens. From this point in the process of learning, there is only the doing. Chapter 4 begins with full rituals to mark the phases of the moon.

Notes

1. For a list of elemental correspondences, see Starhawk, *The Spiral Dance: A Rebirth of the Religion of the Great Goddess* (San Francisco: Harper and Row, 1979), p. 201 ff. The Goddesses named in these invocations were chosen by me and Shekinah Mountainwater for her trysting ritual.

2. Shekinah Mountainwater, *Songs and Chants of the Goddess, Vol. I*, audio tape, Moonspell Tapes (P.O. Box 2991, Santa Cruz, CA 95063). Send $1 for catalog.

3. Diane Stein, *The Women's Spirituality Book* (St. Paul: Llewellyn Publications, 1987), pp. 90-92.

4. Z. Budapest, *The Holy Book of Women's Mysteries, Vol. I* (Los Angeles: Susan B. Anthony Coven No. 1, 1979), p. 5.

5. See Scott Cunningham, *Magical Herbalism* (St. Paul: Llewellyn Publications, 1982), p. 95 ff. for oil information and recipes.

Chapter Four

────────────○────────────

The Moon and Women's Lives

The Goddess and the moon are one, and the moon is the center of women's Be-ing. The 28-1/2 day lunar cycle is the cycle of women's menstruation, fertility and menopause. It was the first form of counting and calendars, the first marking of time beyond that of day and night. The words for moon are both the words for menstruation and the names of the Goddess. Every culture has its Moon Goddess and the Goddess of the moon is the Goddess of women, water, birth, menstruation, the tides, and healing. The Moon Goddess, the Great Mother, is often imaged as a sea-creature, serpent, or mermaid. The beginnings of religion were based on the cycles of the moon, which are also the cycles of women's bodies. Personified, they became the Goddess, who as the "Charge" says, is "Queen of all Women." Women are tied to the moon, are part of her, and the moon is part of all women's lives.

Patriarchy has erased women's cycles and replaced the moon with the sun. (Note, however, that many of the now-male sun gods were originally sun Goddesses.) Men have made the moon into something to shoot at, and used it as a refuse dump. The killing of the dragon in male mythology is a universal metaphor for the destruction of the Moon Goddess and the Goddess matriarchies, and for the suppression of women. Marduk dismembered Tiamat the Great Goddess; Beowulf killed Grendal and Grendal's mother; and St. Patrick drove the snakes out of Ireland. Women's bodies have gone the way of the conquered moon, and menstruation is something shameful in patriarchy, with pregnancy and menopause made illnesses by male medicine. Patriarchal religions declared women's bodies unclean, and used that to justify the enslavement of women. Women even today have been taught to deny their cycles, forcing their bodies to imitate men's or be rejected as people in the male-run world. In the days of the Moon Mother, the days before patriarchy, it was not this way.

The Moon Goddess, the serpent, is creator of the universe and earth in cultures worldwide. The serpent/snake and moon are both metaphors for change, as in the lunar and menstrual cycles. The sea is the source of all life and the moon rules her tides; women's blood tastes of salt and water. In the Near East the Moon Goddess is Tiamat, the sea dragon. In Yoruba West Africa she is Yemaya, described as a mermaid. She is Kwan Yin in China, Rainbow Serpent in Australia, and the Old Woman Who Never Dies in the Sioux culture. Some of her other names are Selene (Crete and Greece), Coatlique (Aztec), Atargatis (Syria), Chalchiuhtlique, Mistress of Rains and Rivers (South America), Jezanna (Africa), Isis (Egypt and Greece), Nina or Nana (Sumer), Izanami (Japan), Shakti (India), Gaia (Greece), and Venus (Rome).[1] These are all water or serpent Goddesses, and there are dozens more of them. In Polynesia, the Moon Goddess, creator of the world is called Hina, which means "moon"; all women are called, in her image, "wahines." In Scandinavia, the creator is Luonnotar, "Luna the Moon," or Mardoll, "Moon Shining Over the Sea."[2]

The Moon Goddess is also the three-form Goddess of Maiden, Mother and Crone — the Waxing, Full, and Waning moons. In her three aspects as the triple Goddess, she is the all-giving and all-taking Mother. She is represented by Goddesses in threes worldwide. As the Moon Goddess, she is Diana (waxing), Selene (Full) and Hecate (waning moon); as the earth, she is Persephone, Demeter and Hecate. The Goddess is both the moon and the earth in many cultures. The three-form Goddess is often fate or karma as in The Morrigan of the Celts (Ana, Badb and Macha), the Greek Three Fates (Lachesis, Clothos and Atropos), or the French Three Maries of the Sea. The Goddess is pre-menarche youth and newness at the waxing moon (Maiden); adult, sexual, powerful and fertile at the Full moon (Mother); and age, wisdom, knowledge and death in the Waning moon (Crone). The phases are menarche, fertility/birth, and menopause. Then the cycle turns and the moon is new again, reborn.

In women's menstrual cycles the phases are clearly seen, as in the ages and changes of women's lives. Before the advent of artificial light women all bled at the same time. The Full Moon was the time of ovulation, the choice of pregnancy or not, and the last days of the Waning moon cycle (when the moon is not visible in the sky) were menstruation. At the New Moon, with menstruation ended or nearly so, the new cycle began. The Greek story of Hera (whose name means "womb") and her renewing pool is a metaphor for the New Moon and new cycle, the end of menstruation. The whole moon cycle, unpolluted and without artificial light, was the heavenly image of women's womb cycle, and of women as images of the all-creating Goddess.

When women lived together in tune with the cycles of the earth and moon, they all ovulated and menstruated at the same time. This has profound consequence, for it meant that women had control of fertility. Knowing that the Full Moon meant ovulation, a woman could choose heterosexual sex to have a child at that time, or avoid it to prevent a pregnancy. Archeologists believe that in most matri-archal communities women lived together separately from men. Even now, women living together tend to menstruate together. Women would have had the knowledge of the menstrual cycle and the connection between sexuality and pregnancy sooner than men knew it. They kept it secret for obvious reasons, a woman's mystery. In cultures where women were viewed as images of the Goddess and the sources of all life, menstruation, birth, and the ending of menstruation at menopause were the most sacred of mysteries.

The early menstrual huts were places for women to go to rest at the Dark Moon phase. They were probably the "old girls' clubs" of their time, where the political and social decisions of the tribe or cul-ture were made. The word "Sabbat" in the Near East and Africa (the Bubbulum) originally meant a day of rest, the menstruation of the Goddess. Women's witches Sabbats were originally at either the Full or the New Moon, became weekly to celebrate the moon phases, and later became the Judaic sabbath.[3] The wiccan Sabbats now extend to include the four lunar and four solar holidays of the year cycle (Candlemas, Beltane, Lammas and Hallows are lunar, the Solstices and Equinoxes are solar), and the word for Full Moon rituals (thirteen in the year, the witches' number) is "Esbat."

The words for *moon, menstruation,* and *time* have common roots in most cultures. In the Latin from which English is derived, *menstruation* comes from *menses,* which means *month,* and *month* is derived from the moon cycle. The Old English word for moon, *mona,* derives from the Indo-European word *me* which means both *mind* and *measurement.*[4] When the Goddess Inanna tricked the *me's* from Enki and brought them to her people, what was she bringing them? They were said to be all the gifts of civilization, abundance and fertility. In primitive cultures, the unborn baby was believed to be formed by "moon blood," since women do not men-struate while pregnant, and both pregnancy and women's bleeding were said to be caused by the moon.

Time-keeping began with women's marking of their menstrual cycles and pregnancies, to know the times of ovulation, menstruation and birth at term. Moon calendars carved on rock appear in archeology as early as 300,000 BCE and were complex calendars by 30,000 BCE. Calendar systems carved on sticks were known from cave paintings as early as 50,000 BCE and as late as Native American portraits in 1828. Such calendar marking sticks were used by Australian, Siberian and Native American women living tribally into modern times. This first magick wand was used by pregnant women or by midwives[5] — ten lunar months marked pregnancy's full term — and birth was of great consequence in matriarchal cultures. The menstrual/birth/lunar calendar stick was the original wand of rulership, power and ritual magick. Women's menstruation, birthing and menopause were the source of all sacredness and power, reflections of the Moon Goddess who created the universe, earth, and all life. Essential functions for personal and tribal survival, these measurements of time and cycle were based on the changing moon.

The marking of time was the beginning of several other aspects of civilization, probably also originated by women. The development of the calendar meant the prediction of the seasons and led to agriculture and domestic animal breeding. It also led to the development of mathematics, astronomy and astrology, and the measurements of distance. Knowledge of the birth cycle led to the skill of midwifery, and knowledge of the menstrual cycle to the control of conception for the promotion or prevention of fertility. These skills were the beginnings of healing and medicine. Menstruation and the moon were the beginnings of civilization. The celebration of the Sabbats, the days of bleeding and rest at menstruation, were the beginnings of ritual and religion.

Women's blood as the source of life, as women's connection with the life-giving and life-taking Moon Goddess, was sacred. Menstrual blood given to the fields increased crop yield, and made the land more fertile. Menstrual blood used as a lure could draw animals to the hunters. Fertility is the source of life, be it the fertility of plants whose grain becomes bread, or of cows who must give birth before women can milk them. The breeding and domestication of animals meant promoting their fertility as well. Abundance for early tribes also meant women's fertility, for without many births in days of high mortality, the tribe could not continue or increase. Fertility beyond childbearing was also held sacred; the woman after menopause was said to withhold her menses, without a pregnancy, turning blood into power. Women's blood and fertility today is seen in context both of women's bodies and women's minds; creation is babies and so much more. But the connection between women, the moon, the Goddess and menstruation remains as important now as it did in matriarchal/prehistoric times.

Women's Spirituality is reclaiming women's blood, as a way of reclaiming women's bodies, and a way of reclaiming women's consquence and Goddess-within. Women are the image of the all-creating Goddess, the developers of civilization and the determiners of their own lives. Women's blood is a reflection of the Goddess-power of women's bodies, and a symbol of women's Goddess-within. The menstrual cycle is a paying attention to life and the life force, to blood shed naturally without wounds or wars, and to a return of women's peaceful values over the abuses of patriarchy.

The patriarchy has separated women from their bodies. The high incidence of dis-eases in women's reproductive organs and the high incidence of premenstrual syndrome among menstruating women is evidence of this. The high use of estrogen replacement therapies for menopausal women — taking away hot flashes by offering cancer — is another evidence. In the Moon Goddess matri-archies, women were part of their bodies, respecting their cycles and living in tune with them. When the matriarchies were con-quered, women's ways were suppressed and women were separated from each other. Women's bodies were made unclean (by men's rape and incest?) along with women's souls. Menstruation became some-thing to hide, women's dirty secret. Pregnancy was something shameful, and labor and delivery were taken away from women by male medicine's mechanics. The high rate of caesarean births is scandalous today, as is the high rate of hysterectomies and mastec-tomies — most of them unnecessary. In the nineteenth century, clitoridectomies were popular as a "cure" for women's sexual feel-ings. The dis-eases were invented by the men, accepted as women lost their moon power.

In modern society there are no moon lodges or menstrual huts where women can rest and have Sabbat on the Dark Moon. Women have lost the connection with their bodies' cycles that is their Goddess-within consequence, and the pain of this loss manifests in the emotional and physical dis-eases men are so eager to cut out and drug. When women bled together on the Dark Moon in moon huts that were the center of the tribe's political strength, there was no such thing as PMS. When women counted due-date on lunar calendar sticks and put their trust in the Moon Goddess and her healer-midwives, pregnancy and delivery were not a dis-ease. When the menopausal woman was seen as holding her moonblood within her for greater power, menopause was not the trauma that modern society makes it today. When women reclaim the Goddess and their own lunar cycles, they reclaim their connection to their bodies and to their power as women/Goddesses.

An important way for women to do this reclaiming is to mark the moon phases with rituals. These were the original Sabbats in the wiccan craft, and are highly important for all women. The non-feminist craft celebrates the thirteen Full Moons and the eight lunar and solar Sabbats (The Wheel of the Year). Women's Spirituality and traditional wicce put greater emphasis on the Wheel than on the moon phases, though many women celebrate the moons, or at least the Full Moon on their own, and some groups do the Esbats (Full Moons) regularly. By marking the moon phases, women grow in tune to lunar energy and learn to know their personal body energy in connection with the moon cycles. These biorhythms are also apparent in moon-sign astrology, a further refinement of the moon phases.

The phases of the moon are the ages of women's lives, and celebrating them in ritual celebrates women's and the Goddess's three ages. The Waxing Moon is the time of the new child, the girl before menarche. She is young and new, innocent and lively, and her energy is growing and hopeful. The Full Moon is the Mother, the adult woman in her power, choosing to be fertile or not for this cycle. The energy here is strong, powerful, sometimes more intense than women feel comfortable holding onto. The Full Moon Mother is the power of women, a power that's scary for women to reclaim. The Waning Moon is the time of the Crone, the woman after menopause who no longer bleeds or gives birth. She holds her power within her, and this inward power lays the roots for the next cycle's beginnings. Her wisdom holds psychic knowledge; she has experience and knows how to do things.

Modern calendars divide the moon into four phases of seven days each, called the quarters. The first quarter is the New Moon, the second the Waxing Moon, the third the Full Moon or fulfillment phase, and the last is the Dark or Waning Moon. For purposes of ritual and closeness to the intent of the craft, I divide the lunar month into three phases. The first section is the Waxing Moon, from Day 1 of the cycle till Day 11 (three days before the Full Moon). The Full Moon is the next phase, the fourteenth day of the cycle, plus three days before and three after the Full Moon date. The last phase is the Waning Moon, from three days after the Full Moon (Day 18) until the cycle begins again. The lunar month is 28-1/2 days, and there are thirteen lunar cycles in a year. Most non-Western cultures are still on the lunar calendar. The three phases are the Waxing Moon, Full Moon and Waning Moon phases, the Maiden, Mother and Crone, and there are rituals in this chapter to honor each of them.

Women who do moon phase rituals learn to live by the moon. They find an attunement between their bodies and the moon calendar that is something new in their lives. Women who learn to flow with this cycle find that their menstrual pain and premenstrual syndromes disappear. Their cycles regulate and they learn to enjoy their bleeding times. They find menarche (first menstruation) in themselves and their daughters something to celebrate. If they choose pregnancy, their children are wanted and the pregnancy, labor and delivery are met with joy. Women who connect their bodies with the Goddess and the moon cycle take menopause as a natural part of living and have less difficulties and discomforts with it, or with growing older. When women are respected in all their ages, and come to respect themselves, being a woman is a gift, not a patriarchal curse.

Women who celebrate the cycles of the moon and the cycles of women's lives discover the beauty and sacredness of being female. This sacredness should be self-evident, but is a truth that the patriarchy has erased for generations of women. By reclaiming the moon, menarche, menstruation, birth, menopause and the Moon Goddess/divinity-as-a-female-with-a-womb, women return to their lives something that has been missing for more than 5,000 years. They return to the time when women had consequence, when women were the developers of civilization and made all the big decisions. They return that consequence to their own self-worth and self-image, their own sense of body image, and they reconnect the sacredness of their bodies to the sacredness/Goddess of their minds. The result of this is women who have consequence again, who make real changes for the better in the world.

The Waxing Moon

This first third of the lunar month is from Day 1 of the cycle (the New Moon) until Day 11 (the first day of the Full Moon phase, three nights before the Full Moon). The Waxing Moon is the time of the Maiden, the girl before menarche. The Maiden Goddess is young, inquisitive, strong in her innocence, and not knowing that life has limitations. In the Motherpeace tarot deck, she is The Fool, the child of all potential and all power, or the Daughter of Swords, the amazon maiden. She is the tomboy climbing trees, delighting in her tough young body. She refuses the word "no."

Anything is possible to the child, and anything is possible (to begin) in the Waxing Moon phase. Some Goddesses representative of this third of the cycle are: Artemis (Greece), Diana (Rome), Pele (Polynesia), Anahita (Persia), Oya (Africa), Hathor (Egypt), Lucina (Italy), Blodeuwedd (Wales), White Buffalo Calf Woman (Native America), Cheng-O (China), and Bast (Egypt). Also for the Waxing Moon phase are foremothers known as warrior-women and freedom fighters. Some of these, of many possibilities, are Harriet Tubman, whose running of the Underground Railroad freed more than 300 slaves before the Civil War; Boudica, a Celtic woman who led her troops across Europe and nearly defeated the Roman Empire after her daughters had been raped by Roman soldiers; or Joan of Arc, the young wiccan woman who fought to free France and was betrayed. This is a phase for daughter Goddesses, daughters and amazons, with an occasional mother in evidence — to protect them.

Use white candles on the altar for the Maiden Moon, she knows more of milk than of blood yet. If there are flowers on the altar, try white ones or pastels, innocent blooms like white daisies of paperwhites. Remember also, that the cycle has just changed, and the innocent daughters bring with them the hint of the Crone. Some of the daughter Goddesses are also underworld Goddesses, like Persephone, Pele and Oya. They have just been reincarnated, just come from the Crone. Don't underestimate their power.

Women's bodies at the New Moon are in the last stages of menstruation or have finished bleeding. This is in the ideal, of course, before the advent of electric light and high-stress living skewed women's cycles so that they no longer bleed together. Some women now ovulate on the New Moon; others have rotating cycles with more or less days than the full lunar month, so that their bleeding moves through all the phases. Each woman's personal New Moon can be a different date. But in celebrating the New and Waxing Moon, women celebrate the cycles of the Goddess, who is all women. Some women who begin to do moon rituals discover their cycles changing to fit the moon's. Anne Kent Rush in her book *Moon Moon* (New York, Random House, 1976) describes ways to self-regulate women's moon cycles by use of controlled light. Whatever the individual woman's body cycles, the metaphor for the New and Waxing Moon is the ending of menstruation and the new cycle.

At menstruation's end, the woman/Goddess is renewed. She has completed the last full cycle, and if she has bled she is not pregnant. If she is past the age for bleeding, her body still knows the cycles and she may feel closer to the moon phase dates. If she is under the age of menarche, she is just learning about her body, and the changes in it to come. On the date of the New Moon, Persephone returns from the underworld. Hera and Diana bathe in their sacred pool, becoming virgin again. The word *virgin* in the ancient world had nothing to do with sex or lack of it; it meant a woman who was free, who owned her body in herself.

Physically, women's bodies at the Waxing Moon are preparing to ovulate again. Menstruation has released unfertilized the last cycle's ripe egg, and now another one is readying for release. This in the menstrual cycle is called the follicular stage.[6] A new egg is readied by one ovary, stimulated by a complex variety of hormones. All of a woman's eggs are present in her ovaries at birth. The egg will leave the ovary and follicle at ovulation, traveling down the fallopian tube to the uterus. The uterus is preparing a new lining to receive it, if it is fertilized and implants. The implanting is a pregnancy. At this stage, the follicle and egg are not ready for fertilizing yet, but the follicle is forming and leaving the ovary. The uterus, cleared of its old lining by menstruation, begins to rebuild.

Women's moods and minds are as connected to the moon as their bodies are, bodies and Be-ings are one. The Waxing Moon is a time for creativity and new beginnings, for starting new things. It's a time for activity, outward-directed and increasingly so as the moon waxes. The energy of the New Moon is strong and often erratic, but it becomes a steady pull of increasing strength as the days move toward the Full. Women use the energy for doing things, for manifesting ideas into new realities. This is the time to take risks, go for change, to make things, write things, start things. The flow is with women who create and take action, and optimism is high. Start new books, new jobs, relationships, or living in a new home at the Waxing Moon phase. Emotions are stable after the first day or two, and positive.

Waxing Moon rituals take advantage of the energy flow for hope, new growth, and reaching out. Rituals enter the labyrinth or spiral, the darkness of the not-yet-visible moon at the New, and emerge into the increasing light of the Waxing phase. Things planted (seeds, actions or ideas) at the New Moon emerge in Waxing to move toward harvests at the Full. Wishes made at this time of the cycle come true at the Full Moon. This is the time of newness and emerging. The Waxing Moon is the Maiden, just starting on her journey to maturity, her whole life's potentials yet unknown and to come.

The Waxing Moon — A Ritual of Beginnings

Spend time at the Waxing Moon making a group altar, or alone making or re-making a permanent altar at home. In group rituals, place a give-away blanket in the center of the circle or in another room. Each woman brings a natural object or something she no longer wants to put on it. In solitary rituals, make a gift to oneself instead or dedicate a piece of moon jewelry, and place it on the altar. Do this ritual on the New Moon or anytime in the Waxing phase. Be sure to include the Self-blessing.

Need

White candles and white flowers on the altar.

Incense. Vervain for healing and protection, frankincense for spirituality, rosemary for purification, or rose for love. Or use a bowl of water for sprinkling instead.

Give-away blanket. Each woman brings an item to give away.

Moon Poem or Invocation. Use the one below or choose another.

A bowl of earth or cauldron and a bowl of seeds or dried beans.

Oils for the Self-blessing and a mirror wrapped in cloth.

Optional: Play the song "Every Woman Born" from Ruth Barrett and Felicity Flowers" audio tape, *Invocation to Free Women* (Circle of Aradia Publications, 4111 Lincoln Blvd. #211, Marina del Rey, CA 90292). Or another piece of music, poetry.

Matches to light candles and incense, charcoal block for loose incense, circle-casting wand.

Outline

Light candles.

Purify — With incense smoke or by sprinkling.

Cast circle/Invoke the Goddess for each element and spirit. These are amazon foremothers, with two Mother Goddesses (Demeter and Hina) to watch over them.

> Earth — Demeter, whose daughter returns at the New Moon (Greece).
>
> Air — Boudica, amazon who fought for women's freedom (Celtic).
>
> Fire — Harriet Tubman, who risked her life to free others (American).
>
> Water — Joan of Arc, a witch who fought to free France.
>
> Spirit — Hina, Mother of the Moon (Hawaii).

Each woman in the circle invites/invokes another hera. Keep

going round till the women run out of names — of women living or not, mythological or herstorical, including relatives or friends living or dead.

Invocation — Read the following Moon Poem Invocation or choose another written piece.

Waxing Moon Invocation
Goddess of our mothers, our foremothers and our selves,
The Moon is new and we are new within her.
Together with the moon we make beginnings,
Set goals and lay the roots for our achievements
To fulfill when the time and moon grow full.

We are women of peace
Attaining our goals in peaceful ways.
What we ask for benefits us and benefits the earth and
    all.
We accept the challenge of manifesting our dreams.
We accept the responsibility for our choices.

We are careful what we ask for,
Knowing it may happen;
We are careful what we ask for,
That we violate no one's free will.

We have the awareness of women
And the power of women;
We are each the Goddess and the changing moon.

With the New Moon we begin and plant our dreams,
And watch them grow and ripen.
As we will it, so it is.

We are the New Moon.
We are Goddess.
We are the changing world.

Body of ritual — Take the bowl of seeds and the cauldron or bowl of earth from the altar. Pass them around the circle clockwise, or place them in the center of the circle. Each woman in her turn says:

"These are my beginnings. I plant these seeds for growth on

the Waxing Moon. I want _____." (She plants a seed in the bowl or cauldron.) "I have (*she repeats her want*)." She makes one wish each time the bowls go round the circle; they continue to go around for as long as women have wishes. Keep the wishes short.

The high priestess says:

"Hecate becomes Persephone on the Waxing Moon, and Demeter regains her daughter. Women come from the past, to now, to the future, making all things new. All dreams come true."

Self-blessing — (See page 58.) This is a good time to use a variety of magickal fragrant oils to fit women's wishes and needs, and a good time to use the cloth-wrapped mirror.

Raise energy — Use songs or chants, or visualize the dreams planted in the cauldron coming to fulfillment. Direct the cone of power to the wishes manifesting (or their equivalents or better, according to free will — says Marion Weinstein), and to the earth for healing. This is a quiet, gentle ritual, not for drums or howling at the moon.

Ground.

Optional — Play the song, "Every Woman Born" from Ruth Barrett and Felicity Flowers' audio tape, *Invocation to Free Women*, or play the whole tape, or any other parts of it.[7]

Open circle.

Hugs.

Give-away.

Suggested chants to use in this ritual include:

>We all come from the Goddess,
>And to her we shall return,
>Like a drop of rain,
>Flowing to the ocean.

or

>Holy Maiden huntress,
>Artemis, Artemis
>New Moon come to us.

>Shining silver wheel of
>Radiance, radiance,
>Mother come to us.

>Ancient queen of wisdom,
>Hecate, Hecate.
>Old one come to us.

> Holy Maiden huntress,
> Artemis, Artemis,
> New Moon come to us.

or

> A river of birds in migration,
> A nation of women with wings.[8]

The Full Moon

The lunar cycle is 28-1/2 days, and the Full Moon is the center and high energy point of that cycle. The Full Moon phase includes the date of the Full Moon (the fourteenth night) plus three nights before and three nights after it for a total of seven days. These are Days 11 to 17 in the lunar calendar (beginning with the New Moon as Day 1) The Full Moon is the time of the Mother and Mother Goddesses, the woman/divinity at the height of her creative power. The Mother Goddess is strong, capable and all-giving. She gives birth from her body, nourishment from her breasts, and has the strength and wisdom to protect and raise her offspring. The Mother's offspring are not only babies, though that is the metaphor of the Full Moon. The Mother's creations include everything from mountains to panthers, books to symphonies, woven rugs to computer programs.

In the Motherpeace tarot deck, the Full Moon Mother is the Empress or Strength card. She is pregnant with ideas, highly sensuous and luxurious, surrounded by young animals who turn to her for protection and nurturing. The Full Moon Mother is capable maturity personified. She is all-powerful, as the human mother seems to the infant, and what she says goes. The Mother of the Full Moon is also the Earth Mother, who needs protection as much as she protects. The Goddess of the moon is immanent on the earth.

Some Goddesses representative of this cycle are: Selene (Crete), Ishtar (Babylonia), Luna (Etruscan), Mary (Christian), Isis (Egypt and Greece), Yemaya (West Africa), Astarte (Semitic), Venus (Rome), Aphrodite (Phoenician), Lilith (Hebrew), Hathor (Egypt), Amaterasu (Japan), Parvati (India), Kwan Yin (China), Hina (Polynesia), Mawu (Dahomey), Demeter (Greece), Hera (Greece), Freya (Scandinavia), Copper Woman (Native America), Luonnotar (Finland), Arianrhod (Wales), Tiamat (Semitic), and Aido Hwedo (Haiti). She is also The Great Mother, The Great Goddess — or just Mother.

Use red candles for the Full Moon phase (or white ones, which are fine for any ritual). Red is for the Mother aspect of the Goddess, red for birth and menstrual blood, for women's wombs. White candles or silver ones are an alternative to red, for the light and illumination of this moon phase. Flowers on the altar are heady and full ones: try red or white chrysanthemums or red proteas, red or white peonies, red roses or red or white hibiscus. Use one color or the other, red or white. Go for the unusual and exotic; braid flower crowns or leis. Lush abundance is a symbol of the Mother on the Full Moon. The Goddess is pouring out her energy, sexuality, creativity and charm. "All acts of love and pleasure are my rituals."

Women's bodies at the Full Moon are in the ovulation stage (in menstruating women whose cycles began at the New Moon). This is fertility and sexuality at its height; the choice of conception or not for this cycle; the choice of joyous sexuality, heterosexual or lesbian. The follicle of the Waxing Moon has burst to release the ready egg. It reaches the uterus, also ready with its lining developed enough again to sustain a pregnancy, through one of the fallopian tubes. If the egg is fertilized on the way, a pregnancy occurs. If the egg is not fertilized, it is reabsorbed and menstruation happens in the next stage of the moon cycle, fourteen days after ovulation. The Full Moon is the time of births and deaths; more of these happen at the Full Moon than at any other time of the lunar cycle. This phase for women, menstrual or not, is a time of choices, births, deaths and fulfillments — the all-giving and all-taking Goddess.

Women's emotional and psychic lives are heightened at the Full Moon, and dreams reflect the cycle. Full Moon dreams are of babies and eggs, pearls, round shining objects, breasts and moons.[9] Full Moon dreams are more likely to be precognitive and psychic ones, and every form of psychic activity is heightened at this time. Divination by scrying, tarot cards, runes, Table of Ifé, or I Ching is powerful. Emotionally, the energy is wired and intense, and many women are made uneasy by it. Women who flow with the moon phases learn to channel this nervous energy into projects or physical activities for a feeling of total aliveness. Sexual arousal is strongest at this time, also with energy that needs to be released in love-making or in other ways. The power of this energy for creating, manifesting, accomplishing and for turning ideas into realities is immense.

Full Moons may have been the first of the witches Sabbats, as women in early times were aware of the moon's power and its connection to ovulation and conception. Full Moons and dark moon menstruation were probably the earliest ritualized acts. In days of no pollution or artificial light to obscure night skies, the rising of the Full Moon was an awesome and beautiful sight. As patriarchy took over, the time and rituals were ridiculed and avoided for their "lunacy." Men, who had no connection to the lunar cycle, feared its female power, and the power of women's fertility and choices became something to suppress. Women today reclaim that power, take that "lunacy" and make creative things of it, returning its energy for women's consequence. Women who draw down the moon in the Full Moon ritual learn how powerful the moon is, how powerful the Moon Mother and how powerful is their own Moon Goddess-within.

Full Moon rituals are rituals of women's affirmation, manifesting, fulfillments and power-within. They take the high energy of the Full Moon Goddess and transform it into things they want to make happen in their lives. In these rituals, women become the Goddess by drawing her power into themselves, and they use the Goddess's creative/conceptive/birth power for taking action and fulfilling wishes, moving the New Moon's beginnings into full growth and active presence. Women ask for money and abundance at the Full Moon, for wishes to come true and love to consummate, and they develop consequence and Goddess-within power in their Be-ing. Fertility/creativity and abundance is the theme of the Full Moon, with the warning "Be careful what you ask for." On the Full Moon you might get it.

Full Moon Wishing Ritual

This ritual for the Full Moon is intended to tap the Goddess's power at its height and make wishes and dreams come true. Women can have anything that they want in their lives and Full Moon rituals are the perfect time for proving it. They take ideas from the psychic plane and bring them down to earth. When women draw the Moon into themselves at the Full Moon and feel the power of the Goddess within them, they know they can do anything, no matter that the patriarchy tells them otherwise. Along with wishes come responsibilities, so think carefully before asking. What you ask for at the Full Moon will surely manifest.

Use lots of candles in this ritual, choosing either red or white/silver for the overall color theme. Place lots of crystals on the altar, to clear them in the Full Moon energy of the ritual and so their own energy will magnify the ritual's results. Put a shiny silver dollar on the altar for prosperity; use a "Susan B." Full Moon rituals are at their most powerful outdoors, where the rising Full Moon Mother can observe, approve and become a part of the proceedings.

Need

Candles — Choose white/silver ones or red for the overall color theme of this ritual, and flowers in the same color.

Crystals on the altar.

A silver dollar for prosperity.

Incense — Use amber for clarity, rose for love, vervain for abundance, or myrtlewood for love, abundance and fertility.[10] Mugwort is a psychic opener.

Tarot deck, rune set, I Ching, Table of Ifé seashells, or scrying bowl/crystal ball.

Mooncakes — Round or crescent cakes or cookies for the Full Moon.

Fragrant oils and mirror for Self-blessing.

Matches, charcoal block for loose incense, ritual wand, altar.

Outline

Light candles.

Purify — With incense smoke or sprinkling.

Cast Circle/Invoke Goddesses of the Moon for the elements and spirit, emphasizing women's rights and freedom.

> Earth — Copper Woman (Native American), for women's free will.
>
> Air — Lilith (Hebrew), for reproductive freedom.
>
> Fire — Erzulie (Haitian), for women's power and passion.
>
> Water — Kwan Yin (China), for self-healing and self-love.
>
> Spirit — Selene (Crete) or Hathor (Egypt), for women's rights everywhere.

Drawing Down the Moon — The high priestess draws down the Moon to herself and the group. (See page 53.)

Charge of the Goddess — High Priestess reads the "Charge" or another woman reads it. Or play Shekinah Mountainwater's sung version on *Songs and Chants of the Goddess, Vol. I.*[11]

Each woman in the circle sings her own name and the group sings it back to her three times.

Body of Ritual — Fulfillments/Wishes/Thanks. Go around the circle. Each woman gives a *fulfillment* that's happened since the last Full Moon, a *wish* to manifest by the next Full Moon, and a *thanks* for something already begun or given. (Or use a *thanks*, a *goal* and an *affirmation* — I want/I have.) Continue going round the circle till the women run out of wishes, then go round once more and ask for one more thanks. Move rapidly, keep it in short phrases.

Pass around a tarot deck, I Ching book, rune set, or Table of Ifé seashells. Each woman picks a card or rune without looking first for a Full Moon message or direction. (Or use a scrying bowl or crystal ball. Or do full divination readings for each other in a small group or if working alone.) Go around the circle, each woman explains her reading, if she chooses to reveal it.

Raise energy. Use humming or howl at the moon, use drums, rattles, faster-moving chants. Full Moons are too high-powered to be quiet. Direct the cone of power to fulfillment of the women's wishes and remember to send some of the energy for earth healing and for women here and in other cultures who have less freedom.

Ground.

Self-blessing/mirrors. Energy may be too high after howling and drums to do the Self-blessing, and this can become a long ritual. Gauge the mood and needs of the group.

Share mooncakes.

Open circle.

Ground again/Group hug.

Potluck dinner.

Some songs and chants to use for the Full Moon include:

> Isis, Astarte, Diana, Hecate,
> Demeter, Kali, Inanna. (by Deena Metzger)

or

> The earth, the air, the fire, the water
> Returns, returns, returns, returns. (by Starhawk)

or

> (Chorus)
> And the Full Moon, is her vagina spread wide.
> And the Full Moon, is her vagina spread wide.
> With a whole wide world of all possibility,
> Every possibility comes pouring out.

> 1. And the New Moon is her waiting womb.
> And the New Moon is her waiting womb.
> With a whole wide world of all possibility,
> Every possibility waiting to grow. (Chorus)

> 2. And the Old Moon is her empty womb.
> And the Old Moon is her empty womb.
> With a whole wide world of all possibility,
> Every possibility returning home. (Chorus)
> (by Peter Sodeburg)

The Waning Moon

The last third of the lunar month is from Day 18 till Day 28, the end of the cycle. As the Waxing Moon is the Maiden and the Full Moon the Mother, the Waning Moon completes the cycle with the Crone. The time in the cycle is that of aging and the positive darkness, ending with menstruation or menopause as aspects and validations of women's consequence. For too long has the patriarchy hidden away women's power in the dark, and then named the darkness evil. For too long has menstruation been "the curse," menopausal women "old bags," old women laughable or worse, and women of color subjected to every racist act men could think of. Women affirm the darkness, the inside of the Goddess's womb, the dark phase of the moon, as whole and powerful, and they honor and reclaim it at last.

The dark is the source of women's consequence and the light could not exist without it. It is the deepest feminine aspect, the labyrinth, the spiral, the Goddess and Goddess-within, the place of emergence into Be-ing, the place of return at death. The darkness is the womb of women, the source of all life. Menstruation is women's power, women's ability to carry new life within their bodies, to bring it forth at term and nurture it until independence. Menopause is women's time of freedom from conception, the time of life of wisdom and experience, when blood not shed is power held within. Old women are the teachers and guidance of the world, the grandmothers who are the mainstay of every child's early days. Black women are beautiful and consequential sisters, strong in their suffering and fighting back, and with much to teach. Misogyny, agism and racism have deprived women of a large part of their heritage and separated women from each other, but no more. On the Waning Moon, women honor the positive darkness, and reclaim what has been lost.

The Motherpeace tarot card for the Waning Moon is the Crone. She is a woman of power, holding a light to guide others on inner paths. The Crone has been there and she knows the way. Among the many Crone Goddesses are: Old Woman Who Never Dies (Native America), Hecate (Greece), Befana (Italy), Baubo (Greece), Mother Holle (Germany), Baba Yaga (Russia), Sedna (Inuit), Spider Woman or Spider Grandmother (Native America), Nepthys (Egypt), Ceridwyn (Wales), Ama No Uzumi (Japan), Kali or Kali-Ma (India), Ala (Nigeria), and Obatalla (West Africa). Goddesses of transformation and change, and Goddesses of the underworld (like Rhiannon of Wales, Inanna of Sumer and Oya of Yoruba Africa) are also Waning Moon Goddesses, as are karmic triple Goddesses like the Three Fates

(Greece) or The Morrigan (Celtic).

On the Waning Moon, the candles for the altar are black for banishing negativity, white for new beginnings, and red for fulfillments. The Crone becomes the Maiden at the New Moon, and the Mother, giving birth, stands in between. Black is for the Waning Moon, red for the Full, and white for the New Moon Maiden, soon to be reborn. White candles are also for pre-menarche, red for menstruation, and black for menopause.

The three-form Goddess appears in all her strength and beauty in this last moon phase. Flowers are not needed on the altar in this part of the cycle, as the Crone is done with blooming and conceptive sexuality. A sprig of evergreen or a single orchid are appropriate, however. Use a cauldron on the altar for rituals with the Crone, she is the womb of transformations, and emphasizes the element of spirit. The Crone's powers of death and reincarnation are total; her powers are of endings that change to new beginnings.

Women who ovulate on the Full Moon are premenstrual at this time in the lunar cycle, and menstruating at the very end. They are shedding the old lining of the uterus, refusing conception for this month; the egg is dead. Very few eggs are ever fertilized, of the 100,000 present in women's ovaries at birth. Women who have premenstrual syndrome find great comfort in affirming the Crone phase and honoring their wombs and moontimes. Learning to value women's cycles is a beginning of releasing menstrual pain or premenstrual symptoms; the patriarchy has taken our bleeding from us by making menstruation into "the curse." Women reclaim it as positive and enjoy their blood.

Those women who have passed menopause or had hysterectomies no longer menstruate. They are free of the burdens and worries of possible conception and free of the role of taking care of children. They have time for themselves now, something to celebrate for sure. Their nurturing, if given, is no longer biological but a choice. Women who feel validated in society/community and have their own lives to live, are not bothered by the patriarchal hype about "worthless old women." In the days of the Delphic Oracle, only women after menopause could become a Pythia, a seer at the shrine. It was believed that the power of the Python Goddess was too intense for younger women to withstand. In some Native American cultures, women after menopause were eligible to become tribal elders. It was these women who chose the famous chiefs. In a menstruation ritual for the Waning Moon, Crone women celebrate their freedom from the Mother phase; they affirm their wisdom and their bodies.

Dreams and emotions are reflected in the Waning Moon cycle,

as they are in other phases. At the Waning Moon, some women's psychic abilities are enhanced, for some women and some skills more so than at the Full. This is a good time for past-life regression work, meditation, healing, and for astral projection. Dreams are sometimes "flying dreams," astral projections with sexual over-tones. Women's power is too full to go unnoticed at this time and dreams often reflect the pain of living in the patriarchy. There are dreams of crones and hags, angry dreams, dreams of power, and sometimes dreams of violence (that seldom manifests, but can be disturbing to the dreamer). There is no safety in living in patriarchy, and no hiding from its realities and dangers in this psychically sensitive time.[12] Divination is especially powerful at this time in the moon cycle, possibly going deeper into the psyche than Full Moon readings. The Waning Moon is a good time to do scrying with a crystal ball, in a pool or candle flame, or in a bowl of water with crystals. Use the information for a deeper understanding of one's Crone self.

Emotionally, the Waning Moon is a time for completions and a time for laying the roots of the next cycle's beginnings. It's a time for banishings and protections, letting go of negative habits and bad relationships, and releasing those who have passed out of one's life or passed over. The Waning Moon is also a time for healing women's rage. The positive rage that allows women to survive against all odds is something to validate, but the anger that holds women back, stuck in a place of pain and "spinning their wheels," is released in the Waning Moon. Women rest at the end of the lunar cycle, letting go of the past and making plans for things to come. They remember the moon huts of the Goddess matriarchies. On the New Moon to come, they begin again.

The Waning Moon — A Menstrual Ritual

This is a ritual to reclaim women's blood. It can be turned into a menopause ritual with more emphasis on the black than the red, or try the Croning ritual in the Rites of Passage section. Decorate the altar in red, with a red altar cloth, a red and a black taper candle, and a thicker white candle for the center. Place menstrual items on the altar, tampons, pads, sponges, blood prints. The women dress in red or are skyclad with red, or red and black, cords (belts) or necklaces. Wear necklaces that represent the moon. At the begin-ning of the ritual, light the white center candle only, the others are lit during the ritual itself. Having each woman bring her own red candle is a good addition to the ritual; or menstruating women can bring red candles and menopausal women black ones. When done as a menopause ritual, each woman brings a black candle, and the color for the altar and ritual emphasizes the black.

Need

Candles — A red taper, a black taper, and a white thicker candle for the center. Each woman brings her own red (or black) candle, if possible.

Incense — Sage, cedar, sweetgrass or frankincense. A sage/cedar smudge stick is suggested. These are incenses for healing, immortality, protection, purification. Or use a whisk broom to stroke auras.

Menstrual items for altar.

Menstrual Poem or Invocation — Read those that follow or pick others.

Bowl of red "gummy coins" (candy coins), available in the supermarket.

Oils or menstrual blood for Self-blessing and mirror.

Optional — Drums or rattles.

Matches to light candles and incense, charcoal block, ritual wand.

Outline

Light candles — Light the center white candle only.

Purify — With incense or sprinkling. Try using a small broom as an alternative to incense and sweep auras. Brooms are symbols of the Crone.

Cast Circle/Invoke Crone Goddesses for the five elements.

      Earth — Hecate (Greece), Crone of the underworld and Waning Moon.

      Air — Old Woman (Native American), Goddess of who we are and will be.

      Fire — Amaterasu (Japan), Goddess of women's power and blood.

      Water — Tiamat (Middle East), Old Woman of the Sea and women's wombs.

      Spirit — Oya (W. Africa), Goddess of immortality and women's changes.

Another set of Goddesses to use is: Earth, Spider Woman (Native American, Navaho), for women's strength; Air, Ceridwyn (Wales), for thoughts; Fire, Oya (W. Africa), for purification; Water,

Sedna (Inuit), for peace; and Spirit, Hecate (Greece), for transformation.

Menstrual Poem or Invocation — See below or use others.

Menstrual Poem
by Felicity Artemis Flowers

I bind myself to my Self.
I am Sacred Woman.
I bind myself to all who bleed
who have bled
and who will bleed to Life.
Sacred Women
I bind myself with Life.
Blessed be.[13]

Menstrual Invocation
by Lynn Andrews

We are born of the first words of the first mother. We are
of the void and we carry the void. Our blood is her body.
It is sacred. It is said she was born of the water and the
earth, and that is why our blood shall return to the earth
and our spirit to the waters of the sacred dream. Her
power shall be honored over all the earth, and all shall
know her as the beginning. . . .

We have transformed our bodies into the womb time;
take care that the blood seed of our first mother is
welcomed in a sacred way, for it is of her body...Bless her
memory for she lives within us. When we eat, it is she
who eats. When we offer smoke, it is she who takes our
message to the faraway. When we bleed, it is she who
bleeds. When we give our body to be divided in love, let
all parts of us be in her name so that her love can be
complete on this great earth.

For too long the memory of who gives us life has been
hidden. We forget that our moon is our celebration time
for her life within us. Women in their moon have set
themselves aside because it is our power time, our time
to look within and feed our inner strength. Women have
certain ceremonies at this time because their power is so
great . . . In the old way there were special lodges for

women in their moon, and most women of the camp would bleed near the same time. This is because our bodies adapt to the harmony of our sisters. . . .

Dream to the great mother. Your laps are her altar. Put your essence into prayers, as we put our blood into her life and ask for balance and understanding in this lifetime. Give of your blood that she may hear us in our dreams and remember us when she wakes.[14]

Meditation — Do a meditation on the womb cycle which is the Waxing/Full/Waning Moon and the ages of women (menarche/ menstruation/menopause and growth/ovulation/bleeding). Experience each age and cycle. Go within your womb and feel its power. Experience your womb power within and then know your power in the world. Come back to now.

Body of ritual — A bowl of red "gummy coins" is passed around. Each woman in her turn takes one and says:

"Here's how I've paid my dues as a woman _____." (She lights her red candle.) "I am powerful as a woman because _____." (She places her lit red or black candle on the altar or in front of her after she speaks. If there is only one red candle, the high priestess lights it after all the women speak.)

The high priestess lights the black candle and says:

"You have the power now; choose something unwanted to banish on the dark moon." (Go around the circle for banishings, then blow out the black candle.) "They are gone. Cycle endings are also cycle beginnings. Choose something begun within and nurture its growth." (Go around the circle again for the women to speak their beginnings to emerge on the New Moon.) "The new is begun."

Self-blessing — Use menstrual blood or oil, and pass around the mirror at the end. For the belly chakra say:

"Bless my womb that bleeds in season, bears children, creates projects, stops bleeding at menopause for even greater power within."

Raise power — Use drums or humming to raise power for new projects, banishings and women's power within.

Ground.

Open Circle/Hugs.

Blow out candles.

Suggested songs for this ritual include:

>We are the old women,
>We are the new women,
>We are the same women,
>Stronger than before.
>
>Hey!

or

>The earth is our mother,
>We must take care of her;
>The earth is our mother,
>We must take care of her.
>
>Hey and a ho, and a hey, ya ya.

or

>Born of water,
>Cleansing, powerful,
>Flowing, healing —
>We are.

Validating women's bodies in ritual is a powerful way to celebrate them back into women's lives. For 5,000 to 20,000 years the patriarchal order, fearing women's womb and Goddess-within consequence, has devalued women and women's life-giving creativity. Women's Spirituality reclaims women as it does the Goddess, and reclaims the value and beauty of women's bodies. Women who ritualize the moon phases learn to appreciate and love their physical Be-ings. Whether their bodies are large or small, fat or thin, of whatever color, able or disabled, young or old, they are beautiful as all women are beautiful. Women and women's bodies are the Goddess. Knowing women's bleeding cycle for the power that it is begins the process of loving women's bodies as they are. This accepting, validating and loving of women's physical selves and life-giving Be-ing is an important part of Women's Spirituality and the Goddess.

The next two chapters celebrate in ritual the wiccan Wheel of the Year, the eight great lunar/solar Sabbat/holidays.

Notes

1. Merlin Stone, *Ancient Mirrors of Womanhood* (Boston: Beacon Press, 1979), stories of these Goddesses throughout, and more.

2. Barbara G. Walker, *The Women's Encyclopedia of Myths and Secrets* (San Francisco: Harper and Row, 1983), p. 670.

3. Monica Sjöö and Barbara Mor, *The Great Cosmic Mother: Rediscovering the Religion of the Earth* (San Francisco: Harper and Row, 1987), pp. 150-151.

4. *Ibid.*, p. 151.

5. *Ibid.*, pp. 144-145.

6. Helen Farias, *The College of Hera: The First Seven Lessons* (Clear Lake, WA: Juno's Peacock Press, 1988), pp. 9-10. Cycle information in this chapter is from this source.

7. Ruth Barrett and Felicity Flowers, *Invocation to Free Women*, audio tape, Circle of Aradia Publications (4111 Lincoln Blvd. #211, Marina del Rey, CA 90292), $12.

8. The songs and chants used in Women's Spirituality have undergone the folk process. Wherever known, I will credit authors; where no author is given, it's because I don't know who she is.

9. Helen Farias, *The College of Hera*, p. 16.

10. Incense suggestions in this book are from Scott Cunningham, *Cunningham's Encyclopedia of Magical Herbs* (St. Paul: Llewellyn Publications, 1985.

11. Shekinah Mountainwater, *Songs and Chants of the Goddess, Vol. I*, audio tape, Moonspell (P.O. Box 2991, Santa Cruz, CA 95063). The divination idea in this ritual is from her, also.

12. Helen Farias, *The College of Hera*, p. 16.

13. Felicity Artemis Flowers, *The P.M.S. Conspiracy* (Marina del Rey, CA: Circle of Aradia Publications, 1986), p. 12.

14. Lynn Andrews, *Flight of the Seventh Moon: The Teaching of the Shields* (San Francisco: Harper and Row, 1984), pp. 77-78. Slightly adapted.

Chapter Five

─────────◯─────────

The Wheel of the Year I
The Waxing Year

The wiccan/Women's Spirituality year is a circle without beginning or end. It follows the agricultural growing cycle through the seasons, and the themes of the Sabbats are themes of passage through life and death. The Goddess is born at Yule (Winter Solstice, December 20-23), is a fragile new hope at Candlemas (February 2), a child at Spring Equinox (March 20-23), a Maiden discovering sexuality at Beltane (May 1), the Mother of all life at Summer Solstice (June 20-23), the maturing matron at Lammas (August 1), in menopause at Fall Equinox's harvests (September 20-23), and the ancient Crone at Hallows (October 31). Candlemas, Beltane, Lammas and Hallows are considered lunar Sabbats and their dates are fixed; they are the cross-quarter days between the Solstices and Equinoxes. The Solstice and Equinox Sabbats (Spring and Fall Equinox, Winter and Summer Solstice) are considered solar Sabbats and their dates change with the solar year. To ritualize the Sabbats is to ritualize life — the life, death and rebirth of the Goddess, of the year, of all growing things, and of women. The essential message of the Wheel is life unending, a process from birth to death and birth again, continual movement and continual change.

In celebrating the Wheel of the Year, women meet together approximately every six weeks to observe the year's movement and its meaning. As the Goddess grows and travels through her rites of passage, women watch the earth change with her, quicken from snow to crocuses, bloom from the tentative beginnings of spring to full summer, grow into rich harvests, and then fade and die into winter again. Each aspect has its other side: the barrenness of Yule reflects the lushness of Summer Solstice; the Maiden's sexual awakening at Beltane reflects her dying at Hallows as a Crone; the harvests of Fall Equinox remember the next spring's planting to

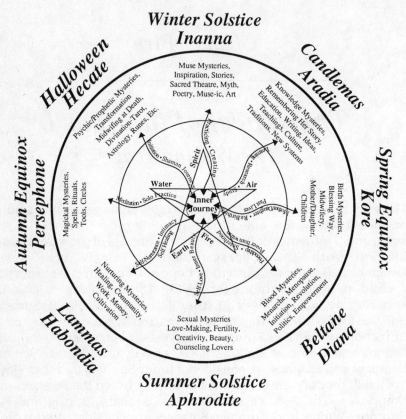

Originally titled "The Gifts of the Priestess," this wheel was made to catalogue some of the many ways a priestess can serve as well as the inner work that supports her skills.

come. Where there is growth and life in the Wheel of the Year, there is fading and death on the other side; where there is fading and death, there is rebirth and blooming when the Wheel turns. The year and all life have two halves, the waxing and the waning, and one cannot exist without the other.

Women who watch the changings of the earth, of the Goddess who is the earth and is women, learn about change and transformation in themselves. They know the year's cycles and know those cycles are present in their bodies, minds and spirits. They know the only law is change, change from within, and learn to use that change to make of their lives all that they can be, all that they want it to be. Women learn about life as an ever-changing never-ending Wheel, and see their place on that Wheel as the hub and center. There is a certainty and centeredness in seeing oneself as part of the plan of the universe and earth, a part of the changing Goddess. There is calm, beauty and sweetness in knowing oneself and one's life as part of the Wheel. Women who know that their existence has meaning are women of consequence in the world.

The beauty of ritualizing the Sabbats is in acting out the life passages of the Goddess, earth and year within oneself. In doing the rituals for each Sabbat as it comes, doing them alone or with a group or coven, women feel the changes of the cycle happening within them. Winter seems less long when the rebirth of spring and oneself is celebrated at its beginning (Yule), and when new growth is nurtured at the coldest part of winter (Candlemas). Summer's heat and sexual maturity have balance when at Summer Solstice women celebrate the change to death and winter. Winters seem less long and dreary, and summers less endlessly hot viewed in this way. The fall's passage from lush harvests into age and death are enacted each year, and the rebirth of spring that comes after. Women who flow with the beauty of the changes see the beauty of those changes in themselves.

There is also a feeling of oneness and community in knowing on each Sabbat (or Full Moon) that women everywhere are celebrating ritual at the same time. For women working alone, this is an awareness against loneliness. For women doing ritual in groups, it's a feeling of family, a feeling of certainty that the world is changing, that women's values are returning to the earth. And they are. To imagine women from all over the world, thousands of them together at the night of Candlemas doing initiations, self-initiations and Self-blessings is an awesome, wondrous thing. To imagine women from all over the world together on Beltane dancing the Maypole, or at Lammas celebrating the harvest or Blessing the Animals is awesome and inspiring, too. Women everywhere come together on the nights of the Great Sabbats to celebrate the Goddess, the earth and themselves, as they come together monthly to do the same on the Full Moons.

While Women's Spirituality rituals for the moon phases are aimed at the short-term cycles of women's wombs, the year cycle has a longer/larger focus. The rituals for the year follow the changing earth through her ages, the year a smaller microcosm of the longterm growth of the earth. The microcosm of the year is also the microcosm of women's life cycles. The focus is on the changing year, but its effects are on women's changes within. Rites of passage rituals focus these changes on the individual, but the Sabbats focus them on life as a whole, on the earth as a whole, and on women collectively.

The structure of the Sabbat rituals is much the same as the structure of the Esbats or moon phases. Drawing down the moon is only used on Full Moons (though I have used it at Summer Solstice), but "The Charge of the Goddess" is used for all the Sabbats (in moon rituals it is only used for the Full Moon). Each Sabbat has its seasonal theme and the altar is decorated for it, using colors of the season. Each Sabbat has its particular purpose and focus that is enacted in the ritual. The overall message of the Wheel of the Year rituals is the idea of ever-changing. The earth continually changes, and so does the Goddess and women's lives. There is no holding on to make a season stay; it keeps on growing, as women keep on growing. The growth of women as Goddess-within is the central theme of the Goddess craft.

A schedule of the eight Sabbats follows. Where the date is not a set one (solar Sabbats), check each year's calendar for the exact date of the Equinoxes and Solstices. The cross-quarter days between (the lunar Sabbats), have dates that do not change. Do rituals on the Sabbat date wherever possible, and where it is not possible, do them before rather than after the exact date. The energy is waxing for that Sabbat until its date, highest on it, and waning away from it toward the next one after. When a New or Full Moon occurs within a few days of a Sabbat, I like to schedule the ritual to connect the sun and the moon. The power of doing so is apparent in the energy of the ritual. Women who work in groups are encouraged to commit themselves to following the Sabbats for a full year's cycle at least; women who work alone are urged to ritualize them, too, however simply, every time.

The Waxing Year	The Waning Year
Yule (Winter Solstice, December 20-23)	Summer Solstice (June 20-23)
Candlemas (February 2)	Lammas (August 1)
Spring Equinox (March 20-23)	Fall Equinox (September 20-23)
Beltane (May 1)	Hallows (October 31)

Yule (December 20-23)

Winter Solstice is the longest night and shortest day of the year. In the turning of the Wheel, the lowest ebb of light means light's returning, and Yule is the return of the sun by the Goddess' rebirth. The idea and theme were taken over by Christianity for its nativity of Christ, but the original idea was wiccan and female, and most sun gods were also originally sun Goddesses. Yule celebrates the birth of the sun child — i.e., Persephone in Greece — whose rebirth brings back the springtime. In nonfeminist wicce, the Yule child is male, and the cycle of death and rebirth is focused on the god. Out of the darkest time of winter comes the promise of spring warmth to come.

Yule rituals re-enact the return of the Goddess and the return of warmth and light. They are essentially rituals of being born and reborn, of the renewal of hope and promise. As rituals, they are quite similar to New Moons, with the same theme of beginnings. The experience of nothingness, of death, is changed to the experience of new Be-ing, where everything is wonderful and possible. Women bring forth life at Yule, and bring forth new ideas, plans for the birthing year. The tarot cards that represent the Sabbat are the Aces, the very earliest starts of projects and endeavors of all sorts. Many women rest in the positive darkness of Yule until the awakening of Candlemas, letting ideas germinate in the underground labyrinth of the dark inner mind. This is a time of hibernation, and of emerging from the womb.

Sun Goddesses of Yule include: Amaterasu (Japan), Igaehindvo (Native America), Sunne (Scandinavia), Lucia (Sweden), Persephone or Kore (Greece), Befana (Italy), Perchta or Bertha (Germany), Rhiannon (Wales), Grianne (Ireland), Unelanuhi (Native America), Isis (Egypt), Tonantzin (Mexico), Akewa (Argentina), Arinna (Anatolia), Coatlique (South America), and Sun Woman (Australia). Archeologist Patricia Monaghan reports that many moon Goddesses, such as Hathor in Egypt, were originally sun Goddesses, and that the idea of a sun god is a late one in most cultures. Fire Goddesses like Pele (Polynesia), Oya (Africa), and Fuji (Japan) are also included as Goddesses for Yule.

Decorate the altar in red, for the return of light and warmth at

Winter Solstice. Use red candles, and a lot of them, the more brightly burning the merrier. Use greens and evergreens on the altar, too; their never-shedding leaves are symbols of rebirth and eternal life. Many cultures have been incorporated into western Christmas decorations, and most of the customs came from wicce. Pine boughs, evergreen trees, holly, poinsettias and mistletoe are quite proper to decorate the altar and room for women's Yule rituals. Holiday foods from many cultures are also the foods to use for Yule; put a candy cane on the altar. Red, dark green and white are Winter Solstice colors.

Yule — A Ritual of Rebirth

The ritual that follows below is a group ritual that is easily adapted for use alone. It is also a good ritual to try for the New or Waxing Moon. Decorate the room and altar for the season, with evergreens, holly and pine boughs, even a decorated fir tree. Place lots of candles on the altar, red ones, and put them at the corners/directions of the room if they are safe there. Use a holiday angel draped in white for an altar Goddess image, or even an image of Mary, who after all, was a Goddess (probably derived from Isis). On the altar are an unlit red, white, and black candle. The whole altar may be dark, candles lit within the ritual, for good effect. Use bells when invoking the Goddesses of the elements and spirit. Yule is a great time for a potluck after the ritual; bring all the holiday foods of every culture, from Chanukah to Kwanza — they are all feasts of returning light.

Need

Candles — Lots of red ones, and red, white, and black tapers for the altar.

Incense — Pine for protection and fertility, cedar for purification, or sweetgrass to call the spirits. Or use sprinkling, or stroke auras with a fir branch.

Solstice Invocation — Use the one below or choose another.

Evergreens, holly, pine boughs on the altar, images of the sun Goddess in white, icicles, and other seasonal things.

Drum — (Optional.) Use bells in invoking the elements and spirit.

Oils for Self-blessing/mirror.

Potluck dinner contributions, for after the ritual.

Matches to light candles and incense, charcoal block for loose incense, circle-casting wand.

The women enter the circle by a birth canal, but cast the circle after everyone is inside. The high priestess and another woman stand at the door of the room, arms held high to make an arch, holding hands. As each woman enters, the women at the door lower their arms around her and say:

"From woman you were born into this world; from women you are born into this circle. Blessed be."[1]

They lift their arms and the woman passes into the decorated room, joining the lengthening chain of women welcomers. The chain lengthens until all of the women are inside the room and the last woman to enter passes through several pairs of loving arms. When all the women are inside, the pairs separate and the circle is formed.

Outline

Candles are unlit, or lit only at the directions and center. Tapers in red, black, and white on the altar are dark.

Purify — With incense smoke, or by sprinkling or stroking auras.

Cast Circle/Invoke sun Goddesses for the elements and spirit.

 Earth — Tonantzin, Sun Goddess, Mother of Mexico.

 Air — Befana, who brings gifts to children on Twelfth Night.

 Fire — Amaterasu Omikami, Sun Goddess of Japan, Lady of the bright mirror.

 Water — Unelanuhi, Sun Goddess of the Hopi, divider to time.

 Spirit — Isis of Africa and Egypt, who wears the sun in her hair as a crown.

Read "The Charge of the Goddess."

Invocation — Use the following invocation and poem, or choose others. The high priestess says:

"We are here to celebrate Winter Solstice, the longest night of the year. This is the time of women's rebirth from darkness, of the Goddess's rebirth. Light comes from darkness, growth from barrenness, and spring from the depths of winter. Persephone leaves Hecate in the underworld and is reborn to Demeter. Yemaya creates the world anew again from her fertile womb. Women are reborn, are new. We are here to bring light to the world.

Yule Poem

birthwatch night of sun
from darkness light
west becomes the east
freezing becomes fire
Goddess Mother Moon
she births the sun
she births the earth
she labors for
the sea and sky
death is granted life
so mote it be

circle closes
circle opens
and the oak fire strikes
bright the earth and sun
bright the newborn sea
bright the infant stars
her glowing earth
winter set aside
with new year naming
"everything she touches changes"[2]
as above us so below.

Meditation — Lead the group in a meditation on change, from the old to the new. Experience nothingness in the womb, experience birth (without pain), be a child, growing up, adult, growing old, experience death peacefully, and be back in the womb and reborn again. Grow up to now, then return to the circle.

Body of ritual — At the end of the meditation above, the high priestess goes to each woman and awakens her to life. She says, "It's a girl! Look it's a girl!," helps her to sit up, then goes on to the next woman in the circle.[3] When each is "born" the women welcome each other to the world by singing each woman's name in turn:

(Name) be well, (Name) be well,
All manner of things shall be well. (by Z. Budapest)

Or sing "Happy Birthday" to each woman, using her name.

Go around the circle, asking each woman what she saw and felt in the meditation and "birthing," and when her name was sung.

Go around the circle three times for three wishes. Move clockwise. Each woman makes a wish to Hecate to affirm *something ending.* After they all speak, the black candle is lit. The second wish is to Persephone, for *something beginning;* then light the white candle. The third wish is to Demeter, to affirm a *goal,* and as the women speak, all the extra red candles on the altar are lit. The altar and room are bright with light and promise now.

Raise the cone of power — Use humming or drums. (Drumming is also good as the women enter the ritual room, and during the meditation and "birthing," if it is a soft, steady heartbeat. Drumming to raise power is stronger and louder, but still controlled for this ritual). Direct the cone toward the women's growth in the waxing of the year.

Ground — Send the excess energy to the earth for healing.

Self-blessing — Use pine-scent oils and the mirror.

Open Circle.

Ground again/Group hug.

Potluck dinner — With or without gift-giving for the season.

Candlemas (February 2)

Candlemas is also known as Brigid, for the Celtic Goddess of fire and inspiration, and Oimelc or Imbolc, which means "new lambs." The Sabbat marks the first beginning of spring, the actual date when the winter's temperatures start rising, halfway between Winter Solstice and Spring Equinox. The Goddess as Persephone is young and fragile at Candlemas, a child still at the breast of her mother. In the Hopi version, Powamu, bean plants are grown in the kivas as the promise of new green to come. Valentine's Day, Groundhog Day and the Chinese New Year are outgrowths of this Sabbat. In the deepest cold of winter, the spring is born and nurtured. Candlemas is a time of light, inspiration and poetry, creativity, the nine muses and graces, smithcraft, healing, dedication and initiation. It is a lunar Sabbat.

In nonfeminist wicce, new members are most often accepted and initiated into the coven at Candlemas, and new covens are formed and named. Acceptance into traditional craft must be made and ritualized by a high priestess of at least second degree, or the seeker cannot call herself a witch. Women's Spirituality has no such hierarchy or study plan. Any woman who chooses to be a witch and calls herself so in thoughtful ways is accepted as a member of the craft. Membership in groups is more likely by consensus than initiation. The woman's intent is the important thing, as no one can name a witch, she must name herself, and no high priestess is needed for initiation. Some women choose to dedicate themselves, at the New Moon or Candlemas, and this Sabbat inspires rituals that are beautiful and empowering. Many groups do dedication/ initiation rituals at this time. The high priestess in women's wicce is chosen for her experience and willingness, or by rotation rather than by initiated degrees. Every woman has consequence, and is who she chooses herself to be.

In the tarot, the card for Candlemas is The Star, Persephone emerging from the pool reborn. The woman at Candlemas has purified herself, cleansed the old from her Be-ing, and she accepts a new order of her own choice. She has trust and hope in what is to come, and certainty on her beginning path. She is innocent and new. The woman who dedicates herself to the Goddess and God-dess-within at Candlemas is making major changes in her life. Take the dedication/initiation seriously, for great inner transformations follow. Goddesses of the Sabbat are Goddesses of fire, light and healing: Brigit (Ireland), Lucia or Lucina (Sweden), Oya (Africa), Pele (Polynesia), Amaterasu (Japan), Juno Februata (Rome), Vesta (Rome), Hestia (Greece), Freya (Norway), Befana (Italy), Perchta or Bertha (Germany), Sul-Minerva (Britain), Igaehindvo (Native America), and Arinna (Anatolia). Sappho, a foremother lesbian poet, has become a Goddess for many women, especially for this Sabbat.

Decorate the altar all in white at Candlemas, for the Sabbat's purity and new light. Use lots of candles lit throughout the ritual, and crystals on the altar. Candlemas is the change of winter to the coming spring, the depths and almost-ending of the barren cold. Women dedicate themselves at Candlemas with open hearts and clear minds, entering new realms of brightness.

Candlemas — Initiation as a Woman and a Witch

For many years, I have done Self-dedications alone at my altar on Candlemas, and it's made this Sabbat the most special and impor-tant of the eight for me. (I like Summer Solstice, too!) This past Candlemas, for the first time, I had a group to lead in the ritual, and after asking each member if they were ready for initiation, developed the following. As simple as it is, it proved highly powerful for every-one involved, as the even simpler self-dedications of many years had been alone. Do this ritual with a group if possible, or do it alone, but if the time is right for naming oneself a witch, dedicating oneself to the Goddess, just do it. Adapt it to individual needs.[4]

Decorate the altar in white and have on it a white candle for each woman participating and a gold (or rose) candle for each. The women can bring their own candles, or the high priestess can provide them. Use central altar candles to light at the beginning of the ritual, but leave the women's candles dark until the ritual itself. Place candles on the altar and white flowers. If a white altar cloth is not available, use a rose or red one instead.

Need

Candles — White ones on the altar, plus unlit at the beginning, a white candle and a gold one for each woman.

Flowers — White flowers and many crystals on the altar.

Incense — Use stick incense for this ritual, myrtlewood or rose for love, self-love and dedication.

Oils/mirror for Self-blessing — Important in this ritual.

Optional — I like to give everyone a kiddie valentine at the end of this ritual. Pick nonsexist ones.

Matches for lighting candles and incense, ritual wand.

Outline

Light central altar candles — Leave the women's white and gold candles unlit at this time.

Purify — Use stick incense, spin it in the darkened room like a sparkler for a wonderful effect of moving light.

Cast Circle/Invoke Goddesses of light and inspiration.

> Earth — Oya, (W. Africa) Goddess of change and free women.
>
> Air — Sappho, (Greece) Mother of poetry, foremother of inspiration.
>
> Fire — Pele, (Hawaii) Goddess of women's passion and power.
>
> Water — Tiamat, (Sumer) Dragon Mother, for emergence of women and of spring.
>
> Spirit — Brigid (Ireland) or White Buffalo Calf Woman, (Native America) receiver of women's vows.

"The Charge of the Goddess" — Read it or play Shekinah Mountainwater's sung version, on *Songs and Chants of the Goddess I.*

Invocation — The high priestess talks about the Sabbat, what it is and what it means, and reads the following invocation and poem, or those of her own creation or choice.

"This is the night of Candlemas, the night of poetry and inspiration when women make their vows to the Goddess. This is the night to choose who you are, name who you are, and become one with the Mother. Choose only in perfect love and perfect trust."

Candlemas Poem

Night of lit white candles
darkness turned to light
"everything she touches
changes"
feast of waxing flame
fire of heart and hearth
fire of the mind
flickering of spark
quickening of air
warming into inspiration
thawing in her innocence
snow into desire

"she shines for all of us
she burns within us all"
spiral heat of life
"she shines for all of us
within us all she burns"
the fires to create
"she shines in all of us
she burns us all within"
awakening arising is her need
"she shines for all of us
she burns within us all"
her candle is our only source.[5]

Body of ritual — Each woman in turn lights a white candle and says (high priestess does some coaching):

"I am (name), daughter of (mother's name).

I am a woman and a witch.

I dedicate myself to the Mother Goddess as a (healer, writer, teacher, musician, mother, poet, priestess, etc.).

I pledge myself to _____ (or says what dedication means to her)." She places her candle on the altar.

Each woman in turn lights a gold candle and says:

"I choose (name) as my craft name and (Goddess) as my Mother Goddess because _____." (She describes qualities to add to her life that are part of that Goddess name/ persona.) She holds the candle or puts it on the altar.

"I invite (that Goddess name's) presence and blessing into this circle and into my life. I ask her help and guidance." Each woman in turn says:

"I initiate myself as a woman and a witch. I dedicate myself to (Goddess name) and (quality)."

Self-blessing. Begin it with "I dedicate myself to the Goddess who is Goddess-within. I initiate myself as a woman."

Use the mirror draped in cloth, a picture of the Goddess, to pass around at the end of the blessing.

Raise power — Use songs, chants or visualization. Visualize what being a woman and a witch means. See how you are changed now. See yourself strong, fulfilled and having purpose in your life. See yourself having all you desire. Send the image out. Feel it return like the light of fireworks, feel that light within. Draw it in. It is done.

Ground.

Open Circle/Hugs.

Pass out valentines, a treat to lighten up the evening.

Some songs to use for this ritual in raising power are:

> Lady, lady listen to my heart's song.
> Lady, lady listen to my heart's song.
> I will never forget you,
> I will never forsake you.

or

> Shine on, darling shine on.
> Remember I love you, shine on.
> And wherever you go,
> Let your sweet spirit show.
> You are loved in the universe,
> Shine on, shine on. (by Karen Mackay)

or

> Celebrate the birth of the sun
> Light the way O Lucina.
> Dance around the altar side.
> Blessed be the Great Mother. (by Kay Gardner)

Spring Equinox (March 20-23)

At Spring Equinox, Persephone returns from the underworld to her mother Demeter, and all the earth blooms with rejoicing. No more is the new Goddess a fragile infant at the breast; now she is a laughing child, inquisitive, and getting into everything. The growing Goddess plays jump-rope and hopscotch and knows a thousand bad jokes to try out on family and friends. Her pockets are stuffed with stones and frogs, bubblegum and plastic spiders. She runs wild through the fields and cities, pretending to be a horse, pretending to be a movie-queen, practicing for being a woman and a Goddess one day soon. Her mother is there to protect her as she learns and grows.

Spring Equinox rituals in Women's Spirituality are a time for reclaiming childhood and the child-within. Too many women never had a chance to be children, to play and have fun. Too many women had responsibilities too early, or were fighting for survival. Too many women have too many things to heal about their girlhoods. In rituals at this Sabbat, women go within to discover their child-selves and to heal the hurts that might still be there. In invoking the child-Goddess, women invoke Persephone as themselves and create a happy childhood if they can't remember one. By having childhood again at Spring Equinox, women return something vital to their lives. It is something important that is all too easily and too often lost.

In wicce, Spring Equinox is a time of renewal and rebirth. Days and nights are of equal length and the year is waxing into warmth, fertility and light. Eggs are the Sabbat's primary symbol, for fertility and fecundity, and also for the great cosmic egg of the Goddess, from which the earth and universe were hatched. This is the time for new lambs, calves, chicks and colts, and for babies and little children. Pastel candles, spring flowers, colored eggs and children's things, stuffed toys and bubblegum, games, charades and kiddie pictures are all part of women's Spring Equinox rituals. In the Motherpeace tarot, the cards for this Sabbat are the Daughters, though they are slightly older than the Goddess and women at Spring Equinox.

Goddesses for Spring are Mother Goddesses, the variety of them shown with children from many cultures. Some of them are: Isis (Egypt), Oddudua (Africa), Hina (Polynesia), Demeter (Greece), Parvati (India), Copper Woman (Native America), Kwan Yin (China), Chalchiuhtlique (South America), Oshun (Africa), Mary (Christian), Lilith (Hebrew), Gaia (Greece), Guadalupe (Mexico), and Eostre (Saxon) or Astarte/Ishtar/Esther (Semitic) — from which the Sabbat gets its other name of Oestre. Easter and Passover are both derived from this Sabbat.

Traditional foods for Spring Equinox are eggs, green growing things and children's foods. The colors are pastels, and the theme is childhood innocence. Use a rainbow of bright colors for this Sabbat, and a playful tone and mood.

Spring Equinox — A Ritual to Heal the Child

Be aware that childhood has traumatic overtones for many or most women, and that in doing a child-oriented ritual with adults, a lot of old stuff can surface. In the following ritual, the tone is fun and silliness, but there will also be sadness to resolve for women participating. It is up to the high priestess to monitor the energy and strike a balance between having fun as grown-up kids and healing the pain that may go with it. When both the light and dark aspects of Spring and childhood are met and resolved in the ritual, it becomes a healing and reclaiming of women's consequence and Goddess-within. The women need to treat each other gently in this ritual, to laugh with each other and have compassion for each other's joys and sadness.

Every ritual that follows the criteria given in Chapter 3 for the Body of the Ritual creates a looking-within for the women who participate. The criteria are: (1) that everyone participate; (2) that elements of healing, change or transformation are involved; and (3) that it be a validation of each participant as Goddess. When these three factors are present in a ritual, as they are in this one despite its light tone, the ritual becomes a ritual of healing. Women need these rituals to repair the damages of living in a patriarchal, misogynist world. Participating in them is a transformative process, as is this ritual for healing the inner child.

The colors and decorations for Spring Equinox are pastels and emphasize childhood. Use candles in light colors, blues or greens, peach, yellow or rose (rose is primary in the next Sabbat, Beltane). Decorate the room with balloons and crepe paper streamers and have a basket of colored eggs on the altar. Use lots of flowers in a variety of pastel colors for this Sabbat. Place a bowl of penny candy on the altar (peppermint cigarettes and candy lipstick went over especially well with my group), a jar of bubble soap, and a variety of children's games, toys, and stuffed animals. Have each woman participating bring some photos of herself as a child and place them on the altar.

Need

Candles — Pastel colors, a pair or more, to light at the beginning of the ritual, and a central candle to light during it. Or have
each woman bring a pastel candle to light in the ritual.

Flowers — Pastel colors, a lot of them everywhere in the room.

Incense — Use flower or fruit fragrances. Or purify by using a
flower to stroke auras.

On the altar — Children's toys, penny candy, bubble soap.
Each woman brings photos of herself as a child.

Kids' games — Jacks, jump rope, paddle ball, kazoos, etc.

Bowl of saltwater.

Potluck contributions — Kids' foods.

Matches to light candles and incense, charcoal block for loose
incense, ritual wand.

Outline

Light candles — Light the center pair, leaving one unlit, or one
for each participant unlit.

Purify — Use incense or sprinkling, or brush auras with a
flower (do not reuse).

Cast Circle/Invoke mother and child Goddesses.

> Earth — Oddudua, Mother of the Gods and Goddesses
> of Africa.
>
> Air — Isis, Mother Goddess of Egypt.
>
> Fire — Copper Woman, Mother Goddess of the Pacific
> Northwest.
>
> Water — Mari, Mother Goddess of the Near East.
>
> Spirit — Kwan Yin, Mother Goddess of China.

"The Charge of the Goddess" — Read or play the tape.

Invocation — The high priestess says:

"We are here to celebrate Spring Equinox, the time of the child.
Persephone has returned from the underworld to Demeter and all
the earth blooms in rejoicing. The newborn Goddess of Candlemas
has grown to a playful daughter. The earth is reborn with her in
springtime, when flowers and trees turn green, and all things are
young, playful and new. Day and night are in equal balance and the
cycle waxes in the spring. All promise is yet young but manifesting;
there is joy and rebirthing on the earth."

Meditation — Go back to your childhood. Be an infant. Be
three years old, six years old, in grade school, in high school.
Remember the joys and if there is pain, watch it but be removed
from it, heal it. Hug, stroke and love the litle girl that you were. Ask

her if she has a message, ask her if she has something for healing for you/her. Hug her again. Shrink her image small, hold it in your hand, open your heart and draw her in.

Body of ritual — Each member of the circle talks about her childhood. Go around four separate times:

1. What she was like as a child. What she liked to do most. Did she have a favorite toy, pet, sister, friend?

2. What she would've liked to change about her childhood. (We're going to heal those things next.)

3. How has she healed, or is she healing, her childhood and inner child?

4. Visualize putting all the bad things about childhood into a bowl of saltwater (or cauldron or candle flame). Pass the bowl around. They are gone.

Light a candle on the altar, or each woman light her own candle, to honor the child within.

Pass around a bowl of penny candy and a bottle of bubble soap. Blow bubbles and eat the candy (make it a good variety), and reassert the good/light things about childhood.

Play children's games — jacks, circle games, Goddess charades. Get silly, let your inner child come out to play. Have a bubble-gum blowing contest. Skip rope.

Raise energy — Use children's songs, nursery rhymes and camp songs to raise energy. Go around the circle for suggestions and as someone remembers something, all join in. Do them at an increasingly faster pace. If someone has a kazoo or a child's drum or grade school percussion instruments to go along, so much the better. This can all get pretty noisy! Direct the cone of power to healing the child within each of us, that young Goddess-within, and to healing all the children of the world who are in need.

Ground.

Open Circle/Group or everyone hugs.

Potluck — Eat children's candies and foods: Spagetti-O's, children's cereals, milk and cookies, peanut butter and jelly sandwiches, jelly beans, gummy bears, birthday cake. Sharing of kiddie pictures may go on all night! Have the women take the balloons, flowers and toys with them, to take the child energy home.

Beltane (May 1)

Beltane or May Eve is the last Sabbat of the waxing year. The next holiday is Summer Solstice, the zenith of the light, from which the year begins to wane. Beltane is the approaching height of fertility and is a feast of fires and flowers; women's passion is its theme, and the Goddess's passion, and the earth's passion to bloom and bear fruit. Brightness and abundance are present everywhere at Beltane, in the greening and blooming of the land, the colors of the Maypole and the candles, and the brightness of the women's clothes. Where Spring Equinox colors were pastels, Beltane's are rose for new love or primary colors that emphasize brightness and fertility.

Persephone has come of age and reached menarche, she is no longer the child/Maiden. Her body changes and she discovers the fires of sexuality, of physical love and self-love, and learns what passion means. She begins, experiments, and changes partners as she learns. The custom of making love in the fields on May Eve was done in wiccan England to enhance the fertility of the growing crops. It may also have been a remnant of the days when women mentruating bled in the fields, for the same reason.

In the Motherpeace tarot, a card for Beltane is the Four of Wands, which is a menarche celebration for a young woman coming of age. Others of the Wands, signifying sexuality, passion and life force energy, are also appropriate for both Beltane and Summer Solstice. The Lovers is a Beltane card, the coming together of two Be-ings. At Beltane love is new and just beginning, still trying-out and emotionally innocent; at Summer Solstice it is mature and in committed relationships. Persephone at Beltane discovers love and passion for the first time, and the earth blooms with her sexuality. "All acts of love and pleasure are the Goddess's rituals." Flowers are female sexual symbols and the symbol of the season, as are the Maypole and the May Eve fire.

The Maypole is a European custom, brought to this country from wiccan England. Decked with flowers and danced/woven by women, it is a female Goddess and fertility totem, the moontree of the Great Mother. Fertility in this Sabbat can be sexual or celibate, procreative or creative in any form. To make a Maypole, where a handy tall tree without low branches is unavailable, use a pole such as a clothesline pole. Ideally the pole should be twice as tall as the dancers, and the ribbons are half again as long as the pole, attached at the top.[6] Have each woman in the coven bring a roll of wide giftwrap ribbon or crepe paper, in all colors. To make the pole stand up unassisted, dig a hole for it a foot deep or more (depending on height of pole), and wedge the base with rocks. Steadying it at the top by crossing two clotheslines also helps. While weaving it in the ritual, remember the weaving of the universe by Spider Woman.

Indoors, this type of Maypole is harder to manage, but a Maypole is still possible. Fasten the lines to a high lighting fixture, if someone can get up there, and don't pull too hard. Or make a weaving frame instead. To do this, take two horizontal poles and string a warp between them vertically. In the ritual, the women use this as a frame for Spider Woman-type weaving. The effect is not the same as dancing a vertical Maypole, but is still creative and appropriate. In this horizontal May weaving frame, use a variety of materials: yarn, ribbon, fabric, lace, beads, bells, shells, etc. to make an interesting tapestry.[7] The indoor weaving frame is also an alternative when women are doing Beltane rituals alone.

Goddesses of flowers and blooming, love, fertility, and the moontree/Maypole are the Goddesses of Beltane. Some of them are: Flora (Rome), Bloddeuwedd (Wales), Bona Dea (Italy), Freya (Norway), Oshun (Africa), Aphrodite (Phoenicia/Greece), Ishtar (Semitic), Asherah (Hebrew), Tonantzin (Mexico), Danu (Celtic), Gwenhwyvar (Wales), Mary (Christian), Mawu (Africa), Ostara (Germany), Belili (Mesopotamia), Kwan Yin (China), Spider Woman (Native America), and Hina (Polynesia). Use rose-colored candles for passion, new love, and first blood. Foods for the Sabbat are sensual ones, strawberries and vanilla ice cream, lady locks, cream puffs, whipped cream and red cherries, red fruit juices and cherry sodas.

The other Beltane custom is the May fire or Bel-fire, jumped over for fertility, health and good luck for the year. Use a candle in a cauldron for this, a hibachi or small charcoal grill, or a real outdoors Beltane fire. Step over it, jump over it, or even walk around it, focusing on wishes to come true.

Beltane — A Ritual of May Weaving

The two themes of this ritual are the weaving of the earth and universe by Spider Woman, and the blooming and passion of the coming-of-age Goddess and earth. The wiccan traditional Maypole and Bel-fire are included, with emphasis on women's ways of looking at this Sabbat that differ from nonfeminist craft. The May Eve ritual is best done outdoors, where the green and flowering earth becomes the setting for it. It is best done with a group of women, as Beltane is a time of celebrating sisterhood and love, but can also be adapted for use alone.

Use rose-colored candles and lots of spring flowers for this ritual. Pink roses are wonderful as are flowers in all the lighter colors. Make the altar at the base of the Maypole, but keep the Belfire a little ways away, out of range of the weaving dancers. If the activity of the ritual could be uncomfortable or physically inaccessible for any women of the coven, make sure a safe space in the circle is provided. Dancing, moving women are careful not to bump or knock over less steady sisters. This is an active ritual, but not a rowdy one.

Need

Candles and flowers — Emphasize rose and pastels.

Incense — Use lighter flower scents like rose, patchouli, myrtlewood, cherry or vanilla — all draw love. Or purify by sprinkling or stroking auras with a broom or flower.

Cauldron with candle inside or other Beltane fire.

Maypole — Described above. Everyone in group brings a roll of ribbon, or items to weave into the weaving frame indoors.

Oils for Self-blessing and a mirror.

Optional — Rattle or drum during Maypole weaving.

Matches to light candles and incense, charcoal block for loose incense, circle-casting wand or use a flower.

Set up the Maypole before the ritual begins, adding each woman's roll of ribbon as she arrives. The Maypole is the center of the cast circle. If a bonfire is used, rather than a portable cauldron and candle, it should be set up at a safe distance from the Maypole and started before the ritual. Designate one woman who knows how to tend fires as fire-witch. Women are seated in a circle around the Maypole at the beginning of the ritual.

Outline

Light candles.

Purify — With incense or stroking auras or sprinkling.

Cast Circle/Invoke Goddesses of love and flowers.

> Earth — Flora, Roman Goddess of beauty and women's passion.
>
> Air — Bloddeuwedd, Goddess made of flowers, from Wales.
>
> Fire — Tonantzin, Love Goddess of Mexico.
>
> Water — Oshun, African Goddess of love and passion.

Spirit — Aphrodite, who rules Beltane and women's
hearts.

Read "The Charge of the Goddess."

Invocation — The high priestess says:

"This is Beltane, the fullness of spring. It's a time to open, to
rise and to grow. Persephone, almost a woman now, reaches
menarche and bleeds in cycle as all women bleed. Her body is
becoming a woman's and is something new. She plays in the flowers
and all her wishes come true in the blooming of the spring. She
attracts a love, the other half of herself, and they learn passion
together. "All acts of love and pleasure are the Goddess' rituals."

May Eve Poem
desire and delight
consummation of the earth
maiden and the fertile year
merry meet by moon of
flowering and merry part
to dance her living dance
choose ribbons of the east
choose ribbons of the south
choose ribbons of the west
choose ribbons of the north
circle in the maypole dance
her rite of love

"thou art Goddess"
in the winding of
this weaving dance
"thou art Goddess"
in partaking
of her rainbow flame
"thou art Goddess"
in her changing
and your seashell change
"thou art Goddess"
"she is shining
in us all."[8]

Meditation — Go on a journey of being born, nurtured, first
smile, first passion. Watch yourself play, grow, grow up, mature to
now. Take lots of time imagining the passion. Make a wish, the most

important thing you want, and see it coming true. Hold its image in front of your heart, and draw it inside. See yourself bloom with full growth, full potential realized. See yourself as Persephone, the Maiden Goddess. Come back to now.

Body of the ritual — The Maypole: the women form two circles, one inside the other, and the circles move in opposite directions. As the women pass each other in the dance, they go *over* the first woman's upheld ribbon, then pass *under* the next ribbon after, over and then under alternating. This makes the weaving around the pole. The movement should be steady but not too rapid, and go with singing, bells and rattle or drum rhythms. Suggested songs are at the end of this outline. There is a great deal of merriment here. The high priestess, as the movement begins, says:

"In the spirit of Spider woman, who wove the earth and the universe, we weave this Maypole of women's desires come true at Beltane. Dance the Maypole for the beauty of the earth, the Goddess and of women. Weave the Maypole to make all wishes come true."

Raising the cone of power — When the Maypole is wound to the bottom, the women go to the Beltane fire. Each makes a wish as she jumps over, steps over or walks around it, and gets in line again. Each jumps the fire for as many wishes as she has, speaking them aloud or not as she does so. The last round over the Bel-fire is for good health and prosperity for the year.

Ground. Send the excess energy for earth healing.

Self-blessing — If the energy is too high, it may not be possible to quiet it enough for the Self-blessing, but it brings the women back to the circle and is positive to do here. Do it if the energy feels right for it.

Ground again.

Open circle/Everyone hugs.

Dessert potluck — Strawberry shortcake, creamy bakery goods, sensuous ice cream, chocolate-covered cherries.

Chants to use while weaving the Maypole include:

> Weave, weave, weave, weave,
> Women weave the web of life.
> Weave, weave, weave, weave,
> Women weave the web.

or

> We are the flow, we are the ebb,
> We are the weaver, we are the web.

We are the weaver, we are the web,
We are the spider, we are the thread.

We are the spider, we are the thread,
We are the witches, back from the dead.
(by Shekinah Mountainwater)

or

Sister, sister,
Let me tell you what I know:
You have given me such pleasure, I love you so.

Love, love, love, love:
Women we are made of love,
Love each other as ourselves,
And I love you so.

The next chapter continues the Wheel of the Year rituals with the rituals of Summer Solstice, Lammas, Fall Equinox and Hallows — rituals for the waning half of the witches/Women's Spirituality year.

Notes

1. As done by Z. Budapest, at the *Of A Like Mind* Dianic Wicca Conference, in Wisconsin, September, 1988.

2. Poem by Diane Stein, quote from Starhawk, *The Spiral Dance: A Rebirth of the Ancient Religion of the Great Goddess* (San Francisco: Harper and Row, 1979), p. 175.

3. Versions of being born at Yule have appeared in a number of books on Women's Spirituality and the process is becoming a tradition.

4. I would like to thank my friend Tanith for our many discussions and her ideas for this ritual.

5. By Diane Stein. Chants are from Starhawk, *The Spiral Dance*, pp. 174-175.

6. Julia Falanga and Helen Farias, "The Maypole: Dance and Feast," in *The Beltane Papers Octava* (P.O. Box 8, Clear Lake, WA 98235), Vol. 3, No. 4, Beltane, 1988, p. 2.

7. Thanks to Rebecca Crystal for this weaving frame idea.

8. By Diane Stein. First published in *SheTotum* (P.O. Box 27465, San Antonio, TX 78227-0465), April-May-June, 1985. Quotes are from Starhawk, chants on page 174 of *The Spiral Dance*.

Chapter Six

────────◯────────

The Wheel of the Year II
The Waning Year

The first four Sabbats of the year, Yule, Candlemas, Spring Equinox and Beltane, are Sabbats of the waxing of the year. This is the time when the days are lengthening, and warmth and growth are increasing on the earth. Winter turns to spring in the waxing of the year, crops are planted and emerge from the earth to bloom. Women's and the Goddess's life cycle is also waxing. At Yule the Sun Daughter is born, at Candlemas she is a fragile infant, at Spring Equinox a growing child, and at Beltane she is coming of age and at menarche. In the Persephone story, the Maiden is returned to her mother from the underworld, and Demeter releases the earth from barrenness to grow again. The cycle is repeated in the story of Isis and Osiris, with the birth of Horus. Women in the rituals for these Sabbats experience the hope of rebirth and new beginnings. The year, the Goddess, the earth and women are in their time of bloom and increase.

In the second half of the year, from Summer Solstice to Hallows, the cycle is reversed. From blooming and lush growth, the earth sinks back into the barrenness and resting of the dark phase, energy concentrated in the roots and seeds. What has been born and grown up in the first half of the year, matures, ripens, seeds and dies in the second half. The Sabbats are Summer Solstice, Lammas, Fall Equinox and Hallows. Persephone enters the underworld at the height of the summer blooming, and all growth ends in harvesting and then decay. The Goddess at Summer Solstice is the Mother, at Lammas she is the matron, at Fall Equinox she reaches menopause, and at Hallows she reaches old age and ending. From the Mother, the Goddess ages to the Crone, descending into the womb of the labyrinth underworld to be reborn again at Yule. When Demeter returns from seeking her daughter in the underworld at

Hallows, Persephone is already present in her womb, readying for rebirth.

The waxing time of the year is followed by the waning time, which is followed in turn by waxing again. The circle has no ending and no beginning; the Wheel of the Year is truly a Wheel. Women who follow the Goddess through the changing seasons and turning cycles learn the rhythm and beauty of the process. In a Wheel without ending there is ever-changing. Living is a process of change, from birth to death and rebirth again. Most women in Women's Spirituality believe in reincarnation and see death not as an ulti-mate ending but as part of a continuing process. They see birth not as a beginning but as a returning.

Where the year does not end with winter and life does not end with death, the outlook is very different from American pop culture attitudes. Women who see life as a process look at spring in the depths of winter and know that it will come. They look at summer as a time of abundance, and also as the start of endings. They see each section of the Wheel for its mirror-half, and affirm and value every part of the cycle. Without the cold of winter there would be no spring; without the darkness and resting time no light or new growth; without the busy times of planting and cultivating there could be no harvest or safe winter's sleep. They see life as a part of the joined cycle of life and death, and death as a natural and necessary part of the cycle, too.

The attitude of moving in flow with the cycles of life and the seasons has consequence for women who live by it. The Women's Spirituality community values women on every step of the path. There is no ageism, no cult of youth, in the Goddess movement, as women and the Goddess are all ages. All the ages are valued for their place on the Wheel and the beauty of what they offer to the whole. The old woman in patriarchal society is written off; in Women's Spirituality she is envied — she gets the freedom of being a Crone at last. The child is seen for her potential, the Mother for her mature sexuality and responsibility, and the Crone for her sense of herstory, her experience and wisdom. All are needed, all are good, all are beautiful and powerful. All are Goddess.

Women's Spirituality sees death in a different way from cur-rent culture, too. Modern western culture has a pathological horror of death, and a great deal of denial. It isolates older people, who are mostly women, in old age homes and senior-citizen apartment complexes, separated from the rest of society. The culture denies the fact of death and aging in bizarre ways — with face lifts and fat suction, heart transplants, life support machines for terminal patients, and with the lack of compassion given women in hospitals and nursing homes who are terminally ill or in need. The quality of life in modern medicine is secondary, clinical existence is the only goal. If the monitors say the woman is not brain-dead, the surgery was a success. A critically ill or dying patient is placed alone in bare rooms and hooked to machines, separated by the "rules" from her loved ones and family, from friends and emotional caring. She is kept alive at any cost, at or against her will, unless she has no health insurance to pay for it. In death, her body is painted and dressed to look alive, embalmd and buried where it cannot decay back to the Earth Mother.

In wicce, the fact of death is taken as a natural part of the Wheel of Life. There is no horror or denial of it. The old are not isolated and separated from the rest of the community, they are a valued part of it with things to teach. A terminal patient is not put on life support, but helped to be loved, comforted and nurtured through the end. She is not prevented from her way if it is her time to leave this world. Death is a transition, not an ending. After the crossing-over comes a new realm, a realm of rest and Be-ing until the choice of rebirth. The spirit or soul does not end, only the physical body, and most bodies after death are cremated quickly and cleanly. When a woman has finished her time and work on the earthplane, and her body is worn out, she leaves it and goes on. She will return in the right time. Life is a series of beginnings, changes, endings and beginnings all over again. There is far more caring and compassion, more emphasis on the quality of life and being truly alive, than in the modern patriarchy. There is no denial of endings, though the grief at losing loved ones is as real.

The year is the model for women's life cycles, from beginning to end to beginning again. The rituals of the Wheel of the year, the eight great Sabbats, are rituals of the process of the life cycle. Beginnings are celebrated at the start of the year, and endings are celebrated in their time as well. There are times of emerging, in the waxing of the year, and of descending into the positive darkness in the waning half. A symbol of the whole is the Chinese yin and yang symbol, in which both halves are part of the larger circle, and a portion of each section is intrinsic in the other. Without starts there are no endings, without winters there are no springs, without death there is no life, and without darkness there can be no light. Women's Spirituality validates and affirms both sides of the symbol, both sides of the Wheel, and both sides of the process of life and death. There is wholeness in doing so, the full circle.

In the waning half of the year, from Summer Solstice to

Hallows, the emphasis is on fulfillments and harvests, and the experience of the underworld/labyrinth of death and return. At each step, the Sabbat's opposite is kept in mind. Summer Solstice has Yule for its mirror opposite; Lammas has Candlemas, Fall Equinox is opposite the Spring; and Hallows is matched with Beltane. For each waning Sabbat there is a waxing one to come. The waning half of the cycle is women's descent into darkness, the experience of aging and the Crone. In the process of the rituals, there is an increasing turning-inward, into darkness, into age and into the self as Goddess-within. As the age of the year advances, so does its power, till the Crone at Hallows is the most powerful aspect of all. Women taste the consequence of who they are as the maturing, aging, waning Goddess and year. It is a new perspective for younger women, one that older ones have come to know. The positive darkness is a new perspective for Caucasian women who have been taught to deny it, and one that women of color have known all along. At Summer Solstice, the height of brightness is reached and the descent into darkness begins. The women meet in ritual to honor the dark side of the Goddess and themselves, to turn the Wheel.

Summer Solstice (June 20-23)

Summer Solstice, also known as Litha or Midsummer's Night, is the longest day and shortest night of the year. At this height of increasing light, the Sabbat marks the zenith of the year's waxing half. From here the days get shorter, the nights longer, and the dark side begins to take over the cycle. This is the time of the Mother at the fullness of her strength, sexuality and fertility. The crops in the fields are in full bloom now, or past blooming, and the grain forms on the stalk and the ear. The harvest is promised, but is still far away in the future; this is the midpoint of the growing season. There is trust in the Mother Goddess to take care of her children, to give proper rain and not too much heat or cold, so the grain can mature to perfection.

At Summer Solstice in the Persephone story, the Goddess at her height of living discovers death. She leaves the earth at this Sabbat to enter the underworld realm of her grandmother Hecate. Demeter, finding her gone, searches the earth for her daughter. Not finding her, she declares an end to all growth and life, and the harvest comes, the crops fade, and death begins on the planet. At Solstice, Persephone has just made the beginnings of her descent;

the Mother doesn't know yet that she's gone.

The Goddess that was born at Yule has reached her maturity at Summer Solstice. She is the Earth Mother, the Empress, Strength or Sun card in the Motherpeace tarot deck. Her children and animals surround her and her image is one of full brightness, abundance, sexuality and fertility. She is pregnant with life and the harvest. The land of milk and honey is literally her body, and the body of the earth.

Goddesses for Summer Solstice include Earth Mothers and Goddesses of beauty and mature sexuality. Some of them are: Gaia (Greece), Tiamat (Semitic), Aphrodite (Phoenician), Ishtar (Mesopotamia), Asherah (Hebrew), Inanna (Sumeria), Freya (Norway), Flora (Rome), Mawu (Dahomey), Spider Woman (Native America), Tonantzin (Mexico), Yellow Land Earth Queen (China), Corn Mother (Native America), Aine (Ireland), Amaterasu (Japan), Hera (Greece), Erzulie (Haiti), Yemaya (West Africa), Iamanja (South America), Anahita (Persia), Oshun (West Africa), Coatlique (South America), and Rhiannon (Wales). These are only a few of the possibilities. Fire Goddesses are also honored at Summer Solstice, as they are at Winter Solstice/Yule; their light is at its highest with this Sabbat. Water Goddesses are part of Summer Solstice, too; all life begins with the Mother Sea.

The themes of this Sabbat's rituals are fulfillment and the turning of the Wheel of the Year. Everything women want is manifested at Summer Solstice, the time to reach high and aim high and ask for the moon and the universe. The Goddess and earth are at their most abundant now, with the most to give. Merging and passion are part of the fulfillment, the life force at its peak. Turning the Wheel is the other theme, the realization at this high point that after the peak comes waning. A beginning of the dark cycle is present at this time of fullness.

Summer Solstice is the best of Sabbats to do ritual outdoors. The weather is good in the northern hemisphere (it is Yule in Australia and South America now), and the least likely time to get cold or rain on the night of the ritual. The Beltane bonfire is also a custom for Summer Solstice, as is the sexual energy that has matured since Beltane. Take advantage of the all-giving Mother and hold a spiral dance outdoors, bonfire and all, for the Summer ritual. This is a good time to bring out all the drums and rattles and do something really exuberant.

The red of passion, the sun, and the summer bonfire is the color of Summer Solstice. For an indoor altar, use red candles and lush, open red flowers like red full-blown roses. For an outdoor ritual, as the one that follows, use the bonfire with the candles, and do it big. Foods for the Sabbat include marshmallows to toast in the fire, s'mores, pizza, and vegetable shish-ka-bobs cooked on the open flame. Also try hot and spicy foods from Asia, Mexico and India for a multi-cultural potluck indoors.[1]

The following ritual for Summer Solstice is an outdoors bon-fire and spiral dance to do with a group. It's perfect for the big ritual at a large women's festival.

Summer Solstice — The Spiral Dance

This is a ritual designed for outdoors, but possible inside with space for movement. If there is no bonfire, place the altar and a cauldron in the center of the circle. The women each bring a red candle to light in the ritual, and a candle holder. Summer Solstice rituals, like Beltane and Spring Equinox, are not quiet. Let the exuberance of the season be reflected in the songs, drumming, dancing and move-ment, and remember to provide a safe space as well. The banishing used in the ritual is a first reminder of the coming dark seasons, but the emphasis for Solstice is still on fulfillment. Think carefully of what to ask for in this ritual; the earth is at her highest point of giving.

Need

Bonfire — Have everything ready and start it before the ritual.

Candles — Red on the altar. Each woman brings a red taper and candle holder.

Flowers — Lush red ones, red full-blown roses, heather, peo-nies, etc.

Incense — Use a smudge stick of sage or sage/cedar.

Invocation and Poem — As below or choose others.

Drums and rattles — Let the drummers have full play.

Matches to light bonfire, candles and incense; circle-casting wand; bonfire wood and starter materials. You may need a fire permit.

The altar outdoors is located at spirit, and a safe space area of pillows and/or chairs is provided there. The drummers sit or stand at the other end of the circle, but anyone with an instrument can join in. Leave some rattles on the altar for anyone to use. The bonfire is at the center of the circle; keep it small enough at the beginning of the ritual so it doesn't dominate it, but let it grow. Lead the spiral dance away from the fire for women's safety. Each woman brings a red candle and holder, unlit at the beginning of the ritual, and matches are available for lighting them at the right time.

Outline

Light candles — On the altar only. The fire is started.

Purify — Use a smudge stick, passing it around the circle. Begin drumming softly, a heartbeat throughout.

Cast circle/Invoke Fire Goddesses. A woman at each of the elements can invoke one Goddess, as elaborately or simply as she chooses. The drummers do a few minutes' interpretation of each element and spirit after it's invoked.

Earth — Mawu, Goddess of earth and fire (Dahomey).
Air — Akewa, Goddess of air and fire (Argentina).
Fire — Pele, Goddess of passion and fire (Polynesia).
Water — Oshun, Goddess of water and fire (West Africa).
Spirit — Sun Woman, Goddess of immortality and spirit (Australia).

"The Charge of the Goddess" — Read it or sing it.

Invocation and Poem — With soft drumming. Use the following or others. The high priestess says:

"This is the fullness of Summer, the reign of the Mother Goddess. Tonight all wants are fulfilled, all wishes come true, all loves and abundance reach full passion. Women everywhere on the planet are gathered together tonight to invoke the Goddess. Our many voices embrace her, awaken her from the long sleep of patriarchy. Listen to her words."

Solstice Poem
by Z. Budapest

Ten thousand years I have been sleeping, and now am being wakened. My heavy eyelashes are the woods, they are beckoning. My heart, the clouds, are surprised because they are calling me, calling me. My Earth-body is bedecked with a thousand flowers; many breasts of mine, the mountains, joyfully rearing their tips. They are calling! They are calling! I want to embrace all the sad and the lost. All wrongs, my hands shall doom to death. I am the defender of every woman as I am the defender of my holy self.

Earth-Mother am I, the Only One; everything springs

from me. I carry the seed of all creation. I, alone am the bestower of life. Oh, oh, . . . Oh, I am awake![2]

Meditation — Done to drumming that increases in speed and intensity with each chakra. The high priestess says:

"Feel the movement and heartbeat of the earth at Solstice, feel the rich, black earth. Draw black into your body, through your feet, legs, vagina, abdomen, heart, chest, throat, head. Feel it enter through your feet, travel through your body, release through your crown. Feel the richness of the Mother Earth." (Repeat with each color, improvise, use color correspondences.) "Feel the color red, the pulsing in the blood . . . Feel the vibrant orange, color of women's passion . . . Feel the active yellow, color of women's will . . . Feel the color green, sympathy and emotion . . . Feel the color blue, throats filled with song and creativity . . . Feel the color indigo, color of psychic knowing . . . Feel the color purple, color of the Goddess . . . Feel the color clear, color of all light. . . ."

The women draw into each chakra the colors in turn; connect the colors with other sensory impressions. After the color clear, tell women to "Draw in what you want from the Solstice: what fulfillments, passions, abundances, Draw them in from the earth, release them to the universe as they manifest." Then, "Feel the colors stop, knowing they are all within you. Know all wishes have been granted. Come back to now."

Give this meditation time, it's very powerful. Allow the drums to enhance and increase the intensity of the meditation. This need not be done in quiet.

Body of Ritual — Immediately after the meditation, lead the women in a spiral dance. They will be ready to move. Keep the spiral moving clockwise steadily, but not at break-neck pace. The high priestess leads, first taking the hand-holding line of women away from the fire, then in a snake chain around the land, then finally coming into a circle, leading the beginning of the circle in on itself until the women are wound tight against each other. Then start moving outward in the opposite direction, unwinding, the high priestess goes to the outside end to do this. When the spiral is unwound, lead the women in a chain again around the grounds and back to the fire circle. Bring the women back into the ritual circle again. Have them sit down; they will be winded. The drumming stops.

Ground — Direct the power raised in the meditation and spiral dance to fulfillments, passion and creativity; the fullness of the light and the beginning of the dark.

Moving clockwise, each seated woman lights her candle at the bonfire, with a match, or from another's candle. She makes a wish, states a banishing, then blows out her candle. After all the women have had their turn, light all the candles again and leave them lit for the rest of the ritual, with the statement, "On Summer Solstice, the Goddess grants all wishes." For this part of the ritual, the drums are silent. The candles are placed in front of each woman.

Self-blessing — It may not be possible to use oils in a large group outdoors; do it without them.

Ground — Send the excess energy for earth healing and good harvests, food for starving people.

Open circle/everyone hugs — The women who invoked the elements and spirit thank and release them.

Toast marshmallows, send for a pizza, or have a potluck dinner.

Some songs to use in the spiral dance include:

> She's been waiting waiting,
> She's been waiting so long,
> She's been waiting for her daughters
> To remember to return. (by Paula Wallowitz)

or

> Air I am,
> Fire I am,
> Water, earth and
> Spirit I am.

or

> Isis, Astarte, Diana, Hecate,
> Demeter, Kali,
> Inanna. (by Deena Metzger)

Lammas (August 1)

Lammas, Lughnasadh or Lady Day is the first of the three harvest Sabbats of the wiccan and Women's Spirituality craft. The time is the beginning of fall and the ending of summer, the early part of the waning cycle. The days shorten and night lengthen, but not drastically yet, and the weather is still summer-hot. Trees and leaves have lost their earlier fresh greenness, and most flowers are past blooming and starting to seed. In some Native American traditions, the time is the green corn dances or first fruits festivals. For the Hopi people, the Flute ceremony alternates bi-yearly with the Snake-Antelope ceremony, the sacred marriage of the Earth Maiden. The earliest ears and stalks in the fields are ready for eating, but the harvest as a whole is only at the start. A lot can happen between now and gathering, and the crops are promising but not yet secure. There is hope for a good harvest at the witches Thanksgiving, Fall Equinox, six weeks away.

Summer has passed her peak and the Goddess who was an infant at Candlemas is a matron now. Persephone has descended to the labyrinth land of Hecate and the dead, and Demeter in despair halts all new growth until her return. Her story is paralleled by that of Inanna, who has left the earth for the underworld, and all life waits for her ascent again. They have not been in the underworld long yet, the waning has just begun. The Sabbat in Ireland is given to the three-form Goddess, The Morrigan, sisters Ana, Badb and Macha, who in Greece are the Three Fates. The thread of life has been spun and now is measured, ready soon for the cutting.

In the Motherpeace tarot, cards for Lammas are Justice and The Wheel of Fortune, both representing the workings and balance of karma or fate. Ideas that women have already set in motion are now reaching consequence, and the cause and effect of natural law is being felt. What women asked for at the Summer Solstice spiral dance is ready to happen. The women of the coven celebrate their closeness to the earth and their oneness with all living. They experience the life cycle, the lives of animals and growing plants, learning oneness with the changing earth. They celebrate the first fruits harvest.

Goddesses for Lammas include corn and grain Mothers, and Goddesses of fate and fortune. The Three-form Goddess is present at this Sabbat. Some names include: The Corn Mothers (Native America), Ceres (Rome), Demeter (Greece), Tailtu (Ireland), Habondia (Italy), Mawu (Africa), Chicomecoatl (South America), Huruing Wuhti (Native America), Oddudua (Africa), Tonantzin (Mexico), Changing Woman (Native America), Rhea (Greece), Gaia (Greece), Juno Augusta (Rome), The Morrigan (Ireland), The Three Fates (Greece), the Norns (Scandinavia), Guadalupe (Mexico), and Yellow Land Earth Queen (China). The Sabbat also honors the Goddess as Lady of the Beasts: Epona and Rhiannon (Wales), Bast and Bau (Egypt), Rainbow Serpent (Australia), and Artemis (Greece).

The altar at Lammas uses colors for the almost-harvest. Candles are dark green, yellow, golden, or orange. Flowers in these colors, including chrysanthymums and heather, are on the altar. This is the Sabbat to make corn dollies, to decorate the altar with ears of the still-green corn and wheat, and whole fresh vegetables. Late summer veggies, like foot-long zucchinis and corn on the cob are the start of Lammas potlucks. Make sumptuous dinners of green salads, stir-fried veggies with brown rice, vegetable shish-ka-bobs, corn on the cob, and fresh fruits for dessert.[3]

The ritual below is an honoring of the Lady and her animals, a thanks-giving for the gift that animals bring to women's lives all year. It is based on the October fourth Blessing of the Animals ceremonies held in Mexico, and the World Day for Animals celebrated the first Sunday in October. I have moved it to earlier in the harvest season. The women in the ritual can use photographs of their pets or bring the pets themselves. Most women have animals (or have had them at some time), and many bring them to coven rituals. My own coven brings as many as four dogs to all the Sabbats, where they supervise the proceedings and enjoy the potluck dinners best. This ritual is also done easily alone, at home with one's dog or cat familiar.

Lammas — Blessing of the Animals

This ritual has the potential for great beauty or great chaos when a group of women bring live animals to the circle. Here are some suggestions and ideas to keep the Sabbat orderly. First, only bring animals that are used to coming out in public, ones that are housetrained and happy visiting, and that like other animals. In some covens, the animals come along for all the rituals, and these are the best pets to do this ritual with. Decide before the ritual if the circle will be for dogs or cats, and do two separate rituals on separate nights if consensus says both. Don't mix dogs and cats in the ritual unless they already live together peacefully. If a woman has a pet that she wants to bring to the ritual, but she knows it will fight or be disruptive or unhappy, she brings its photograph instead. If the women feel that their pets would not like each other or are not socialized enough for group rituals, they can decide together to place everyone's pet photos on the altar and leave the animals themselves at home. The animals of the house hosting the ritual could represent all the women's pets.

In the circle, the animals are held by their women, dogs on leash if they are not used to being together, and kept calm and under control. Encourage the animals to sleep through the proceedings, anywhere in the ritual room. Do the ritual quietly and with little movement, speak quietly. In raising power, avoid loud music, and if singing, sing softly. This is not the time for drums, dancing or strong rhythms. If someone's dog or cat would rather sleep on the couch in the next room than come to the ritual and participate, let her do it. Remember the concept of free will. If someone's dog or cat is disruptive, put her in a carrier or out of the ritual space gently. Animals move in and out of the cast circle freely, without changing its energy. Keep lit candles off the floor.

Need

Candles — Use early fall colors of darker greens, yellow, gold or orange.

Incense — Try protection scents, use stick incense of frankincense, sandalwood, lavender or rosemary. Or stroke auras with a corn shuck or wheat ear, or use sprinkling with corn meal or water.

Flowers and altar decorations — Use green corn ears, corn dollies, green wheat stalks, vegetables, fall flowers, and animal images.

Oil for animal blessings — Use a magickal Protection Oil, Blessing Oil, clear salad oil, or a bowl of corn meal.

A larger bead, charm or gemstone with ring or tie for each animal; place them in a bowl on the altar. The women can each bring these.

Photos of pets or pets themselves.

Optional — Audio tape by Kay Gardner, *Avalon: Solo Flute Meditations* (Ladyslipper Music, P.O. Box 3124, Durham, NC 27705), 1989.

Potluck dinner contributions/pet treats.

Matches to light candles and incense, ritual wand.

The altar is set up and ritual is ready before the women bring the animals into the room. Allow them to be interested and get settled before starting. They will probably go to sleep.

Outline

Light candles.

Purify — With incense, corn shuck, wheat ear or sprinkling.

Cast circle/Invoke animal Goddesses for the elements and spirit.

> Earth — Epona (or Rhiannon), protector of horses (Wales).
> Air — Bast, Goddess of cats large and small (Egypt).
> Fire — Bau (Gula Bau or Hecate), guardian of dogs (Egypt).

> Water — Rainbow Serpent, Snake Goddess (Australia).
> Spirit — Artemis, Lady of all Animals, Lady of the Beasts
>   (Greece).

Read "The Charge of the Goddess."

Invocation — Use the following or choose another.

"She is the dark night and the black soil that holds within itself the intense powers of light, the secrets and the forces of all life. She is the mouth, the vagina, the passionate and wise source from which all comes and to which all returns. . . .

"The black-winged night laid a silver egg (the moon) in the womb of darkness, in the dark waters. The divine one resided in that egg during a whole year. Then she by herself alone divided the two halves and out of these halves She formed heaven and earth."[4]

The high priestess says:

"We are here to turn the Wheel once more, and honor the Lady's beasts. We are here to give thanks at this first harvest for the creatures who are our companions. We welcome them to this circle. Blessed be."

Meditation — "Imagine yourself as the she-wolf running free, leading the pack, high priestess of animals. Scent the air, nurse your puppies, call your mate . . . Imagine a dog or cat on the street, struggling to survive. See the world from her view for awhile. Be that dog or cat and give her love, comfort and blessing . . . Then imagine yourself as your own pet. See her life and your life from her eyes. Be a cat or dog taking care of her human. Realize how she takes care of you. Send her love. Come back to now."

Body of ritual — Each woman talks about her experiences in the meditation, then about her relationship with her own pet. She faces her pet (or holds up its photo) and says:

> (Name), I thank you for being in my life because _____.
> I honor your Be-ing.
> I wish for you a long, peaceful and happy life.
> I ask you to be _____ in my life as my partner and
> companion. (Touch animal's third eye with oil or corn meal.)

The woman presents her charm to her pet, to be put on its collar later or kept for her. She blesses the charm in the name of the Goddess of the Animals, Lady of the Beasts, charging it for protection.

Raise power — Play the flute music of Kay Gardner's audio tape *Avalon*,[5] or a live flute or recorder, as the women raise power silently. Visualize a circle of blue light surrounding you and your animal and visualize the two of you together. Be Goddesses, Diana and her hound, Bast and her cats, etc. Make your pet a gift of every wish you want for her, health, long life, prosperity, happiness. Offer it to her as the charm from the ritual. Let the music play awhile before stopping it. Direct the cone of power to making those gifts manifest and to protection for your pet.

Ground — Send excess energy to homeless animals, animals in need, for comfort and safety.

Open circle/Hug pets and each other.

Give out pet treats.

Potluck dinner.

Fall Equinox (September 20-23)

The Fall or Autumn Equinox is the witches Thanksgiving and the source, in its Native American version, of the national holidays in Canada and the United States. The Sabbat is also called Mabon, for Queen Mab of the Faery People (Maeve of the Celts). This is the time of the actual harvest, the promise made at Solstice and Lammas now fulfilled. The Earth Mother gives to her children great nourishment and abundance, the means of surviving the barren time of winter soon to come. The fruit and grains gathered in are the last stores of life: with the death of the plants is the birth and the mystery of the seed. All growth is held in suspension and silence within. At the harvest season of Fall Equinox, women remember the sprouting of the seeds in Spring, springs of the past and to come, and remember the earth that produced them.

The Goddess born as the Yule Child has reached menopause; she no longer bears and she ages. Inanna approaches the last gate of Erishkegal's palace, all but one of her jewels removed, the last to be taken at Hallows. Persephone is in the underworld, and Demeter stops all life on earth until her return. In the Eleusinian Mysteries, celebrated until the fourth century in Greece at Fall Equinox, a single stalk of wheat was presented as symbol of the sacred mystery of Demeter and her daughter: life gone into death until the miracle of rebirth. The cycle of Persephone, Demeter and Hecate was the central religion and religious mystery of the world for nearly two thousand years.

The women's mysteries at Eleusis were open to all, peasants and nobles, slaves and freeborn. The initiation and rituals were so powerful they were described as life-changing, yet so sacred that no one in all the centuries ever divulged their secrets. The rituals have

never been described in full. The Lesser Eleusinian Mysteries
happened at Spring Equinox, with the Greater Mysteries at Fall
Equinox. They were based on the Persephone-Demeter cycle:

> The ceremonies continued for eight days. On the first day, a procession
> of women carried the sacred objects, including the comb of Demeter,
> her mirror, a snake figure and some wheat or barley, to the temple. On
> the second day, the initiates purified themselves in the sea, which was
> bonded to the Goddess "in the very ancient sacred legends," and put on
> new linen garments. On the third day, offerings were made to the two
> Goddesses. On the fifth day, the procession returned to the temple, for
> sacred dance and song. On the next day began the secret rites, of which
> we know almost nothing. Probably the following night brought the cul-
> minating experience of the initiation, the sacred vision. In a crowded
> hall, in perfect silence, something occurred which so changed the lives
> of the initiates that it was described as eliminating the fear of death.
> Some occurrence on the psychic plane, some collective vision left an
> indelible impression on everyone present.[6]

The stalk of wheat presented in silence, was the week's most sacred
culmination. The mysteries have been lost.

Themes for Fall Equinox in today's women's craft include
thanksgiving, healing and earth healing. In this era of great danger
to the planet's ecology, the body of the Goddess, women work on
concrete and psychic levels to make changes. The damage done to
the planet is also damage done to women's bodies and Be-ings. The
following ritual of earth and women's healing is a way of reclaiming
consequence for women and the Goddess/planet. It goes along with
activism in changing things.

Tarot cards for Fall Equinox include Judgement and the
World. The World is everything achieved, the harvest of dreams and
realities rewarded for hard work. Judgement is the healing of the
earth, universe and women's lives. Goddesses for the Sabbat in-
clude grain and corn mothers, three-fold Goddesses, mother God-
desses and Goddesses of healing. Some of them include: Persephone,
Demeter and Hecate (Greece), Proserpine and Ceres (Rome), Mawu
(Africa), Ata Bey (Caribbean), Spider Woman (Native America), The
Corn Mothers (Native America), Tonantzin (Mexico), Chicomecoatl
(South America), Baubo (Greece), Gula (Babylonia), Amaterasu
(Japan), Ishtar (Semitic), Isis (Egypt), Freya (Norway), Inanna and
Erishkegal (Sumer), Changing Woman (Native America), The Morri-
gan (Ireland), The Three Fates (Greece), The Norns (Scandinavia),
Fortuna (Rome), Sarasvati, Parvati and Lakshmi (India), Yemaya
(West Africa), Kwan Yin (China), and Mary (Christian).

Candles for the altar include fall colors of dark green, gold, orange, brown, dark red, and yellow. Decorate the altar with fall leaves, dried corn, gourds, wheat stalks, fall flowers and a bowl of fall fruit. Foods for the Sabbat include apples, grains, root vegetables, nuts and squash. Put a pomegranate[7] on the altar to eat after grounding in the ritual. Use a globe of the earth in the ritual that follows.

Fall Equinox — Planetary Healing

This is a ritual involving any of the many healing methods used in Women's Spirituality craft. Touch-healing/laying on of hands is extremely simple and powerful. The women place their hands lightly, palms down over the chakras of a woman receiving the healing. They rest their hands gently or hold them just above the woman's body, and keep them in place for a period of up to five minutes for each chakra or placement.[8] Each woman touches one chakra, and the women work with each other in pairs, or several women together as a group in each healing. The woman receiving the energy lies on her back, completely relaxed. The healers touch no private parts of the body, and do no pushing, pulling or other forceful movements. The women may be clothed or skyclad, and they take turns in the ritual at receiving healing energy from each other or the group.

Need

Candles — Fall colors of dark green, orange, gold, brown, dark red.

Incense — Use rosemary, sandalwood, vervain or myrrh for healing, or purify with sprinkling salt water or aura stroking.

Flowers — Red leaves, corn dollies, dried corn, gourds, wheat stalks, fall flowers (mums, marigolds, etc.).

Place a bowl of fruit or nuts on the altar, and/or a pomegranate.

A globe of the world.

Invocation/Poem — Use the one that follows or choose others.

A pitcher of water and some glasses.

Matches to light candles and incense, charcoal block for loose incense, ritual wand.

Outline

Light candles.

Purify — With incense smoke, aura stroking or sprinkling.

Cast circle/Invoke Earth Goddesses:
  Earth — Tonantzin, Corn Mother who feeds her children
      (Mexico).
  Air — Nuit, Goddess of the night sky whose body shields
      the planet (Egypt).
  Fire — Pele, whose fire builds continents and can de-
      stroy them (Polynsesia).
  Water — Yemaya, ocean of all life, the womb (W. Africa).
  Spirit — Gaia, the Great Mother Earth (Greece).
Read "The Charge of the Goddess."
Women in the circle chant each woman's name in turn:

(*Name*) be well, (*Name*) be well,
All manner of things shall be well. (by Z. Budapest)

Invocation — High priestess reads the following:

Kore Chant: Fall Equinox
by Starhawk
Her name cannot be spoken,
Her face was not forgotten,
Her power is to open,
Her promise can never be broken.

All seeds she deeply buries,
She weaves the thread of seasons.
Her secret, darkness carries,
She loves beyond all reason.

She changes everything She touches, and
Everything She touches, changes (Repeat chant).
Change is, touch is; Touch is, change is.
Change us! Touch us! Touch us! Change us!

Everything lost is found again,
In a new form, in a new way.
Everything hurt is healed again,
In a new life, In a new day.[9]

The high priestess says:
  "The fall is a time of healing. Women of the Hopi enter the kivas
for the fall healing ceremonies, and women of the circle work to heal

themselves, each other and the Goddess Earth. Each woman tonight gives healing and receives it, and she shares her blessings in a healing for the planet."

Meditation — Travel in a rocket ship or on your own wings up into the sky and out of the earth's atmosphere. Fly into outer space and look down on the planet from above. See all the things on earth that need healing and changing. See them and observe them with compassion. Circle the earth flying and with each circle make a circle of light to surround the planet. With every circled flight, see some wrong healed, some illness of the earth made well again. Circle the planet flying until all the ills are gone. Fly back to the circle and come back to now.

Body of the ritual — Each woman in turn goes to the center of the circle for healing. She lies on her back quietly, and the women of the group place their hands on her body, over the chakras, and over any pain area, moving from head to feet. They place their hands over her heart for emotional healing, on her head and both feet for connection with the universe and earth. Use Reiki positions, polarity placements, laying on of stones or crystals, touch-healing methods. The women hum to raise energy while holding their hands in place for up to five minutes on each position. They visualize her happy and well while touching her. When they complete the healing, the woman rises slowly, rejoins the circle, and the next woman comes to the center. Repeat for all of the group. Have a pitcher of water and some glasses in the circle, the women will want water after their healings. Keep the room relatively warm, especially if working skyclad.

In the circle again, pass around a small globe of the earth. Each woman places her hands on a part of the earth or over the whole globe, sending healing through her hands, and speaking of what needs to be healed (Africa, China, South America, Alaska, the United States government, pollution, famine, the rain forests, AIDS, oil spills, dolphins, apartheid, etc.). All visualize the earth healed, green, peaceful, and her people and animals all healed, well-fed and safe.

Raise power — Use songs or chants to raise the cone of power. Send it to selves for healing, others, the planet.

Ground — Pass around the bowl of fruit or a pomegranate cut in half on a plate. Each woman eats a piece of the fruits of life, death and healing. The seeds are in the womb of the Mother.

Open circle/Hugs.

Have a potluck or give-away.

Some songs to raise power for this ritual include:

> The earth is our mother, we must take care of her,
> The earth is our mother, we must take care of her.
>
> Hey and a ho, and a hey, ya ya.

or

> The river is flowing,
> Flowing and growing.
> The river is flowing,
> Down to the sea.
> Mother, carry me,
> Child I shall always be.
> Mother, carry me,
> Down to the sea.

or

> I circle around, I circle around,
> The boundaries of the earth.
> Wearing my long wing feathers as I fly.

or

> May Artemis protect you,
> and Hera provide you,
> and the woman-soul within you.
> Guide your way home. (by Z. Budapest)

Hallows (October 31)

Hallows, Hallowmas, Samhain or All Hallows Eve is the ending and beginning of the year cycle and the witches' New Year. This is the night to turn the Wheel to a new start by descending into death to be reborn. The veils between death and living are thinnest on this night, with possibility for connection with those passed over. It's a good night for scrying, divination, contacting spirit guides, and contacting dead foremothers, pets, or loved ones. In entering the labyrinth of death on Hallows night, women also enter the womb of reincarnation and rebirth. The cauldron of Ceridwyn, the womb that separates death from life and connects them again, is the central symbol of this Sabbat.

At Hallows, Persephone in the underworld is visited by Demeter who pleads for her return to earth. The mother leaves Hecate's death realm with Persephone in her womb, growing toward rebirth at Yule. Inanna has been in the underworld dead for three days at Hallows, when her faithful friend Ninshuber goes into action to release her. The descent into the labyrinth has reached its bottom-most darkness and ascent is about to begin again. The meaning of endings in the wiccan craft is new beginnings. The Wheel of the Year is a circle, and circles have no end.

The Sabbat is also a night to remember foremothers, both of women's family lines and of women's cultural ones. Foremothers are named and invited into the circle, and a remembrance of the World War II holocaust in Europe and the Burning Times of the thirteenth to seventeenth centuries is made. In the Burning Times in Europe, an estimated nine million witches and healers were executed by fire and hanging, driving the Goddess religion deeply underground and decimating healing knowledge and women's cul-ture. In Italy, hundreds of women walked into the sea to drown, rather than allow the Inquisition to jail and burn them. Many Women's Spirituality participants have past-life recalls of these times; many women alive today were incarnated then. The empha-sis at Hallows is not on bitterness, but on love and compassion, and the understanding that what is gone is not lost, what dies is reborn. It's an understanding and affirmation of women's herstory and personal pasts, and a deep honoring of those gone before.

The Motherpeace tarot cards for Hallows include The Crone, the Nine of Discs and the Death card. Hallows is an honoring of old age and solitary work; Demeter at Hallows is alone on earth waiting for her child to return. Persephone is in the underworld/womb still. The Yule Child of last winter is an ancient Crone, readying for death and renewal. The Death card means letting go. honoring and affirm-ing endings to make way for new births. After death in wicce, birth soon follows.

Goddesses for the Sabbat include Crone aspects, the ancient grandmothers of every culture. These are some of the most powerful Goddesses known to the Wheel of the Year. Some of them are: Hecate (Greece), Kali (India), Oya (Africa), Sedna (Inuit), Copper Woman (Native America), Spider Grandmother (Native America), Baba Yaga (Russia), Yellow Land Earth Queen (China), Yemaya-Olokun (West Africa), Inanna and Erishkegal (Sumer), Ceridwyn (Wales), Nepthys (Egypt), Tara (Ireland), The Morrigan (Ireland), Hella and the Norns (Scandinavia), The Furies (Greece), The Fates (Greece), The Old Woman Who Never Dies (Native America), Persephone (Greece), Proserpina (Rome), Mother Holle (Germany) and Isis (Egypt).

In Mexico, the Sabbat is dedicated to Tonantzin/Guadalupe as

El Dia de las Muertes (Day of the Dead). Lasting a week, the series of ceremonies honors those who have died, including Las Angelitas, a day for remembering dead children. In Egypt, the Sabbat is the Isia, Isis' search for Osiris and mourning for his death and loss. In Ireland, Hallows is the Day of the Banshees, spirits who wail when a death occurs, and in Scandinavia it is the Rites of Hella, asking the Goddess of the underworld to raise and release the dead. The Hopi third women's healing ceremony, Owaqlt ("Melons on the Vine"), honors women as the receptacles for seeds of new life. The observance has sexual connotations.[10]

Decorate the Hallows altar with fruits and flowers of late fall, pumpkins, nuts, dried corn ears, a pomegranate, pinecones and apples. Use a scrying bowl in the center of the circle for a cauldron, a bowl filled with water and a crystal at the bottom. Another bowl holds salt water, and a third bowl seeds, acorns or nuts in the shells. The candles for Hallows are black and white. Foods are pumpkin pie, popcorn, candy-apples, the candy skulls used in Mexico, and favorite ethnic/traditional dishes. This is a good Sabbat to hold a potluck.

Hallows — A Ritual of Endings

Hallows is a Sabbat to use incense for, rather than other methods of purification. Do not neglect purification on this Sabbat. One of the bowls in the ritual, incense burner or scrying bowl particularly, should be a larger cauldron type, as a cauldron is the primary symbol of the Sabbat. Place the scrying bowl in the center of the circle. This is a quiet ritual and a highly powerful one. Drums can be used softly, as a heartbeat raising power, but use them in controlled ways. Where death is celebrated, life is particularly important. The nonfeminist craft does The Great Rite at Hallows, the ritual of making love. Do a potluck dinner after this Sabbat's ritual, or some other form of celebration to lighten the contemplative mood.

Need

Candles —White candles on the altar, lit at the start of the ritual, and a central pair of black and white candles not lit until within the ritual.

Incense — Use sage or cedar smudge sticks, or rosemary, frankincense or sandalwood loose incense for purification and protection. Try sweetgrass to call the spirits of ancestors into the circle.

Flowers — Flowers and fruits of late fall, chrysanthemums,

pinecones, dried seed pods, nuts, apples, pumpkins, gourds, dried corn ears; a pomegranate is traditional for this Sabbat.

Bowl of water and salt.

Bowl of seeds, acorns or nuts in the shell.

Scrying bowl — Dark-sided bowl containing clear water and a crystal, or use a crystal ball or dark mirror.

Oils for Self-blessing/mirror.

Optional — Play these selections on audio tape: Charlie Murphy, "The Burning Times," on *Catch the Fire* (Good Fairy Productions, P.O. Box 12188, Broadway Station, Seattle, WA 98102), and/or Catherine Madsen, "Allu Mari Mi Portati," on *The Patience of Love* (Wormwood Productions, P.O. Box 6167, E. Lansing, MI 48823).

Contributions for potluck dinner.

Matches for candles and incense, charcoal block for loose incense, ritual wand.

Outline

Light candles — Leave a central black and white candle unlit.

Purify — Use incense, sweetgrass or a smudge stick.

Cast circle/Invoke Goddess of death, rebirth and immortality.

> Earth — Hecate, Goddess of endings and beginnings (Greece).
>
> Air — Ceridwyn, Goddess of rebirth and karma (Wales).
>
> Fire — Kali, Goddess of death and re-claiming (India).
>
> Water — Yemaya-Olokun, Goddess of the all-taking sea (Yoruba West Africa).
>
> Spirit — Spider Grandmother, Goddess of the web of immortality (Native America).

Read "The Charge of the Goddess" or play Shekinah Mountainwater's sung version on *Songs and Chants of the Goddess, Vol. I.*

Go around the circle, each woman naming herself and her foremothers, as far back as she knows their names:

"I am _____, daughter of _____, granddaughter of _____, great-greatgranddaughter of _____. I honor my foremothers and invite them to this ritual."

Go around the circle again, each woman inviting the presence of other positive Be-ings, living or not, human or animal, into the ritual. Say a few words of who each is, but keep it short.

Invocation — Use the following or choose others. the high priestess says:

"This is the night of the grandmothers, Goddesses of death and immortality. We invite them into the circle: Ceridwyn, Old Woman, Hecate, Copper woman, Mother Kali and Oya. We welcome them as friends, celebrating the connection between death and life."

Invocation Poem

They who are dead were as alive as we and we have not forgotten. We too will die and we will not be forgot. In our ceaseless file from mystery to mystery, through the veil of life and death and soft November dusk — Are we all alive or like the dead? Let no one say.

I am the seed of the husk that lies dead; I am the husk of those the seeds to come. The corn I plant is the bond between us all; and may our earth attest there be no stop.[11]

Meditation — This is the best night of the year to do past life regressions. Find the procedure in any number of books on the subject.

Body of Ritual — The high priestess passes around the bowl of salt water and says:

"This is a cauldron for banishing fears. Give them to Hecate, to Ceridwyn or Oya, as a purification and banishing of the ending year." The women name their fears and put them into the bowl. The bowl goes around until all the fears are banished.

The high priestess passes around the bowl of seeds, nuts or acorns, saying:

"Take a seed. In the seed are the beginnings and hopes for the new year, for goals and wishes coming soon to replace the fears that were banished." The women each take a seed, and name a hope.

The women move close to the scrying bowl at the center of the circle. In a short meditation, the high priestess says: "Go to a place of joy in the past, a place of joy in the present, and a place of joy in the future." (She gives them time to experience each.) "Invite (don't command) a foremother, spirit guide or Goddess to join you. She has a message or a gift for you, receive it. When you have received her gift and her blessing, come back to now and the circle." (She gives each step time to happen fully.)

The high priestess lights the black candle, then the white one. "These candles symbolize the old and the new, the banishing of fear and the invoking of hope, the harvest and the plantings to come, death and life. At Hallows we turn the Wheel of the Year and death becomes new life."

Play the audio tape of Charlie Murphy's "The Burning Times" or Catherine Madsen's "Allu Mari Mi Portati," and take a moment of silence, honoring and remembrance for the women who died in the Inquisition and the Holocaust, for all who have died for what they believe, and for all who have died of AIDS. These songs could also be used as the invocation for this ritual.

Raise power — Use humming or drumbeat, or Starhawk's chant, "She changes everything She touches, and everything She touches changes" (*The Spiral Dance*, p. 88), to raise power. Send the energy toward banishing evil in the world, banishing women's fears, banishing patriarchy, and invoking hope and peace.

Ground.

Self-blessing/mirrors.

Pass around a pomegranate, cut in half on a plate. Everyone eats some of it. Persephone ate four pomegranate seeds and therefore lives in the underworld four months of the year. The seeds are death in life and the fruit is the womb.

Open circle/Ground again.

Group hugs.

Potluck dinner.

The Wheel of the Year begins again with Yule, which is the next Sabbat, the Goddess's rebirthing six weeks away. (Some traditions place the beginning and ending of the Wheel at different Sabbats.) Women who celebrate the Sabbats regularly, following the Wheel for at least one full year's cycle, see major changes in their lives and in their attitudes. There is a great sense of peace and certainty, a great sense of women's power and consequence, in becoming a part of the Wheel. Celebrating the cycles of the earth brings women into oneness with all Beings, with the sources and cycles of the Goddess life force and that life force in themselves.

The next two chapters deal with Rites of Passage rituals, in which a woman's own life is celebrated and ritualized from birth to death.

Notes

1. Lynn Langsoeur, "Holiday Foods," in *Sage Woman Magazine* (P.O. Box 5130, Santa Cruz, CA 95063), Vol. II, No. 7, Fall 1988, p. 18.

2. Z. Budapest, *The Rise of the Fates: A Mystical Comedy in Eight Acts* (Los Angeles, CA: Susan B. Anthony Coven No. 1, 1976), pp. 85-86.

3. Lynn Langsoeur, "Holiday Foods," in *Sage Woman*, Fall 1988, p. 18.

4. Monica Sjoo and Barbara Mor, *The Great Cosmic Mother: Rediscovering the Religion of the Earth* (San Francisco: Harper and Row, 1987), p. 55.

5. Kay Gardner, *Avalon: Solo Flute Meditations,* audio tape (Ladyslipper Records, P.O. Box 3124, Durham, NC 27705), 1989. Send for the Ladyslipper catalog.

6. "The Eleusinian Mysteries," in *The Crescent* (Re-Formed Congregation of the Goddess, P.O. Box 6021, Madison, WI 53716), Vol. I, No. 3, September 1988, pp. 1-2.

7. Lynn Langoseur, "Holiday Foods," in *Sage Woman,* Fall 1988, p. 18.

8. See Diane Stein, *All Women Are Healers* (Freedom, CA, The Crossing Press, 1990), Chapters I-II for more information on this type of healing work.

9. Starhawk, *The Spiral Dance: A Rebirth of the Ancient Religion of The Great Goddess* (San Francisco: Harper and Row, 1979), pp. 88-89.

10. Diane Stein, *The Goddess Book of Days* (St. Paul: Llewellyn Publications, 1988), October 27-November 1 entries.

11. Adapted from Frank Waters, *The Man Who Killed the Deer* (New York: Pocket books, 1971, original 1941), p. 33.

Chapter Seven

───────────○───────────

Rites of Passage I
Birth to Bonding

Modern society has a great affinity for machines and money, but very little for human concerns, especially concerns that are primarily women's. It has become inappropriate among most groups of people to own or show feelings, and real values are often lost in a quest for material things that attempts to fill the great emotional void. When women are hurting they often have no one to talk to about it; when women reach life changes they often do it alone. Buying a new car is something to celebrate in today's society, but reaching menopause is kept hidden and is not. Taking an island vacation is a cause of envy and much discussion, and a status symbol, but declaring life-bonding with one's lover (particularly if lesbian or gay) is considered inappropriate to make a fuss over. A new pair of status-brand tennis shoes is a topic for conversation at the office, but the death of a friend is something not talked about.

Women lose the most in the yuppie revolution, as it is women's concerns and values that are left by the wayside. In order to hold a fast-track career job in today's society, a woman forfeits family and children and most of her evenings at home. To be one of the boys in a boys' world, women forgo their femininity — menstrual cramps or their daughter's chicken pox or a lover in the hospital have to be ignored. Patriarchy has forced women into a male mold for the sake of "passing" and surviving, for the sake of getting ahead where women are not valued or wanted. The dilemma is even more intensified for women of color, who have to overcome racism to enter the system at all, in addition to the problems of being there. Despite the gains of the feminist movement in terms of women's opportunities and equality, women still earn only sixty percent of what men earn, work twice as hard to earn it, and have lost their souls in the earning. And this is in the wealthy and free Western world, where conditions are the easiest.

The patriarchy has done its utmost to separate women from each other. Work is a male forum, where women enter and exist at the system's or a boss' whim. Home for the housewife is an isolation cell. She is dependent and has children to raise but is lacking connection and community. Women on welfare have it both ways — they are dominated by the system and isolated within it — and face crushing poverty besides. The women's and feminist communities are more autonomous but have lately bought into prevailing values, accepting money and gadgets as the measure of all worth, and forfeiting caring and compassion. Among feminists, the rationale is that women have been exploited too long for their caring. The days of networking to help others are mostly over, and competition over cooperation is too much the rule. In the Women's Spirituality communities caring, networking, compassion and real values are still very much evident. The members of this community are primarily women who were there at the beginnings of the women's movement, have grown up with it actively, and see the forest for the trees. "The personal is political" is still their rule, and the personal and political are also Goddess.

In the early matriarchal societies where women were seen as images of Goddess and the sources of all life, values were very different from today's. Where women celebrated the Wheel of the Year, the phases of the moon, and the individual life passages of members of the community, the focus was not on money or material possessions. The ancient equivalent of the new car was a lot less important than the birth of a new baby. The passage into menopause, power held within to use in wisdom, was a more important event than the right type of shoes. If a woman in the community was in childbirth, sick or dying, all the women of that community took time to be available and help. A society that values life is a far different one than what we have today: a patriarchy that bases its worth/ship (worship) on money, war, one-upmanship, misogyny and death.

Early societies revered women as the life force, and revered life as the most basic of values. All the stages of life from birth through passing over were equally honored, as women of each age group had specific contributions to bring to all. There wasn't time in a communal society to envy or compete for what someone else possessed, everyone had much the same. It was a waste of energy to compete with someone else's skills, as each woman had her own and all the skills were needed. Effort was placed on making the culture function smoothly, and on food, shelter, clothing,and safety for everyone.

Women's skills and values, considered inappropriate and so much denigrated by the patriarchy, are the skills and values that make civilization possible. Video games and VCRs are not life-essentials; the growing and gathering of food is. Money and status fall by the wayside when placed against the importance of midwifery to bring babies to birth safely. The right brand of car loses out to the value of caring for others, whether as someone who listens to a friend in need, someone who mothers, or someone who offers care to the elderly. Without women's values and discoveries, without women's compassion and caring, there would be no society worth saving. The patriarchy cannot bleed monthly or give birth, and so places its values on a parody of it — bloodshed by war. It has erased women and women's values and threatens to blow up the planet or make it ecologically uninhabitable. Only the life-blood shed by women can reclaim us all.

In the matriarchal Goddess cultures, every woman was an image of the Goddess, and every woman as that image had worth and value to herself and to her community. The issue of women's self-worth and consequence, so crucial in reclaiming women and women's values today, was self-evident in the old cultures. Where every woman was Goddess, the changes in the lives of women were important. They were something to notice, to celebrate, affirm and ritualize. Births were important because life was valued, the mother's and the child's. No child was a product of rape, and resources were available to feed every Be-ing. Bondings were important because the members of the community cared about each other, valued love with each other, and because it could lead to new births. Same-sex bondings were as respected as heterosexual ones. Menarche made a girl into a woman, a full-fledged contributing member of the community, and menopause, as the end of menstruation, gave a woman entrance into the society of the governing and the wise. Death was ritualized as both ending and beginning, a way of comforting those remaining and helping them to deal with grief.

With every rite of passage and rite of passage ritual came the message, "You are cared about and loved. You are valued. You have worth in this community. You are wanted and needed here." This sense of belonging and having a place, a purpose in the world, is the major thing missing from women's lives in today's value-deprived culture. When women's rites of passage and ages are marked with communal gatherings and rituals, women feel wanted and needed. A woman who has that feeling has self-worth, and her ability to contribute meaningfully to society goes with it. A woman of consequence and worth in society is a woman who has the strength to make changes in her world.

Rites of passage today are only bare remnants of what they once were. Birthdays are times for gift-giving and sending cards, but can also be very lonely when without personal closeness. Most see birthday celebrations as children's events. Weddings are heterosexual-only in modern Western culture, unlike in the Goddess matriarchies. Women who bond with other women often hide it to survive in the patriarchal world, and lack communal celebration of their love. Heterosexual weddings are less love rituals than family spectacles, costing fortunes to produce and designed to maximize the bride's intake of gifts and money. Menarche and menopause are a public embarrassment, things not mentioned, to the pain and confusion of those experiencing them as life-changing. Burial in modern society is a travesty, a frantic and expensive way of denying death or turning it into a party, with little to offer the bereaved or the one that's gone. When rites of passage are celebrated today, they are celebrated monetarily and superficially, with gifts and parties not always connected to caring or emotional fulfillment. Women make the passages from birth to death with a feeling that something is lacking, often something they can't define. They lack a feeling of belonging in the world, of having a place and purpose in a central plan.

As the Women's Spirituality movement develops, women are turning their attention to individual rites of passage rituals, to honoring women and women's life changes. By doing so, they are discovering how powerful these passages are when celebrated in ritual, how important an event each passage can be with community or as self-validation. They are discovering how much this validation adds to self-worth and their sense of consequence. Women doing and experiencing these rituals also are reclaiming real values in a value-starved world. They return caring, compassion, love for others and self-love to society for the fulfillment and good of all.

The rituals in this chapter and Chapter 8 are women's rites of passage rituals. They are designed to validate a specific woman at specific times of her life, to offer her caring and love at those peak times. They are also designed to connect the woman/Goddess-within to the Wheel of birth, growth, maturity, aging and death. By connection to these cycles, women experience their lives as meaningful, as having purpose in a universal way. By saying to a woman at her changes, "You are Goddess. You are loved," rites of passage rituals help to reclaim the Goddess matriarchies.

Wiccaning

In the nonfeminist craft, wiccaning is a ceremony to present the new baby to the Goddess and God and to ask their blessings and protection for the child. A Goddessmother and Godfather come forth, vowing to protect the child until she is old enough to choose her own path. In feminist rituals of all sorts, only the Goddess as mother is invoked (the major difference between feminist and traditional wicce), and a Goddessmother may be present for the wiccaning. The infant is welcomed and blessed, and the child's mother has equally earned honoring. The pregnancy ritual that begins Chapter 8 also focuses on the mother.

Birth is a celebration of reawakening. The baby has returned to the earthplane from the place where souls go at death; she has been reincarnated, has chosen to return for another round of learning at life in a body. The child's mother is the vehicle for that incarnation and is part of the mother and child's life agreement. The mother has gone to the underworld in the birth process, the labyrinth of death and life; there she has fetched the child's soul for her returning, at risk to her own survival. It's the story of Demeter and Persephone. In the ritual, the baby is blessed, protected and welcomed to the earthplane, and the mother is honored for her descent and their safe return.

Giving birth in today's culture is a high-tech experience. There are machines and monitors, the mother is forced to lie down and be strapped down in an unnatural position, there are a variety of drugs, and the high rate of unnecessary cesarean sections too often makes it major surgery. Women's bodies and wombs are taken away from them and their birthings are given to doctors and hospitals at medicine's scheduled convenience. Birth in modern culture is an illness to treat, not something natural and powerful to celebrate. Many women ask for natural childbirth but not as many receive it. Midwives often work underground, or are so legally restricted that they cannot prevent the medical system's abuses to the mother and infant. Many women come through the childbirth experience traumatized, and many babies are born traumatized as well.

In a gentle and natural birthing, the baby is delivered at home by a midwife, without machines, monitors, drugs, or surgeries. Episiotomy is often unnecessary and is not routinely performed. The mother is surrounded by people she asks to be there, people she trusts and loves, to help her bring new life into the world. She is free to move around. The baby is received with love, sometimes born underwater, and protected as much as possible from feeling fear and shock. Such babies are happier and healthier infants and their mothers are happier and more empowered as well.

A wiccaning ritual is a validation of the birth process for the mother and child. If they have been subjected to the terrors of technology, the ritual is a reclaiming of gentler ways. If they have been able to experience a pleasant natural birthing, the ritual continues that positive energy. Women after the birth experience need validation and attention; they are tired, have come through a life-changing experience, and most of their family and friends' attention is now focused on the baby. The infant may or may not care about the ritual or the blessings she receives, but the blessings go to both the child and mother.

In the story of Briar Rose, twelve good fairies each bring blessings to the girl at her birth, the thirteenth fairy offering her death instead. In a Goddess reclaiming of that story, the last gift is the one that makes all the others possible, and the thirteenth fairy is not evil, only realistic. The gift of death is also the gift of reincarnation. Thirteen has always been a magickal number in the Goddess craft; there are thirteen full moons in a year, and the full moon is begun by the thirteenth night of the cycle. There were traditionally thirteen women in a coven, twelve and the high priestess. Was it the high priestess of the evening who presented the thirteenth gift to Briar Rose?

The wishes for the new baby in this ritual and to the infant's mother all are blessings. They welcome the child and celebrate the mother's survival of her birthing. The child's chakra blessing is similar to the Self-blessing and opens the baby's energy centers for balance, well-being, connection to Goddess and psychic opening. The baby is carried to the four elements and spirit and is presented to the Goddess, to the earth and universe in the circle, invoking protection and blessings for her life. The women in the ritual celebrate new life and the process of birth as a remembering of the Goddess birthing the universe. As Goddess-within, they see the ritual as a protection and blessing for the child, the child's mother, the Goddess, and themselves. What is given in blessings, too comes back three- (or ten-) fold.

Decorate the altar with abundant flowers in white and pastels and light several pastel candles. The altar is very bright and colorful. If there are gifts for the baby, place them on the altar, too. In traditional wicce, the child's first gifts are often her first magical tools. The mother and child rest on a soft chair in the center of the circle. Goddesses for this ritual are mother Goddesses and Goddesses of childbirth. Some of them are: Kwan Yin (China), Yemaya (West Africa), Isis (Egypt), Mary (Christian), Ix Chel (South America), Tonantzin (Mexico), Lucina (Italy), Lucia (Sweden), Carmen or Carmenta (Rome), Artemis (Greece), Oddudua (West Africa), Erzulie (Haiti), Guadalupe (Mexico), Parvati (India), Chalchiuhtlique (South America), Changing Woman (Navaho), Demeter (Greece), The Norns (Scandinavia), and Astarte (Semitic). The Motherpeace tarot cards for this wiccaning are the Aces for new births and beginnings, and the The Fool for all potential. Foods for afterwards are reminders of fertility: beans, green salads and sprouts, milk and decorated eggs.

A New Baby Ritual

Decorate the altar in pastels, with light colored flowers and candles. A bowl of eggs makes a good fertility symbol, dye them colors, and place gifts for the baby on the altar. Make sure the mother and infant are comfortable in the circle's center and that the room is warm enough. The naming and chakra blessing are done by the high priestess, or any other woman chosen for it. The chakra blessing is a version of the Self-blessing. Handle the baby quietly and keep this a quiet, gentle ritual.

Need

Pastel flowers and candles on the altar. Try daisies for this ritual.

Incense — Rose for love and trust, or amber for clarity. Use stick incense, billows of smoke are not appropriate. Or purify using a flower or sprinkling with salt water.

Blessing oil — Use a magickal Blessing Oil, Protection Oil, rose oil or clear olive oil, natural oils only.

A bowl of colored eggs to decorate the altar.

Gifts for mother and baby, if any, are on the altar.

Invocation and Poem — Use those below or choose others.

Comfortable armchair in center of the circle for mother and baby.

Place a lit candle or small altar with candle, at each of the directions of the room, with a symbol for that element. Use a crystal for earth, a candle for fire, a seashell for water, and a feather for air. Use an empty dark-sided bowl for spirit.

Matches to light incense and candles with, ritual wand (or use a daisy to cast the circle).

Outline

Light candles — On altar and at the elements and spirit.

Purify —With incense, sprinkling, or stroking auras. Do the purification on the infant, but keep incense a little away from her.

Cast circle/Invoke mother and child Goddesses.

> Earth — Oddudua, Mother of the Goddesses (Africa).
>
> Air — Lucina, midwife of new births (Italy).
>
> Fire — Demeter, Mother of Persephone and the world (Greece).
>
> Water — Isis, Mother Goddess (Egypt).
>
> Spirit — Kwan Yin, protector of mothers and children (China).

Other Goddesses to invoke include: Earth – Befana, protector of children (Italy); Air – Artemis, Midwife Goddess (Greece); Fire – Tonantzin, Mother Goddess (Mexico); Water – Ix Chel, Midwife Goddess (South America); and Spirit – Demeter, Mother of Persephone and the earth (Greece).

Invocation — The high priestess says:

"We are here to celebrate (*mother's name*) safe childbirth and welcome (*child's name*) back to the earthplane. The Goddesses of childbirth — Eileithia and Artemis, Ix Chel and Yemaya — have blessed them and us to make a new mother and a new infant. We celebrate (*mother's name*) for her courage, for her successful journey to the underworld. In Sparta childbirth was equated with going to war. We celebrate (*child's name*) for her courage; she has left the safety of the Summerland for a new incarnation. We welcome this child to the earth and a new body and welcome her to this circle of women."

New Baby Poem
(of the Kwakiutl Indians)

When a girl is born by her mother, she is washed by the midwife who takes care of the woman who has given birth. After she has washed her, she wraps her in warm covers. Now the mother of the child takes a little mountain goat wool and she takes a narrow strip of cotton cloth. She takes a little wool and puts it on the narrow strip of cotton cloth. Then she prays to it and says, "Now great supernatural power of the Supernatural-One-of-the-Rocks, look at what I am doing to you, for I pray that you, please, have mercy on my child and that you give her success in picking all kinds of berries on the mountain; and this, that she may have success in obtaining property and be rich like you, great Supernatural One; and this, that you protect her that nothing evil may happen to her when she goes up (the mountain) picking berries on the mountain; and this (against) sickness. Go on, please, listen to my prayer to you, supernatural power of the Supernatural-One-of-the-Rocks," says she.[1]

Body of ritual — The high priestess takes a drop of oil and does the chakra blessing (Self-blessing ritual) first on the mother, then on the child. When beginning the child, she first names her.[2]

Touching the baby's crown, the high priestess says,

"I name you _____, and dedicate you to a life of peace and love."

She touches the child's third eye, "that you may see your way clearly."

The baby's throat, "that you may speak truth."

Her heart, "that it be open."

Her solar plexus, "that your will and strength be strong."

Her belly chakra, "that your sexuality be joyful and loving."

Her vagina, "the gateway of lives and creations to come."

Her hands, "that they may do the Goddess' work and your own."

Her feet, "that they may walk in the Goddess' path and your own."

She touches the child's crown again, "Bless this child, who is Goddess and herself, bless her, protect her and give her a joyful life."

Go around the circle. Each woman invokes three blessings for the infant:

May you be (*wise, gentle, prosperous, joyful*) etc.

May you have (*abundance, patience, love, good learning*) etc.

May you give to others (*healing, teaching, blessings, love*) etc.

And one more blessing for the mother: May she (*sleep all night, always be well, bring you joy*) etc.

The high priestess or another woman carries the baby and holds her up to each direction/element and spirit. She introduces her to each Goddess, asking her protection and blessings for the infant. "This is _____, may she always have the Goddess's love."

The women of the circle present gifts to the child and mother, earthly or symbolic. They can be a crystal, a poem, diapers, a blessing charm, etc. Go around the circle clockwise for this.

Raise energy — Use humming or songs and direct the cone of power to the child's bright growth and the mother's joy.
Ground.
Self-blessing — For all the women of the circle.
Open circle/Hugs.

Some songs to use in this ritual might include:

> Safe now, centered I know,
> At one with the mother
> And touching the flow
>
> Of Spirit, gentle and deep,
> Reclaiming our power
> A promise to keep. (by Yarrow)

or

> Blessed be and blessed are
> Those who work in silence.
> Blessed be and blessed are
> The dreamers and the dream.
> Blessed be and blessed are
> Those who scream and shout.
> Blessed be and blessed are
> Those who have returned.

or

> We give thanks
> For unknown blessings
> Already on the way. (Christa Heiden)

Menarche

My first menstruation was a traumatic one. I was older than most girls, almost sixteen, but still had no idea of what was coming. When I began to bleed, I thought I had hurt myself masturbating and was ashamed to tell anyone. I finally went to the gym teacher who provided me with a gauze belt, two pins and a pad that felt like riding a saddle and that itched. She asked me if I knew that I would do this every month and that it meant I couldn't take swimming. I just nodded; it was the first information I had had. When my mother, doing laundry, saw the stain on my clothes, she asked me if I had had my first period. When I said, yes, she inexplicably slapped me on the face. She said that was to remind me I could make her ashamed now, and I shouldn't sit on boys' laps. (I wasn't the least attracted to boys, except to fight with them.) Then she asked me if I knew the "facts of life." I didn't but I said "yes." I was in college a year or two before I found out. The slap, I learned, was traditional for Russian-Jewish mothers to do at their daughter's first menstruation. My mother didn't know why it was done. That was my menarche. It took twenty years and the women's and Goddess movement for me to start enjoying bleeding. It took the early women's movement consciousness-raising groups to learn that most other women of my age had similar experiences.

Girls today are reaching menarche at younger and younger ages, from ten years old on. Better nutrition is given as the cause, but there is also the high incidence of hormones fed to meat and poultry food animals, which may be a factor. Girls today have a better knowledge of their bodies and how they work, and few are as surprised by menarche as I was. Most know about birth control even before they start to bleed, and the bulky, itchy external menstrual pads are almost gone. Girls today know where babies come from, and hopefully learn some Goddess-within respect for the capabilities of their wombs. In this still patriarchal society, daughters of Goddess women are very lucky for the changed attitudes.

In non-Westernized cultures, menarche is the young woman's change from childhood to being an adult. After her first blood and her coming-of-age ritual, she is a full member of the tribe or society, and possibly ready for marriage or for after-childhood training. After her menarche ritual, a girl is an adult woman with women's responsibilities. The only vestige today of these rituals in the West, other than in some practicing Native American groups and in wicce, is the Jewish Bat Mitzvah ceremony from which much of the meaning has been lost. Menarche is unmentioned in it, though was its original root, and fewer girls than boys are given this expensive coming-of-age celebration. Presents and catered parties are the emphasis, and often the girl experiencing it feels it's for family and not really for her at all. The boys' bar mitzvahs came later; but probably the ancient ritual was at menarche and for girls only.

Women who participate in Goddess spirituality are aware of the changing cycles of life and death, and of individual growth along the Wheel. In Women's Spirituality, women's bodies are valued and validated, reclaimed from the negative treatment of five thousand years of patriarchy. A woman who raises her daughter with wiccan values has raised a young amazon. The daughter is aware of herself as Goddess-within, aware of her growing consequence, and has an autonomy and knowledge that her mother probably didn't have till many years and many hard-won experiences later. The girl has knowledge of her body processes and of the benefits and problems that they bring in a misogynist world. She has been taught to value her bleeding and her potential for responsible new life. At her coming-of-age, the young woman has something to celebrate, and turns to the women of the circle to celebrate it with.

Menarche is a ritual in which women celebrate the youth, newness and beginnings of their own and others' daughters. The girl at menarche is biologically an adult, but may be still a child emotionally; she has a developing body, but is not quite yet a woman. She has all her life with its pleasures and pain before her, and a great innocence and hope about what lies ahead. She is maturing sexually, but has only a beginning idea of what that means. Menarche celebrates the amazon in all women, the daughter of power and innocence just coming into her own. The girl is learning her strengths but probably not yet her limits, and the women encourage her to exceed her grasp and to grow.

In a Woman's Spirituality menarche/coming-of-age ritual, the focus of the ceremony is the girl who is celebrating it. This is not a party for grown-ups, but a ritual of meaning for the girl. The young woman sits in a place of honor at the center of the circle, and may wish a girlfriend or two to be with her. The women of the circle make her the center of attention for the whole evening, validating her as a new woman and accepting her as a woman among themselves. Emphasis is placed also on being admitted to women's secrets, mysteries and responsibilities; she is a woman herself now and has a right to know them. The women of the circle offer her knowledge and information, herstory and meaning, awareness and laughter in her new role. The daughter's mother, who has raised her this far and continues to guide her, is a major participant in the circle.

Use red and white as the colors for this ritual, in candles and flowers. Red and white chrysanthemums or carnations make good flowers for the altar; she is not quite ready for red roses. The girl may or may not feel comfortable with menstrual objects as part of the decorations, tampons and pads, belts and premenstrual remedies. Decide what's appropriate, or ask her, but don't make her feel embarrassed. The tarot cards for this ritual are the Motherpeace Daughters, young, exuberant women who haven't learned "I can't." They rush into situations headlong and are protected in their innocence. There are four of them in the deck, one for each suit: cups, discs, wands and swords. The Four of Wands is the card for menarche, depicting a young woman's coming-of-age ceremony.

Goddesses for this ritual are amazons and moon Goddesses. Some of them include: Artemis (Greece), Diana (Rome), Anahita (Persia), Persephone (Greece), Athene (Greece), Pele (Polynesia), Oya (Africa), Hathor (Egypt), Lucina (Italy), Blodeuwedd (Wales), Yngona (Denmark), Changing Woman (Native America), Ix Chel (South America), Lilith (Hebrew), Inanna (Sumer), Erzulie (Haiti), Star Girl (China), Ata Bey (Caribbean), and Kore (Greece). Some amazon foremothers are Boudica and Maeve (Mab) of the Celts, Sojourner Truth, and other herstorical women. Foods for a menarche ritual are red-dyed eggs for fertility of body, mind and spirit, and any foods the daughter chooses for her feast.

Menarche Ritual — A Daughter's Coming of Age

Decorate the altar for this ritual in red and white, red for blood, menstruation and the Mother aspect, and white for innocence and the Maiden Goddess. Use red and white candles and flowers, lots of crystals on the altar, and a red chair or cloth in the center of the circle for the girl to sit on. Have a moon necklace for her, a red stone or clear crystal, or pendant shaped like the moon or a Goddess aspect. The girl wears a crown of red flowers in her hair. This is a ritual in which the girl participates fully, she does not just sit and watch. The daughter may wish to choose the songs and invocation poem, or be involved in designing, creating or leading the ritual.

Need

Candles — Use red and white ones for the Mother and Maiden.

Flowers — Red and white flowers, try chrysanthemums, carnations, tulips. Flower crown of red flowers for the girl.

Incense — Use a red flower to stroke auras, or myrtlewood incense for fertility.

Moon pendant or crystal pendant for the girl.

Bowl of corn meal.

Oils for Self-blessing/mirror. Or use corn meal.

Invocations and Poems — Use the following or let the girl choose others that she likes.

Gifts for the girl, or have a give-away.

Pot-luck dinner contributions.

Matches to light candles and incense, charcoal block if using loose incense, ritual wand (or cast circle with a red flower).

Outline

Light candles — On altar and at each of the elements and spirit.

Purify — Use a red flower to stroke auras, or incense smoke.

Cast circle/Invoke amazon Goddesses. Ask the girl for her favorites when planning the ritual.

> Earth — Changing Woman, Goddess of women's bodies (Navaho).
>
> Air — Athene, Goddess of action and women's wisdom (Greece).
>
> Fire — Pele, Goddess of youth's love and passions (Polynesia).
>
> Water — Yemaya, Goddess of women's blood and the sea (W. Africa).
>
> Spirit — Hathor, Goddess of the moon and women's moontimes (Egypt).

Invocation — The high priestess says:

"We are here to celebrate (*name*), who has now become a woman. We welcome her into women's mysteries and the sisterhood. Women come into their full power in their moontimes, and (*name*) has begun her knowledge of that power."

Body of ritual — Go around the circle. Each woman sings the girl's name and a welcome for her or uses her name as a chant.

Go around the circle. Each woman talks about her own menarche, what it was like, what it meant, how things are different now. (Make it funny, make it not too long for each woman to speak, make it positive.) The girl talks about her own first blood next.

The high priestess takes the girl's moon necklace from the altar, handing it to the first woman in the circle. Pass it around the circle, each woman holding the pendant and sharing *a secret of being a woman* and *a blessing* for the girl. The girl's mother puts the pendant on the girl and talks about her daughter's growing up, and what it means for both of them. If others have gifts for her, they speak next and give them to her.

The girl reads the "Daughter Chant" below, then talks about what being a woman means to her:

Daughter Chant
from the Navaho Puberty Ceremony
Watch over me.
Hold your hand before me in protection.
Stand guard for me, speak in defense of me.

As I speak for you, so do ye.
As you speak for me, thus shall I do.
May it be beautiful before me.
May it be beautiful behind me.
May it be beautiful below me.
May it be beautiful above me.
May it be beautiful around me.

I am restored in beauty,
I am restored in beauty,
I am restored in beauty,
I am restored in beauty.[3]

The high priestess or the girl's mother talks briefly about responsibility — she can have a child now, be sexual with men or women. Talk about how to take care of herself (birth control, safe sex, etc.). Passion is an act of the Goddess, but use free will and balance, it's not a power to take lightly. Talk about how the girl's body will change, is changing, what to do for cramps, etc.

The girl's mother walks her to each of the four elements and spirit and presents her as a new woman. The high priestess touches the girl's third eye with corn meal or oil and blesses her as a woman in the name of the Goddess of each element.

Self-blessing — Ask the girl to lead it and all to participate.

The high priestess says:

"From this month on you are a member of the women's moonlodge. You have joined the cycles of the Moon Goddess as women have done for untold centuries. We hope your monthly bleeding will be a time of joy, a time of reverencing your womanhood and Goddess-within, a time of reverencing life. We hope that you will flow with the changes of your body and the moon, resisting the negativity that patriarchy places on women's blood. We welcome you and bless you as a woman. So mote it be."

Raising power — Use songs to raise the cone of power and direct it to the girl for blessings and for her protection, good life and happiness as a girl and as a woman. Visualize the energy of the cone cascading back into the circle as a waterfall of red light, filling the circle with life and positivity. Breathe the light within.

Ground — Send the excess energy for earth healing, or to women at menarche everywhere.

Open circle/hugs.

Do a potluck or give-away.

Some songs to include in raising power for this ritual are:

> She is the spirit,
> She's like a mountain,
> Tall and strong,
> She goes on and on and on. (by Naomi Little Bear)

or

> The earth is a woman
> And she is rising.
>
> The earth is a woman
> And she is rising.
>
> We all live in her.

or

> I see the Moon
> And the Moon sees me.
> The Moon sees somebody
> I'd like to see.
>
> Goddess bless the Moon
> and Goddess bless me.
> And Goddess bless the
> Somebody I'd like to see.

Bonding

Women in the Goddess craft see relationships and love commitments in a way far different from the patriarchal norm. In the male world, women are mothers and housekeepers, often little else. In the women's feminist community, women are fully autonomous, and a relationship is one of equality and mutual caring. When and if that caring ends, the relationship is over. The nurturing, sharing, passion, trust and respect that women have for each other in a feminist or lesbian bonding is a model for the rest of society. Women in the craft, heterosexual or lesbian, are doing real work at revising commitment expectations and maintaining stable, loving, often life-long relationships. Children are raised together, homes are created, work and love are shared, and the meaning of family is extended and opened for the benefit and joy of all.

Patriarchal marriage vows commit the woman to "love and obey till death do you part." Many women refuse the implications of this, and the high divorce rate is a reflection of its modern unreality. Women in wiccan bonding rituals, called a tryst (from the word "trust") or handfasting, put careful thought into what they want to promise each other. A tryst or bonding ritual can be legal for the heterosexual couple — a few high priestesses have that state authority — but legal or not, a vow made before the Goddess and the circle is one to take seriously. Lesbian trystings *are* serious, the relationships long-lasting, and the ceremony is the only public validation lesbians have of their love and commitment to each other. Women who choose to be trysted have often already been together, lived and created a life together, for a number of years, and the ritual has great meaning for them. Some women who are not in the craft will also seek the validation of a trysting. The ritual below is designed for two women, but can be adapted for heterosexual use or for use by gay men.

Women's relationships are based on equality and mutual respect, not on the ownership model of the patriarchy. What women choose to promise each other in a trysting is usually long-discussed beforehand. The ceremonies involve input from both women and from the high priestess they have chosen to lead the ritual. This is a ritual where the planning can start months in advance, where the focus is on the couple in every part of it, and where the women either write their own ritual or have close involvement in the writing and development. The women seldom promise to be together forever and love each other for life, unless their relationship is a long-established one. Taking vows before the Goddess and circle seriously, a high priestess discourages women from taking all-inclusive vows lightly or before their time.

In the nonfeminist craft, a handfasting is considered binding for a year and a day, unless the couple ask the high priestess for release from it sooner. After that time the vows can be renewed, and eventually made permanent. In some covens, the ceremony is the same as a marriage, and in some it is permanent from the beginning. The permanence is very permanent, the couple promising to love each other and stay together through this life and many lives to come. It's a karmically serious vow with far-reaching implications. In Women's Spirituality, the couple seldom has access to repeating the ritual, unless they do it together alone, and the promises are chosen realistically for each couple's situation. There is no year and a day limit, or any limit. A high priestess is not needed to dissolve the commitment, only the women's choice to do so. In women's trysts, the women are usually experienced enough or have been together long enough to know what they want; many lesbians have been too burned by past marriages to enter the bonding ritual thoughtlessly.

When women have been together for only a short time and they ask for a trysting ritual, I advise them to promise that they will stay together for as long as it's positive for both of them, and to care about each other always, as lovers or not. When the relationship has proven the test of time and living together, they may choose to promise more. When women have been together longer and the event is a carefully thought-out and planned one, the women's promises to each other can be extensive and are tailored to the couple's individual needs. Shekinah Mountainwater's Tryst Agreement with her partner Brown follows, and gives some idea of the extent, care, thought and seriousness that goes into the ritual and the vows.

About Our Tryst
by Shekinah Mountainwater

Patriarchal society is based on oppressor/victim relationships between people who control or are controlled by one another through manipulation, coercion, or scarcity. A free society is based on free relations between free people who give to one another and take from one another openly, willingly, and lovingly, with mutual agreement on all sides. When people feel victimized and helpless in the system, the tendency is to turn around and oppress or victimize themselves or someone else, in order to vent their anger or get what they need. Russia and the U.S. are engaged in such a dynamic, as are most interpersonal relationships.

Free relations between free women creates a new reality, which we can develop among ourselves. Trysting is a revolutionary step in this direction, opening the way for free human interaction on a personal level. As feminists have taught, the personal is political, and when we develop free relationships we are contributing to the larger picture.

A tryst is not a wedding as we have been taught, which is based on ownership of one person by another. It is a meeting of two free lovers who have come together in openness, as independent individuals who seek to share with one another, in order to know the pleasure, fulfillment, joy and richness such sharing can bring. It is a coming together, but it is also an acknowledgment of the individuality, autonomy, and freedom of both members.

We have already made tryst agreements with one another privately, and now exchange them again before you, our community of sisters, that you may witness our love, give it your blessing, help us to stay strong as friends, sisters, and lovers with your visualizations and supportiveness.

True love between women is a foundation stone of sisterhood. It can also be a fragile thing, opposed as it is on all sides. We therefore turn to you, our sisters, for the help and love only sisters can give. In return we agree to stand by you as friends, sisters or lovers, as the case may be. Thus we will build our tribe and liberate ourselves and change the world. So be it. Blessed be.[4]

Tryst Agreement
by Shekinah Mountainwater and M.E. Brown

O Aphrodite, force of passionate love, Goddess of ecstasy and creative inspiration, power that moves the universe and awakens desire . . . please be with us now as we share our vows to one another. Blessed be.

Sisters, beloved women of our community, please be with us now and hear our vows and bless our love.

In the name of the Love that lives between us, I agree:

To stand by you and be loyal to you as a friend and sister always. To be loyal to you as a lover for as long as the fiery passions of Aphrodite flow between us. May it be forever!

To be monogamous with you unless both change in this regard. Should this time come I agree to engage in other love connections with fairness and consideration towards you, and to support your freedom to do the same.

To preserve the magic in our relationship and uphold its sacredness.

To support and respect your spiritual process, be open to learning about it, and to share mine with you.

To give a fair share of my energy, time and space, be it Love, Information, Skills, Money, Touch, Pleasure, Affection, Magic, or other resources.

To support your need for time, space and energy to yourself, and to accept your support of mine.

To support your need for privacy and separateness, as well as intimacy and sharing, and to accept your support of mine.

To give a fair share of house care and the work of other practical needs as they arise, and as my time, energy and skill permit.

To support your creative and professional potentials and achievements, and to accept your support of mine.

To communicate as clearly, openly, and honestly as I can about all things connected to our relationship. Should I need to withhold for a time out of diplomacy and tact, I will take responsibility to bring up issues in due time, and respond honestly to those you bring up.

To recognize and appreciate your value as a woman, and of the many different kinds of energy you give. To accept your recognition of me in the same way.

All of these I give without rancor, without resentment, without being coerced or manipulated, but freely, openly, and lovingly.

I ask the same from you; that you give me all of these without rancor or resentment, or being coerced or manipulated, but out of freedom, openness, and love.

I will stay by your side and/or share our daily lives for as long as this agreement stands, or until a better one is made between us, or until both decide to move on. May that time never come, and may our love flourish and flower always. So be it! Blessed be![5]

As high priestess of their ritual in November, 1986, we learned together what trysting means for women. The ritual that follows is based on that trysting, and on one co-priestessed with Shekinah at the Gulfcoast Women's Festival in March, 1989. In a group trysting ritual at a women's festival, where advanced planning is difficult, the women are asked to make their promises to each other, being aware of implications and of the reality of keeping what is promised.

The major symbol for this ritual is the witches' broom, a highly decorated heather broom used as the primary tool for the trysting. The handle is tied with brightly colored ribbon streamers, beads, bells and flowers. The broom is used to purify, to cast the circle, to make an arch (sometimes with two brooms), and is used as something for the women to step over as a symbol of the ritual's completion. This unlikely object has consqeuence in women's herstory as a magickal tool.

In the days of the Burning Times, when so many women/witches died in the Inquisition, it was dangerous to possess ritual tools or have them visible in one's house. The legend goes that the high priestess' circle-casting wand was a rod disguised as the handle of a broom. In nonfeminist craft a bonding or handfasting ritual is referred to as "jumping over the broom," the broom being a symbol of fertility. The broom is also a symbol of the Roman Goddess Vesta or Hestia, protector of the hearth and home, and in every culture the broom is a women's household tool.

By using the decorated broom in a women's bonding ritual, several symbols are incorporated. One is an honoring of the women lost to the witch-burnings, our foremothers. Next, since women's

love for each other in a patriarchal culture is as dangerous/
tabooed/revolutionary as being a witch was and is, the broom is a
symbol of women's freedom to validate their love despite the haz-
ards and problems of doing it under patriarchy. This insistence on
validating what is right over what is culturally accepted is an
important thing for women. The broom becomes a ritual tool of
women's consequence by this alone. When the idea of trysting is
presented to them, most women know it as "jumping over the
broom" and the act of doing so in the ritual takes on importance by
their expectation. In further symbols, as an object sacred to Vesta
or Hestia, the broom represents a safe and loving home, and the
loving things that happen in the home. Whether the lovers live
together or not, the symbol is meaningful. The broom as a women's
tool is also a validation of the importance of women's work in
making a home, a relationship, or a civilization.

Decorate the broom before the ritual; heather brooms are
easily available in arts and crafts stores. Use imagination and make
it elaborate with colors, textures and sounds. Streamers and bells
add to the interest and make the tool more magickal and feminine.
The high priestess may wish to make this special broom her
bonding gift to the couple. Use red or rose-colored candles and lots
of flowers on the altar, especially pink or red roses. Place a large
chalice on the altar, filled with water or fruit juice, and put a crystal
or rose quartz gemstone in the bottom of the glass. The couple's
gifts to each other are on the altar, and a bowl of honey. Use rose
incense, and rose essential oil for the Self-blessing.

The Goddesses to invoke in a women's bonding ritual are love
Goddesses, of course. Some of them are: Aphrodite (Phoenicia),
Ishtar (Mesopotamia), Oshun (West Africa), Freya (Scandinavia),
Erzulie (Haiti), Chalchiuhtlique (South America), Isis (Egypt), Inanna
(Sumer), Astarte or Asherah (Semitic), Shekinah (Hebrew), Kwan
Yin (China), Shakti (India), Sappho (Greece), Venus (Rome), Blod-
deuwedd (Wales), Flora (Rome), Hina (Polynesia), Cybele (Anatolia),
Anahita (Armenia), Ruth (Hebrew), The Snake Maiden (Native
America), Vesta (Rome), White Buffalo Calf Woman (Native Amer-
ica), and Chih-Nu (Japan).

In the Motherpeace tarot, cards for a trysting are the Two and
Ten of Cups, The Lovers, The Empress and The World — abundance
in nurturing, family, relationship, passion and fulfillment. The
World is having everything women want, total joy and well-being,
and this is the wish for the lovers being trysted. The Ten of Cups is
the double rainbow. Foods for after the ritual include melons,
cherries and strawberries, passion fruit, very rich ice cream, creamy

pastries, and exotically decadent desserts and sweets. The theme of the ritual and the celebration after it is women's love.

A Women's Tryst (Bonding Ritual)

A tryst is a festive gathering, as festive as any in the Women's Spirituality movement. The couple, guests, and high priestess dress in bright colors and decorate the room and altar brightly. There is an abundance of flowers, emphasizing red or pink roses, and lots of red or rose-colored candles. As the high priestess is lighting the candles, she explains the meaning of the trysting broom. The couple to be bonded sit or stand together at the altar or in the center of the circle. In a group trysting, the couples come forward after the Invocation, but are part of the circle until then.

Need

Candles — Use red or rose, red for passion, rose for trust and love.

Flowers — Red or pink roses are traditional. Strew loose rose petals around the circle and on the altar.

Incense — Purify with the trysting broom, but light rose incense on the altar, also.

Decorated trysting broom — Or use two to make an arch.

Chalice of water or juice — Use a large one, or have more fluid available in a pitcher for refilling.

Bowl of honey.

Couple's gifts or rings for each other.

Invocation — Use the poem below or others that the women choose.

Flute music, guitar music, love songs. Optional: Try Ferron's song "Testimony" on her *Testimony* audio tape (Ferrisburg, VT: Lucy Records, 1980), available from Ladyslipper, P.O. Box 3124, Durham, NC 27705.

Oil for Self-blessing/mirror — Use rose oil.

Matches for candles and incense.

Desserts for after the ritual.

Outline

Light candles — High priestess talks about the meaning of the broom.

Purify — Sweep the women's auras with the broom. The high priestess moves around the circle clockwise from the inside to do this. Use brisk strokes.

Cast Circle/Invoke love Goddesses — The high priestess uses the broom to cast the circle, either by gesture or by sweeping the ground around the circle from outside of it. Move clockwise.

> Earth — Flora, Goddess of beauty. We invite your presence to this ritual and to these women's lives.
>
> Air — Sappho, Goddess of poetry and love's inspiration. We invite your blessings to this ritual, and to these women's lives.
>
> Fire — Amaterasu, Goddess of women's passion and power. We invite that power to this ritual, and your passion to last forever in these women's hearts.
>
> Water — Yemaya, Goddess of peace and women's healing. We invite your blessings to this ritual, your healing to women's love and lives.
>
> Spirit — Spider Woman, Goddess of immortality. We ask that these women's love be immortal, and your blessings for their bonding.

"The Charge of the Goddess." — This blessing is generally used only for Full Moons and the eight Sabbats, but it feels right to use it in a trysting ritual. Read it or play the sung version on tape.

Invocation — The high priestess leads the women in a chant of names of love Goddesses: Aphrodite, Yemaya, Oshun, Flora, etc. She brings the chanting to an end, then reads the following poem:

Mothering and Nurturing
by Anisa Gamal

Oh, my sisters, we must be
The illusion we imagine.

If we need someone to come home to . . .
If we need badly to be nurtured,
If we need someone to sew on a button, or . . .
Someone to call on in the middle of the night . . .

We must be that for each other.
Forever and always we must make the time,
Right when the time arises.

Forever and always . . . without strings and conditions.

Anything else is madness. Madness.

Cherish your sisters, for Goddess sake.

We are the saviors of Life itself.[6]

Body of Ritual — The high priestess brings the women to be trysted to the center of the circle. The group chants the names of the women. They face each other and make their promises to each other, aloud or not, and/or read the Tryst Agreement they have written. (In a group trysting, the couples face each other and make their promises to each other only.)

The women exchange hugs and/or gifts, describing what they offer each other. Gifts do not have to be material things. If the women have chosen to exchange rings, these can be their gift exchanges.

The high priestess brings the bowl of honey, placing some on both women's lips. "May your lives together be sweet," she says, as they kiss it from each other. In a skyclad ritual, honey can be placed on other places, too. (Ask how shy the women are, and let them put it on each other.)

The high priestess brings the chalice from the altar, and the women sip from it, holding it for each other. "May you never thirst,"[7] she says. She passes the chalice around the circle, and each woman drinks to the couple's love. Then pass it around again, to drink to women's love. (The high priestess stands by with the refill pitcher.)

Love songs — Live or on tape, are good to play while the chalice is going around. Ferron's song "Testimony" is a women's favorite.[8]

The high priestess holds the broom, or two women hold it or two brooms, in an arch and the circle of women pass under it, the tryst couple first and last. (In a group trysting, only the couples being trysted pass under the brooms.) When the tryst couple (or last group-tryst couple) approaches the broom for the second time, the broom is lowered to the ground and the women being trysted step over it together. They then move around the circle receiving the hugs and congratulations of the women. Make sure the circle moves clockwise, the direction of making and invoking, and hold the broom low enough to prevent tripping on it.

Raise energy — Use songs, and send the cone of power to the lovers for happiness, and to all the women of the circle for their own love and happiness. Visualize the women having every blessing — long and peaceful lives together, joy together, fulfilling passion, great abundance, dreams come true. Women looking for lovers and women with lovers visualize it for themselves also.

Ground.

Do the Self-blessing — The high priestess makes it a blessing for the couple's love and anoints the tryst couple herself at each step. The women in the circle repeat it with her, anointing themselves with the rose oil. Pass the mirror wrapped in cloth around as "a picture of Aphrodite."

Open circle — When thanking and releasing the Goddesses, ask that they remain in the women's daily lives, in the couple's lives, and that they come to the lives of women who need love.

Ground/Group hug.

Dessert. Tease the couple about their "wedding night" and watch them blush!

Some songs to use in raising power for a women's bonding ritual are:

> Make for yourself a power spot,
> Bring you a spoon and a cooking pot.
> Bring air, bring fire, bring water, bring earth,
> And you a new universe will birth.

> Make for yourself a cozy nest,
> Bring you the one that you love best.
> Twine arms, twine legs, twine bellies and breasts,
> And you will know that you are truly blessed.
> (by Shekinah Mountainwater)

or

> When all the women in the world
> Will have their hearts set on freedom,
> When all the women in the world
> Will dream the sweet dream of peace,

> When every woman in every nation,
> Young and old, each generation,
> Join hands in the name of love,
> There will be no more war.[9] (by Karen Mackay)

or

> Sister, Sister,
> Let me tell you what I know,
> You have given me such pleasure,
> I love you so.

> Love, love, love, love,
> Women, we are made of love.

Love each other as ourselves.
I love you so.

Notes

1. "The Treatment of a First-born Girl Among the Kwakiutl Indians," in Penelope Washburn, Ed., *Seasons of Woman* (San Francisco: Harper and Row, 1982), pp. 4-5.

2. Kelly Weaver, "Wiccaning Ritual," in *Circle Network News* (P.O. Box 219, Mt. Horeb, WI 53572), Winter, 1988-89, p. 9.

3. "Navaho Puberty Ceremony," in Penelope Washburn, Ed., *Seasons of Woman*, pp. 20-21.

4. Used by permission of Shekinah Mountainwater.

5. Used by permission of Shekinah Mountainwater and M. E. Brown.

6. Anisa Gamal, "Mothering and Nurturing," in *Thesmophoria* (P.O. Box 11363, Oakland, CA 94611), Vol. 7, No. 8, May Eve, 1986, p. 2.

7. Z. Budapest, *The Holy Book of Women's Mysteries, Vol. II* (Los Angeles: Susan B. Anthony Coven Co. I, 1980), p. 66.

8. Ferron, *Testimony*, audio tape (Ferrisburg, VT: Lucy Records, 1980). Available from Ladyslipper, P.O. Box 3124, Durham, NC 27705.

9. Karen Mackay, "If Every Woman (No More War)," on *Annie Oakley Rides Again!*, audio tape (West Virginia Woman Records, 1984). Order from Ladyslipper, P.O. Box 3124, Durham, NC 22705.

Chapter Eight

———————◯———————

Rites of Passage II
Pregnancy to Passing Over

Rites of passage rituals continue in this chapter with the waning half of the Wheel of women's lives. In Chapter 7, the rituals were from beginnings and birth to the fullness of women's bonding, the Maiden to the Mother. In this chapter, the rituals move from maturity, the Mother aspect of the life cycle, through the Crone phase and the great transition known as death. As in the eight Sabbats of the Wheel of the Year, the Wheel of Life has its waxing and waning halves, mirrors that reflect upon each other. As death and winter in the Wheel of the Year proceed to birth and growth again, so do women's physical births proceed to growth, maturity, aging and death — before life begins again. The waxing phase is followed by the waning, and the waning by new births into new lifetimes.

In Women's Spirituality, maturity and aging have equal value and consequence with beginnings and youth. Death and birth are equal miracles, and both are equally endings and beginnings. The Maiden, Mother and Crone have equal and shared power, the power to begin, maintain, and end creation on a personal, tribal, global and universal level. In the pop culture of the 1960s, the beginnings of the women's, New Age and wiccan movements, the slogan was to never trust anyone over thirty. Now the amazon children who created the sixties love, peace and women's movements have grown up; they are women in their forties creating new revolutions in world consciousness, still active and making changes.

As these daughters of the World War II baby-boom grow older, Western populations age and the focus shifts from youth. Women's values, matriarchy, the Goddess and the honoring of old age return. This reaction to the patriarchal coldness of the youth and money-oriented yuppies is not a new idea. In matriarchal societies, age and responsibility/maturity were valued. Only women after menopause were eligible to be tribal elders in some Native American groups, or oracles at Delphi in pre-Hellenic Greece. In ancient China and in many other cultures, the oldest woman was the matriarch/leader of her clan. In some societies, a woman had to prove her physical or emotional maturity to be accepted into the governing of the tribe. Value was more placed on responsibility and experience, maturity and reliability, than on youth, sexual desirability, money or material status. In a society that values women's consequence, the Crone has the most consequence of all.

Responsibility is the key word for the waning half of the Wheel of Life. At its beginning is pregnancy and the entrance into motherhood, based on the mother rather than the infant of the wiccaning ritual. At pregnancy, the women has chosen to create new life, to accept the role of the Mother Goddess. Her choice is not only for the nine months of gestation and the labor and risks of childbirth, but for the twenty years and more of child-rearing, protecting, teaching, and nurturing that follows. The decision marks the end of the Maiden phase of a woman's life for those women who choose to be mothers. Other acceptances of responsibility create this life passage for women who decline physical motherhood; women can mother more than children. For some women it may be entrance into careers, the choosing of a committed relationship, the co-parenting of a partner's child, or the purchase of a home. Some women retain the Maiden aspect longer than others, entering gradually into the Mother phase, with or without childbearing. Some women enter childbearing late, having already made the passage into adulthood, placing careers, relationships or homes first.

The Crone aspect comes at the end of childbearing potential, whether the woman has chosen motherhood or not. Some women define passage into the Crone at age fifty-six, the second Saturn return, or at the completion of menopause, the ending of menstruation. Other women feel their adoption of the Crone role at neither of these times, but when they are psychically ready for it and decide to choose it. Some women mark the death of a parent for their initiation as a Crone, their retirement from careers, hysterectomies, or when their daughters become mothers, making them grandmothers. The age can be any physical age. The emotional aspect of the Crone is that of a woman of experience, someone who has knowledge and wisdom gained by a lifetime of learning and doing. The Crone is no longer a mother involved with the raising of her children, and her first responsibility is to herself. If the woman has been a mother, she can think of herself and her own needs before anyone else's for the first time in decades, and live her life finally as she wants to. If she has retired from a mainstream job, her time is her own at last, she has some financial autonomy, and her creativity is free to flower. If she has worked on her own, she can continue to on her own schedule. Younger women with careers, commitments and child-raising responsibilities have reason to long for Cronedom.

The last rite of passage of the waning phase is death or passing over. Modern culture's denial and horror of death does not extend into Women's Spirituality. The Goddess movement sees death as the ultimate adventure, the great transition, the entrance into the idyllic Summerland, the return to the Goddess. As women's Be-ing begins incarnation with birth, it ends it with death, and death is the beginning of reincarnations to come. The cycle ends and begins again and the soul goes on to new lives and new evolutions of consciousness.

A vast number of women have made psychic contact with someone who has passed over, usually someone they loved. Some African and Asian cultures place great value on ancestor worship, the concept that those passed over protect and guide those currently living. Every Be-ing comes into the world with the companionship of spirit guides, souls from the other world who protect, teach and comfort throughout life. Many women have psychic awareness of entities or "ghosts," and/or contact with passed over loved ones, ancestors or spirit Be-ings (human or animal). It was not meant for women to lose contact with the world that exists between death and rebirth. Past-life regression work and regressions into the after death/prebirth process add further information that death is not an ending, as do the many accounts of women's near death experiences.[1]

Death in Women's Spirituality is seen as another rite of passage on the Wheel of Life, not an ending but a new phase and transformation. Rituals are designed to help the newly dead make the transition from the earthplane into the other world more smoothly and easily. They celebrate and honor the life accomplishments of the woman who has gone over. The rituals offer comfort to those left behind, a reminder of the continuing Wheel, and a promise of reunion later and in other lives. They help with the grieving process, with going on. Like waning year rituals in the Wheel of the Year Sabbats, passing-over rituals validate and affirm the cycle of birth, life, death and rebirth. They honor women's passages and the turning Wheel.

These three rites of passage are the focus of the waning half of the Wheel of Life — motherhood, croning and passing over. The emphasis is on maturity and experience, rather than on the earlier development and growth of the waxing half — though development and growth continue throughout life. They validate age and wisdom, the taking on of responsibility, and responsibilities met and completed. While the rituals are serious, they are by no means lacking joy. The Goddess and her women have three aspects, the Maiden, Mother and Crone, and the cycle that begins with birth ends with death and begins again in reincarnation. The pattern is a circle, rather than the patriarchal line, or more properly a spiral from the center. The center is the center of all Be-ing, the Goddess, women's consequence and Goddess-within. In the second half of women's rites of passage, the daughter has grown up. Persephone becomes Demeter and then Hecate, and as she sheds each role, each skin, each life-phase, she becomes more and more her Goddess self.

Pregnancy

Women today have more choices than at any time since the ending of the matriarchies, but even in Western cultures women are far from free. Western women are instilled from birth with the values of patriarchy that place them as second-class citizens, despite the gains of feminism. Ultimately, a patriarchal order wants women in the home to be dominated, not in the workplace or the government to take active, decision-making roles. Women's fight to gain and maintain control of their own bodies is representative of this patriarchal force. Issues of women's rights to choose conception, contraception, and abortion are central in the feminist struggle and would not have been issues at all in the matriarchies. Issues of child custody and support, the rights of single or lesbian mothers, day care and Aid to Families with Dependent Children (AFDC) become battles as sinister in the West as those of the veil in Arabic countries and footbinding in the past in China. Though Western women are freer, they are not free until these issues are returned to women's control and consequence.

Women have the right to determine their own lives, to choose childbirth in or out of marriage in their own time, or to refuse motherhood entirely. Lesbians and disabled women have as much right to motherhood if they choose it as do women who are heterosexually married and/or able-bodied. Black women and other women of color, Native American women and women born in other countries have the same rights as Caucasian American-born women to freedom of choice. Conception/contraception information is a right, safe abortion is a right, and freedom to have children or not is a right for all women. The restriction of contraceptive information and availability, the restriction of low-cost or free, safe abortion, and the abuse of sterilization surgeries violate the rights and freedoms of women in the West as much as in less free countries. They are some of the legacies of patriarchy.

As I write this, the Supreme Court of the United States is reviewing the constitutionality of the *Roe v. Wade* decision that made it illegal for states to restrict abortion. If *Roe v. Wade* is declared null by the conservative court, women's ability to obtain safe and legal abortion could be seriously restricted or even totally denied. The religious right wing, more obnoxiously vocal than an actual majority, and the right-wing rule in federal government favor the ending of legal abortion in the United States and in other countries. Their attempt to gain control of life, of women's bodies and Be-ings, is nothing new in patriarchal history but bodes no good for women. Older women remember the days of back-alley abortions, high prices and serious risk of physical/emotional damage and death. Women's reproductive freedom without exploitation is a major women's issue of our time.

In days and places as recent as Europe before the witch burnings, the situation for women's reproductive freedom was much different. From the time of the matriarchies until the establishment of the misogynist Christian Church and Inquisition, women worldwide had control of their bodies via the midwife/healer of each village. Herbal knowledge was available in every culture to facilitate conception if wanted, prevent it if unwanted, and abort an unwanted early pregnancy safely. The information was part of the skill of the midwife, who also knew how to prevent miscarriages, ease morning sickness, hasten labor and delivery, increase breastmilk and stop hemorrhaging in childbirth. The midwife knew how to help a woman through every aspect of pregnancy and delivery and how to best protect the life of the fragile newborn. She knew how to prevent unwanted pregnancies and increase wanted ones. The question today is why don't women take that information back again, away from the control of governments, churches, and the male medical profession? The information is available; there are women who have the knowledge and the willingness to share it. The herbs for safe, effective abortion and contraception grow wild in every climate. The return of women's control of reproduction to themselves would be a great step forward in women's rights, women's consequence and matriarchal power. Conception, contraception, abortion and pregnancy belong fully in women's control, along with the ability to regulate their own sexuality.

The Goddess religion takes a totally pro-choice stance on the issue of abortion. There is no rule or ethic that says that every fertilized ovum must be gestated to a birth, any more than that every fertilized chicken egg must become a chicken. In this era of fragile ecology and overpopulation, runaway fertility of women — or chickens — is something to look closely at. Women are born with 100,000 eggs in their ovaries, each potentially a birth. It is no more expected that a woman will produce 100,000 babies in her lifetime than that she will produce one, two or a dozen. The creation and Mother aspect of the Goddess takes many forms, childbirth being only one of them. There is no stigma on the woman who has ten children, and no stigma on the woman who chooses to have none. There is no more or less value placed on the children of black women than white women, able women than disabled women, single women than married women, heterosexual women than lesbians. All children are valued and hopefully chosen. The emphasis is on responsibility, autonomy, choice and the freedom of women to self-determine their lives.

The Goddess's reverence for all life emphasizes the quality of life. No child should be brought into the world to be unwanted, abused or exposed to incest. No child brought into the world should be hungry or lack love, shelter, or medical care. No woman should be forced into bearing children she does not choose to have, or be prevented from bearing children she wants. Birth is women's ability to create new people, as it is the Goddess's ability to create the world. When a birth happens, the destiny of the mother and child are joined karmically, and what is sent out returns to the sender many-fold. The child's Be-ing and the mother's have agreed to come together. If conception is refused, the child's soul leaves, to return in another pregnancy if and when it is time to incarnate, or the Be-ing of the child may choose another mother. No soul or Be-ing is wasted or lost. When birth happens, it does so for the good of all.

Modern western culture has taken the process of childbirth away from women, as it has women's right to choose pregnancy. Male medicine treats childbirth as a dis-ease with machines and drugs, and takes all initiative, action, control and decision away from the birthing mother. Infertility-as-a-dis-ease exaggerates this even more. In many cases, most of them unnecessary, cesarean sections make birth into major surgery, to the detriment of mother and child. In the days before the Inquisition killed the witch midwives, birth was in the hands of skilled women and was a joint effort between the mother and her healer. Babies entered the world gently, and mothers and babies experienced the process without trauma. The rate of mother and infant mortality has actually increased in the West with the advent of medicine's invasive methods and machines, and the United States has the highest infant mortality rate of any developed country. Many women today are reclaiming the birth process as another way of reclaiming women's consequence and bodies. The older Goddess craft was linked inextricably with midwifery, and is becoming so again. With the return of gentle childbirth, women and infants regain another portion of women's heritage.

A women's pregnancy ritual is the Women's Spirituality equivalent of the modern baby shower, but with far more depth and meaning. The ritual recognizes the mother-to-be's choice to make a life-changing rite of passage, her entrance into motherhood as the Mother Goddess. The women offer her blessings for "a safe birth, a strong child, and happiness in motherhood." The ritual can be designed to bless the start of any new project or new creations such as writing a book or starting a new career. All are women's rites of passage into the realm of the Mother. The themes of the ritual are fertility, creation and change. Shower gifts may or may not be included in the ritual or the celebration after it.

Goddesses for this ritual are mother and child Goddesses. Some of them include: Oddudua (Africa), Lilith (Hebrew), Parvati (India), Kwan Yin (China), Yemaya (Africa), Mary (Christian), Ix Chel (South America), Tonantzin/Guadalupe (Mexico), Isis (Egypt), Demeter (Greece), Lucina (Sweden), Artemis (Greece), Diana (Rome) and Spider Woman (Native America). The Motherpeace tarot cards include the Seven of Discs for pregnancy and waiting and the Ten of Discs, which portrays a birth in the circle of women. Foods for after the ritual are the colored eggs on the altar, green vegetables for rebirth, and round fruits for fertility and abundant nourishment. Milk and honey, symbol of breast milk and the womb, is an optional choice, as is the pomegranate for the womb and the cycle of birth, death and reincarnation.

Pregnancy — A Ritual of Creation

This is a ritual for a woman who is pregnant or who wants to ask for conception/fertility. The woman has chosen the rite of passage of motherhood, and the circle validates the great changes coming to her life as a result of her decision. The ritual can also be adapted for other forms of creation — the beginning of writing a book, the recording of a music tape, the start of a business or career. To do this, the baby symbols are changed for those meaningful to the woman and occasion.

For a pregnancy ritual, decorate the altar with baby toys, bottles, diapers and baby clothes. If there are gifts for the mother, place them on or around the altar, and put a bowl of colored eggs on the altar as well. Use pastel candles and flowers, and a baby rattle to purify. As another way to decorate, try a birth/rebirth theme with baby photos of the women of the circle, photos of foremothers/ancestors, and candles in red, white and black (birth, life and reincarnation). Use a feather to cast the circle, and a bowl of eggs that are red or white.

Put a malachite pendant or shaped gemstone on the altar as a gift for the mother; it hastens labor and is not to be worn until labor begins. Or use aquamarine or emerald to prevent miscarriage, carnelian or orange/red coral to stimulate conception, or agate to help morning sickness. (In a creativity ritual other than pregnancy, choose other appropriate gemstones. Chrysocolla is general creative stimulant.)

Need

Pastel flowers and candles on the altar. (Or in rebirth theme, use red and white flowers; red, white and black candles.)

Incense — Purify by shaking a baby rattle around the women's auras. (In rebirth theme, use sage or myrtlewood incense for immortality.)

Baby toys, diapers, bottles, baby things on the altar. (Or use photos of the women as babies, photos of foremothers.)

Bowl of multi-colored hard-boiled eggs (or red or white ones).

Pendant or gemstone for mother — Malachite or other choice.

Gifts for mother and baby, if any, are on and around the altar.

Invocation/Poem — Use the following or choose others.

Comfortable chair in center of circle for the mother-to-be.

After-ritual foods or potluck dinner contributions.

Matches to light candles and incense, charcoal block for loose incense, ritual wand (or use a feather to cast the circle).

Outline

Light candles.

Purify — With baby rattle or incense.

Cast circle/Invoke mother and child Goddesses. Use ritual wand or feather to cast the circle.

> Earth — Oddudua, Mother of the Goddesses (Africa).
>
> Air — Lilith, who makes children laugh in their sleep (Hebrew).
>
> Fire — Parvati, Mother Goddess (India).
>
> Water — Isis, Mother Goddess (Egypt, Africa and Greece).
>
> Spirit — Demeter, Earth Mother, mother of us all (Greece).

Invocation — The mother-to-be sits in the chair at the center of the circle. High priestess says:

"We are here to honor (*name*) who will be a mother. As she makes the passage through pregnancy and labor, she becomes the Mother Goddess and her life will change forever. No more the Maiden, and mature as a lover, she takes on the care of another life with her own. We are here today to invoke the Goddess in wishing (*name*) a safe birth, a strong child, and happiness in motherhood."

Creation Poem
by Monica Sjoo

The most holy one created the world like an embryo, as an embryo grows from the navel, so she began to create the world by the navel, and from there it spread, grew, multiplied in all directions . . . she was both seed and flower, both primordial and final. The first vibrations of the egg of the world which unfold to the edges of the universe are both expanding and contracting, emerging from the source and pulsing outward to disappear into a spherical vortex. The still center (the heart) is the axis of creation — the universal continuum perpetually unfolds, pulses outward, contracts — perpetually spinning through its own center.[2]

Meditation — The high priestess leads the women in a meditation on pregnancy and birth. Watch the egg divide, become the fetus, and grow inside the womb. The fetus develops and becomes a child. She is born, grows into yourself, grows up. The cycle starts again with a child in the womb of the mother-to-be. Ask the child for a message, send her blessings and love. Wish her well in her beginnings and come back to now.

Body of ritual — The high priestess takes the malachite gemstone from the altar, passing it clockwise around the circle. Each woman who holds it puts three blessings in it:

> For easy childbirth.
>
> For the mother (I wish you — happiness, joy, lots of breastmilk, etc.).
>
> For the baby (I wish her — happiness, health, curiosity, good grades in school, the ERA, etc.).

The malachite is given to the mother, but not to be worn or held until she is in labor. Other stones — emerald, aquamarine, agate — may be worn throughout pregnancy.

Go around the circle again. Each woman shares her own stories of birth or stories from their mothers. Make them positive ones. Share remedies for morning sickness, easy delivery, tips on newborn care, etc.

If the mother-to-be agrees, the women together put their hands in healing and blessing on the pregnant woman's abdomen. Do Reiki, touch healing, polarity healing (gentle touch only) for several minutes, offering blessings and well-being to the mother and child.

Pass around the dyed hard-boiled eggs. Each woman takes one as a symbol of fertility, birth, creation and reincarnation.

Raise energy — Use the sound of the baby rattle, chants or songs to raise the cone of power. The women visualize a safe and easy delivery, a healthy baby and a smiling mother. Direct the energy to these things manifesting.

Ground. Send excess energy to the earth for healing and new growth.

Open circle/Hugs.

Present gifts to the mother-to-be.

Have a potluck dinner, after-ritual celebration or food sharing.

A song suggestion for this ritual is "Goddess Has Risen," to the tune of Cat Stevens' "Morning has Broken." Lyrics are by Shekinah Mountainwater and Lunea Weatherstone:

> Goddess has risen,
> Now is her season,
> She gives us reason
> to be and to give.
> Praise for the Maidens,
> Praise for the Mothers,
> Praise for the Lovers,

loving to live.

Sweet comes the Maiden,
dancing through flowers
rejoicing in powers
so free and so bold.
Praise for the sweetness
of her light laughter,
returning after
Winter's dark cold.

Mother's love showers
over the green Earth,
She brings us a rebirth
of fruit and of grain.
Praise Her abundance,
Praise Her creations,
All lands and all nations
Shall feast once again.

In Summer the Lovers,
lips red with berries,
come singing so merry,
come laughing so gay.
Give thanks to the Maiden,
and thanks to the Mother,
for blessing each lover
with passion's sweet play.

Goddess has risen,
Now is Her season,
She gives us reason
to be and to give.
Praise for the Maidens,
Praise for the Mothers,
Praise for the Lovers,
loving to live.[3]

Croning (Menopause)

Modern culture in America makes it very hard for women to remember their power-within, Goddess-within consequence. No woman is as devalued by the patriarchy as the Crone, which indicates how powerful the Crone really is. Men fear women's power, and no woman is more powerful than an older one. In Native American cultures, the woman who was past menstruation was someone to revere. She held her power within her and could use that power to govern the tribe. In Greece, the priestesses of Gaia who served the Delphic Oracle were post-menopausal women, the power of the oracle considered too much for younger women to withstand. Women live longer than men, and in matriarchal societies the longest-living woman was the leader of the group. By her years of experience and knowledge, her wisdom and power, by her very survival to old age, she was someone to turn to for guidance.

When a woman reaches mid-life, she is beginning a new life. The astrological mid-life crisis that happens around age forty is the start of great transformations. The process eventually changes the Mother to the Crone, leading her to inner growth not possible for someone younger. When she reaches her second Saturn return at age fifty-six, the croning is completed; the woman has passed the many inward tests and emerges as the Wisewoman, strong and deep in her power, confidence and consequence.

Patriarchy keeps the Crone in her place — she is something men can't control or tame — by ridicule and negative stereotyping. Mother-in-law jokes are only the beginning of the abuse done to older women in modern misogyny. The picture drawn by patriarchy is of a fussy, prudish, ineffectual figure in a sloppy dress who goes to church and bingo, is a hypochondriac and a meddler, and who is waiting to die. Nothing could be further from the truth, as Crone women are the ones on the protest lines, the movers and the shakers who make the world change. Imagine Golda Meier in the boys' stereotype, or Bella Abzug, Jean Mountaingrove, Mother Jones or Florence Kennedy. In the face of all that strong and wise Crone power, the men quail.

Take another look. Here is the strong grandmother, hera of little girls' childhoods, making beautiful things with her always-working hands, cooking complex ethnic foods, and always ready with a word of comfort. Here is the village midwife/healer, the woman who knows all the herbs to ease suffering and pain, the woman who knows how to listen and to make most things well. Here is the strong leader, directing meetings, organizing actions, insisting on peace amidst men's eagerness for war. Here is the Crone, the woman who holds her power within her and uses it for the good of all.

When a woman reaches her Crone phase, she can feel very alone in the patriarchal world. Her children are grown and autonomous, and the job she has hated for thirty years or more has finally ended with retirement. All the things she's wanted to do but never had time for are ready for her now, but she doesn't know how to change gears. It's been so long since she could focus on herself that she's probably forgotten where to start. Her friends are in the workplace, her children in other cities, and her lover is going through her own reevaluation. Her body is changing and new ways of doing things need to be devised. It's a time of transformations and changes, even down to everyday living, and the Crone feels isolated and tentative. She will make new patterns and new ways of living; a new life is beginning for her, but she needs some reinforcement. She won't get it from the mainstream culture with its patriarchal devaluation of older women. She needs it from her circle.

A croning ritual is a way to help the woman at menopause begin her new life. It's a validation of who she is and a recognition of a milestone, of her achievement in living long enough to be someone new. A croning is a way to combat the negative stereotypes of patriarchy, to tell the woman she is someone of special consequence, and to remind her of her own power as Goddess-within. The ritual emphasizes her power, her new admission into a sisterhood of the wise, her new beginning as a Wisewoman. It reminds her of her value and consequence, of all that she knows and has accomplished, of how much her wisdom and input are needed by other women. A croning ritual shows her that she is Goddess, that she has a place on the Wheel and is wanted in the universe. A woman's croning is a peak rite of passage on her life path.

The theme of a Women's Spirituality croning ritual is women's wisdom and power. The high number of Crone Goddesses in matriarchal cultures is an indication of the high esteem they held. Some Crone Goddesses are: Oya (Africa), Hecate (Greece), Mother Holle or Holde (Germany), Befana (Italy), Ceridwyn (Wales), Old Woman Who Never Dies (Native America), Baba Yaga (Russia), Sedna (Inuit), Spider Grandmother (Native America), Nepthys (Egypt), Ama No Uzumi (Japan), Baubo (Greece), Kali or Kali-Ma (India), Obatalla (Africa), Yellow Land Earth Queen (China), Yemaya-Olokun (Africa), Hella (Scandinavia), The Three Fates (Greece), The Norns (Scandinavia), The Morrigan (Ireland), and Copper Woman (Native America). The Motherpeace tarot card for a croning ritual is, of course, The Crone.

Colors for a croning are the white, red and black of the three-form Goddess, as the Crone has passed through the Maiden and Mother phase and entered the oldest mystery. She has passed menarche and motherhood and now reaches menopause, bringing with her the wisdom of a lifetime of experience and learning. Foods for the ritual are ethnic foods, the things grandmother taught her daughters and grandaughters. Include something red in the feasting, a pomegranate or one red egg to mark the end of motherhood and bleeding. Decorate the altar with special thought and care for this ritual: this is a very special rite of passage. Include an image of the oldest Goddess the women of the circle can find. Choose flowers for their heady scent, exotic species and open fullness; a woman reaches Cronedom only once.

Croning — A Menopause Celebration

There are various definitions of when a woman reaches croning and is eligible for a croning ritual. She may choose to celebrate when she reaches menopause, or wait until her second Saturn return at fifty-six years. She may want her ceremony when her last child leaves home, at retirement from her career, when she has become a grandmother, or at any other time she feels ready for it. If no circle is available, she may write and priestess her croning ritual alone. The woman may be long past the rite of passage transition when she decides to have a croning ritual — honor her wishes. Any time that a woman chooses to validate her consequence and Goddess-within power is a good time for a ritual.

Need

Candles — Use white, red and black candle on the altar.

Incense — Frankincense, sage, cedar or sweetgrass are incenses of immortality and the Crone. Or use a feather to stroke auras.

Flowers and altar decorations —Red flowers of strong scent, evergreens, exotic flowers, red chrysanthemums and carnations. Put a pomegranate (in season) on the altar or one red egg. Use an image of an ancient Goddess.

Oils and mirror for Self-blessing.

Optional — A scrying bowl or crystal ball on the altar.

Invocation/Poems — Use those below or choose others.[4]

Drums and rattles.

Contribution for give-away blanket and/or gift to Crone.
Potluck dinner contributions.
Matches to light candles and incense, charcoal block for loose incense, ritual wand.

Outline

Light candles.
Purify — With incense or stroke auras with a feather.
Cast circle/Invoke Crone Goddesses.

> Earth — Copper Woman, wise Crone (Pacific Northwest).
> Air — Baba Yaga, grandmother Goddess, the wise witch (Russia).
> Fire — Oya, mother of age and transformations (Africa).
> Water — Sedna, Old Woman of the Sea and women's power (Inuit).
> Spirit — Hecate, Crone Goddess of immortality, of life, death and reincarnation (Greece).

Go around the circle. The women invoke to the ritual other Crones, women's mothers and foremothers, herstorical figures. Go round the circle again, invoking to it attributes to bring to the new Crone — wisdom, patience, laughter, power, etc.

The high priestess says:

"At age fifty-six or at menopause, or whenever she feels herself ready and powerful, a woman becomes a Crone. We are here tonight for the croning of (*name*), to welcome her to the sisterhood of ancient women's wisdom."

The high priestess draws down the dark moon into the woman celebrating her croning, or the woman does it for herself. "May the power of the Crone serve you fully and well." The high priestess touches the woman's heart chakra with her ritual wand or feather, invoking the Goddess into her.

Body of ritual — The high priestess (or a woman of the circle) reads:

Crone Invocation I
by Lee Lanning and Nett Hart

> At croning, "we become more of our female selves. . . . We encourage our crones and the crones within each of us. We know the community's need for wimmin of all ages and abilities." At (*name's*) croning, "we come together to remember. We gather to hear the stories we all have to tell: those who have experienced more have more to tell,

but all share. We laugh much. Some stories bring tears of respect as we witness the strengths of us and the struggles we have endured. . . .

"We tell stories to share how we see ourselves, how we see the world, how we envision the future. We are brought together by each wommon's stories."[5] We share our knowledge as women and as crones with (*name*), who is newly a crone today.

Go round the circle, each woman sharing a story of her life, background, foremother's lives, etc. The new crone needs to find her wisdom — she speaks her own story last.

The high priestess reads:

Crone Invocation II
by Lee Lanning and Nett Hart

"We bring our medicine pouches and share what we know of healing, what we have gathered, what we have learned to do. We share how we are healing our pain, how we leave behind suffering, how we soothe any wrongs done us or by us. We care for one another, responding to one another's needs. We make sure everyone has enough. . . .

"We exchange 'grandmother gifts,' thoughtful deeds or materials we give to others as we perceive their use for them. Anyone may give a gift to anyone else; we do so without thought of return."[6] But our foremost gifts are for (*name*).

Go round the circle again, each woman sharing a healing herb, skill, poem, how-to for the new Crone. Use menopause remedies, arthritis remedies, teas for feeling good, resources, creativity suggestions, etc.

Each woman presents the new Crone with a nature gift, an herb, seashell, poem, crystal, etc., explaining what it is. The giveaway blanket is in the center or outside the circle, with additional gifts for all.

The new Crone moves to the center of the circle. Go round the circle, the women each bestowing a blessing on her (long life, great wisdom, many grandchildren, the Nobel Prize, great happiness, etc.). The new Crone makes a speech or gives a blessing in return, at the end.

Raise energy — Use a drum, rattles, or Crone wisdom songs. Direct the cone of power for blessing the new Crone and validating her coming into her Crone Goddess consequence.

Ground — Direct excess energy for earth healing. The earth is a Crone Goddess, too.

Self-blessing/mirror.

Optional — Do a scrying meditation with the crystal ball or scrying bowl. Ask to see a vision of Crone wisdom or a Crone Goddess. Ask her for a message to return with.

Ground again/Open circle.

Everyone hugs the new Crone.

Give-away blanket, potluck dinner, or both.

Some songs for a croning ritual include:

> We are the old women,
> We are the new women,
> We are the same women,
> Stronger than before.
>
> (Hey!)

or

> Mother, I feel you under my skin.
> Mother, I feel your heartbeat.
>
> Hey-O, Hey-O, Hey-O
> Hey-O, Hey-O, Hey-O.

or

The Crone's Song
> She gave to me a witching ring,
> a wraith of clouds, a song to sing,
> a whispered voice in the leafing tree
> the melting waters of an ice cold sea.
>
> The winter's gone, the hills are bare.
> The rabbit wakes from her darkened lair.
> My heart is hungry and my soul is free —
> O Goddess, give a sign to me.
>
> A bird in flight, so black of wing,
> across my path in the early spring,

She casts her eye, she holds me fast;
I see Her shadow in the tangled grass.

O Hecate pale, your call I know;
my hand grows cold like the nettle's sting;
the blackbird turns, and lets me go;
She gives to me another spring.

The chilly wind a-rushing free,
the pale green veils of the willow tree,
the circling hills, the melting snows,
the sheltered rock where the crocus grows.

The Beltane fires will burn once more,
like fifty summers I've known before.
The ice blue sky, the fallen rain . . .
She gives me back my life again.[7]
(by Doris Henderson)

Passing Over

Death is as inevitable as being born, and Women's Spirituality wicce
views it as a part of the Wheel of Life. In a religion that holds
reincarnation as a primary belief, death is not the final ending, but
only one ending of many. After death comes the other world, the
spirit world, a resting and learning place before rebirth. The child
emerging from the womb emerges from that other world, that
Summerland, and everyone who dies returns there.

Writers Helen Wambach (*Life Before Life*, Bantam Books, 1979)
and Raymond Moody, Jr. MD (*Life After Life*, Bantam Books, 1975)
conducted past life regressions through the death process and into
rebirth. Both concluded that the place of Be-ing between death and
rebirth is a pleasant place, that death is easier than being born, and
that most Be-ings leave the other world for rebirth only reluctantly.
That evidence, added to the many accounts of near-death experiences and psychic connections with those gone beyond, make death
for New Age wiccans something different from what mainstream
Western culture paints it. Most women in Women's Spirituality have
some past-life regression knowledge, sought after or spontaneous,
that indicates that they have lived before. Many have remembrance
of others in their lives, important to them now, who were present
and important to them in past incarnations. Many women are in

contact with spirit guides, a direct connection to that other plane.

Western culture has a pathological fear and denial of death and the death process. The medical system's insistence on preserving clinical life by heroic means (partly for the lure of high fees) encourages ghoulish procedures and surgeries on dying people. The woman who watches her friend, lover or parent die on life support, with respirators, dialysis, tubes, machines and blinking lights attached, sees death at its most distorted and most horrible, and not what it was meant to be. Patriarchal medicine has no concept of the quality of life, and its efforts to defeat the death Goddess are at best inhumane and futile. Often during the heroics, the Be-ing of the woman dying has already passed over. She wants to be released and free to go.

Patriarchal religions encourage this attitude toward death. Judaism says that there is no afterlife, and Christianity threatens the living with the fear of hell. In Protestantism, a woman is "saved" or not by predestination, and the "not" is too horrible to contemplate. No wonder most people in the West fear death beyond any other fear, and deny and fight it fully when it approaches for themselves or a loved one. The Goddess religion recognizes both the all-giving birth Goddess and the all-taking death Goddess, and recognizes that both are positive. One cannot exist without the other; without death there is no birth or rebirth. Hecate becomes Persephone again by emergence from Demeter's womb.

Memorial rituals in Women's Spirituality are the final rite of passage, and they are directed at both the Be-ing now freed of incarnation and at those left in bodies to mourn her passing. The emphasis is on remembrance of the never-ending Wheel, the cycle of life, death and reincarnation, and on sending the soul to the other world with love and blessing. The ritual creates a sacred space of beauty, a place between the worlds that is a bridge to that other world, and that affirms both death and rebirth. Rather than mourning the passing of a loved one, her life is celebrated, and all the things she gave to those who knew her are remembered with joy. Grief is not denied, but is met with hope. Loved ones will meet again. Death is not an ending but a new beginning, a transition to another place of Be-ing.

Decorate the altar in white, with white candles and flowers and use some evergreens in the room. White, or rather clear, is the color of the transpersonal point chakra, the Be-ing's connection with Goddess beyond the physical plane. Evergreens are a reminder of rebirth, as is a pomegranate or bowl of hard-boiled eggs. There is a bowl of seeds, beans or nuts in the shell on the altar, a cauldron/

bowl of earth, and a white flower and white candle in a holder for each member of the circle. Use a lot of candles on and off of the altar, a lot of light for this ritual, and emphasize the beauty of the altar and the ritual space.

The Motherpeace tarot card for this ritual is the Death card, which shows a snake shedding her skin. The message is letting go of the old and outworn and going on to new paths of consciousness. Goddesses for a memorial ritual include all Goddesses of death, rebirth and the underworld. Some of them are: Hecate (Greece), Ceridwyn (Wales), Inanna (Sumer), Oya (Africa), Kwan Yin (China), Spider Woman (Native America), Befana (Italy), Tara (Ireland), Isis (Egypt), Nepthys (Egypt), Erishkegal (Sumer), Mother Holle or Holde (Germany), Sedna (Inuit), Kali (India), Freye (Scandinavia), Old Woman (Native America), The Fates (Greece), The Morrigan (Ireland), The Norns (Scandinavia), The Furies (Greece), Aido Hwedo (Haiti), Persephone (Greece), and Rhiannon (Wales).

Do a potluck dinner after this ritual, it is comforting and grounding to the mourners to eat and be together. Use green vegetables and grains to suggest rebirth and new growth, and foods that the woman who passed over especially enjoyed. Remember to put a bowl of eggs on the table, a reminder of the promise beyond death.

Passing Over — A Memorial Ritual

A Women's Spirituality memorial ritual will probably be held after the traditional patriarchal funeral. That's how it is currently in mainstream society's denial of alternative religion, but this will not always be the case. Rather than fight it, the woman's circle holds a separate ritual for her as soon as possible, private to the coven. The ritual may be needed as a healing from the patriarchal funeral for the women, and a release for the passed over spirit from the holding-on of the funeral and mourners. The ritual's beauty and dignity, its affirmation of women's love and the power of Be-ing, life and death are designed to be healings for all involved.

Wiccan women are much encouraged to think ahead to their own deaths. A Living Will prevents the medical system's use of life support or other abused heroics on the body of a woman facing death. A Power of Attorney prevents the woman's lesbian or nonlegal lover or chosen family from being pushed aside by relatives. A Last Will and Testament designates and enforces what the woman wishes for her funeral and personal belongings, and also protects her lover in a joint relationship. Copies of the documents go to women who will be there in a crisis, and families are notified of their existence. Not enough women make use of these protections, which are relatively inexpensive legal safeguards against patriarchal abuse, and when they are needed it can be too late.

Need

Candles— White candles on the altar, and a white candle and holder placed in front of each woman in the circle.

Flowers — White flowers — try daisies or chrysanthemums — and some evergreens or a potted green plant. There is a single flower for each woman in the circle, put them in a separate vase within reach.

Incense — Avoid scents used in patriarchal churches, try myrtlewood for love and peace, sage for immortality, amber for clarity or sweetgrass for the spirit world. Or use the feather of Maat, symbol of immortality, to stroke auras.

Place a photo of the woman passed over on the altar, if possible.

Bowl of seeds, dried beans or nuts in the shell.

Larger bowl/cauldron of earth in the center of the circle.

Bowl of hard-boiled eggs, to be eaten after the ritual.

Oils for Self-blessing/mirror.

Invocation/Poems — Use those below or choose others.

Optional — Audio tape of Karen Mackay's song "Arms of the Goddess," on *Annie Oakley Rides Again!* (Available from Ladyslipper, P.O. Box 3124, Durham, NC 22705).

Contributions for potluck dinner.

Matches for lighting candles and incense, charcoal block for loose incense, ritual wand.

Outline

Light candles — First on the altar, then the high priestess goes around the circle lighting the candles in front of each woman.

Purify — With incense or the feather.

Cast circle/Invoke Goddesses of the underworld.

> Earth — Hecate, Mother of endings and beginnings (Greece).
>
> Air — Inanna, Goddess who descended and returned (Sumer).
>
> Fire — Oya, owner of the cemetery (Africa).
>
> Water — Kwan Yin, gentle mother of rebirth (China).

Spirit — Spider Grandmother, Goddess of creation and
immortality (Native America).

Each women invites to the circle an ancestor, friend or loved
one who has gone before.[8]

Charge of the Goddess — The high priestess reads the "Charge."

Invocation — "This is a ritual of passing and memorial for
(*name*), who was born on (*date*) and died on (*date*). She has passed
before us to the Summerland to await rebirth."

Inanna's Ascent
by Deanna Emerson

I have seen the piercing eyes
of the dark goddess
as she stands naked in the silent shadows
planting the seeds of vision
reached into the arms
of my deepest sorrow   and
looked into the eyes of death
yet the world dance did not cease.
By the light of the waning moon
I have seen the faces
of the shining ones   and
taking the sword of wisdom
cut the cords that bind me.
Armed only with love
I have entered the healing
power of the moon
drawing it down around me
to enter the sacred womb
of the dark goddess   and
turning pain into power

I have returned.[9]

Meditation — Experience the approach of death, experience
dying. There is no pain, only awareness and beauty. Experience the
process of letting go of the body, of being mourned, being received in
the other world. Experience and meet your spirit family, explore
and experience the spirit world. Now choose to return: enter the
womb, experience birth — there is no pain, only awareness. Grow to
now. Return to the circle.

Go round the circle three times. Each woman speaks and then

takes a seed and plants it in the cauldron/bowl of earth. She speaks three times and plants three seeds. She speaks of:

1. Her memory of the woman passed over, something to remember and celebrate her life. (Plants seed.)

2. Her memory of her first loss or knowledge of death, and what she lost when that person (or pet) died. What that person gave her. (Plants seed.)

3. Her memory of a past-life experience, near-death or past-death experience, her spirit connection with someone gone, her experience of a spirit guide, or her positive knowing of what is beyond. (Plants seed.)

Go round the circle once more. Each woman speaks her own name and plants a flower in the bowl.

The high priestess says:

"As seeds grow to flowers, so do flowers die into seeds; each of us dies and is reborn. We plant our seeds to remember (*name*) and all those we have lost. We ourselves are the flowers that bloom from the seeds, till we become seeds to die and be reborn ourselves. Leave your grief with the seeds till they bloom again in joy."

Optional — Play the audio tape of Karen Mackay's song "Arms of the Goddess," on *Annie Oakley Rides Again!* (Available from Ladyslipper Records, P.O. Box 3124, Durham, NC 22705).

Raise energy — Use humming. Direct the cone of power to the spirit of the woman departed, sending her on to rest, peace and rebirth.

Ground.

Self-blessing/mirror.

Ground again. Direct excess energy as love for the woman passed over, and love and healing for the earth.

Open circle/Hugs.

Potluck dinner.

Some songs for a memorial ritual include:

> Safe now, centered I know
> At one with the Mother
> And touching the flow
>
> of Spirit, gentle and deep,
> Reclaiming our power
> A promise to keep. (by Yarrow)

or

We all come from the Goddess,
And to her we shall return
Like a drop of rain,
Flowing to the ocean.

or

Arms of the Goddess
by Karen Mackay
Chorus:
Fly away into the arms of the Goddess, Sweet Woman,
Fly away into the arms of her pure blessed love.

Fly away into the arms of the Goddess, Sweet Woman,
Toward the light that's shining brightly
through the darkness above.

1. The silver cord is broken
    From your body you are free,
    Still I feel your presence strongly
    I know you're here with me.

    Are you frightened, lonely?
    How could it be?
    Tryin' in vain to comfort those
    Who neither hear nor see. (Chorus)

2. Where are the ones whose task it is
    To guide you on your way?
    Are you blinded by your earthly love,
    Your passion and your play?

    You know I'll always love you,
    Forever and a day,
    But you must listen to the priestess,
    Hear the words she has to say. (Chorus)

3. There's light that's shining brightly
    In the distance over there.
    It's time to cross the River Jordan,
    Time to climb the golden stair.

    I'd like to keep you with me,
    The burden I cannot bear,

And you must turn away no longer
From the Goddess and her care.

Chorus:
Fly away into the arms of the Goddess, Sweet woman,
Fly away into the arms of her pure blessed love.

Fly away into the arms of the Goddess, Sweet Woman,
Toward the light that's shining brightly
through the darkness above.[10]

Notes

1. See Diane Stein, *Stroking the Python: Women's Psychic Lives* (St. Paul: Llewellyn Publications, 1988) for more on these subjects.

2. Monica Sjoo, *The Great Cosmic Mother: Rediscovering the Religion of the Earth* (San Francisco: Harper and Row, 1987), p. 55.

3. Shekinah Mountainwater and Lunea Weatherstone, "Goddess Has Risen," in *Sage Woman* (P.O. Box 5130, Santa Cruz, CA 95063), Vol. III, Issue 9, Spring, 1989, p. 21.

4. This ritual suggested by Lee Lanning and Vernette Hart, *Ripening: An Almanac of Lesbian Lore and Vision* (Minneapolis: Word Weavers, 1981), p. 150.

5. *Ibid.*

6. *Ibid.*

7. Doris Henderson, "The Crone's Song," in *Sage Woman*, Spring 1989, p. 39.

8. This ritual was suggested by Penina Adelman, *Miriam's Well: Rituals for Jewish Women Around the Year* (Fresh Meadows, NY: Biblio Press, 1986), pp. 36-41.

9. Deanna Emerson, "Inanna's Ascent," in *The Beltane Papers' Octava* (P.O. Box 8, Clear Lake, WA 98235), Vol. 4, No. 4, Beltane, 1989, p. 7.

10. Karen Mackay, "Arms of the Goddess," on *Annie Oakley Rides Again!* audio tape (West Virginia Woman Records, 1984). Order from Ladyslipper, P.O. Box 3124, Durham, NC 22705.

Chapter Nine

───────────○───────────

Other Rituals

The moon phases, eight Sabbats, and rites of passage are the basic occasions for ritual but are not the only occasions. Once women begin celebrating change, changes of the moon, the year and their lives, ritual becomes a habit, something to turn to at other important times. Any time of change is a time for celebration and ritual, any time of choice or taking of power or consequence. Many women celebrate some form of ritual nightly, doing a short meditation, affirmation series or candle spell before bed. Any point of movement along the Wheel of Life is an occasion for rituals done alone or with a group.

The four rituals in this chapter are samples of the many occasions and times a ritual can be used. The four included here are house blessing, connecting with spirit guides, group bonding and a letting-go ritual. They are only a sample, as the possibilities are infinite, and by giving a sample I hope to encourage women to go further and create their own. As with the other rituals of this book, these are open to interpretation, change and entire redesigning to fit women's personal needs.

As women develop the habit of living with the flow of their internal/moon phases, with the earth seasons and the Wheel of Life, they discover women's place in the universe and universal plan. This discovery is the returning and reclaiming of women's consequence and power-within Goddess. The habit of doing ritual to mark special occasions continues women's living by the flow of the never-ending Wheel. A ritual makes an event special, and a special event deserves recognition by a ritual. Whether done alone or with a group, these rituals give life specialness and an increase of meaning. Any number of events and occasions can be recognized with a ritual.

The rituals from this book can also be adapted for other than their designated occasions. The Fall Equinox ritual for planetary and women's healing can be done at any time that a woman needs healing for herself, and the planet needs it always. The Full Moon wishing ritual can be used whenever a woman needs abundance or to manifest something in her life. The pregnancy/baby shower can be adapted to mark the beginning of any new project or creation. The Self-blessing can be done nightly, and is a good way to develop self-image, and the Candlemas self-dedication/initiation can be done at any time the woman wants self-dedication or her coven has occasion for the initiation ritual.

Rituals that are not done at Sabbats, Full Moons or life passages are usually solitary rituals, and any group ritual can be adapted for solitary use or for use by a couple or a few friends. A woman working alone can use a full ritual or any parts of it to meet her needs. Solitary rituals are often less formal and less elaborate than group rituals. To cast the circle, for example, the woman may simply invite the four directions and spirit, without doing formal invoking or naming them, or even without tracing the circle to cast it. She may say a few words of what she is feeling or what she intends, instead of reading or developing a written passage. The solitary ritual is no less powerful for being simple.

No occasion that is meaningful to a woman's life is too trivial to create a ritual for. While moving into a new house or apartment is a less momentous occasion than commemorating a death or a daughter's menarche, it is still an important time in a woman's life. Starting a new job is an occasion that may be worthy of ritual to the woman beginning it. A new relationship is a time when the two involved may want a ritual. This is not as formal as the trysting they may choose later, but is an occasion meaningful to them. Even birthdays, so trivialized and silly in modern culture, can be given real meaning by ritualizing them.

The first of the rituals of this chapter is a house blessing. Where a woman lives and the quality of her life there are essential for her well-being. She needs a place of safety and abundance, a place that feels her own and feels good to be in. The building of a living-together relationship or the conditions for women's creativity are contingent on this, on having a home that feels comfortable and secure. The whole quality of women's daily lives is based on it. Being homeless is among the most stressful things that could happen to a woman, and moving is a stressful event. A new home is chosen for its best possibilities as a place of peace and positivity.

In doing a house blessing ritual, the woman makes the

affirmation that her new home has all the qualities she needs. She notifies any negativity or negative entity that it must leave and invites to the house, to her living there, all the things that are meaningful to her in a living space. Vestiges of the last occupants are removed, leaving the house fully hers. Protection is invoked, love, comfort, warmth, low utility bills — whatever she chooses as important. The home becomes what she needs and wants.

In a ritual for meeting spirit guides, women make connection with the other world, the world we came from at birth and go back to after death. We were not meant to lose that connection with other realms. Though the results are powerful, the ritual itself is a simple meditation, an example of the things that can be accomplished in meditation work. It is basically a solitary ritual, though possible with a group.

The group-bonding ritual is designed for women beginning a coven. It's a help in bringing women together, getting them to know each other and to know what each has brought to the circle. It defines what women want from the group, what they are willing to bring to it, and starts the process of bonding that makes ritual work and coven work so powerful. A coven is a woman's chosen family, and beginning it with clearly defined goals and some basic knowledge about each other is a starting place. While the closeness takes time to develop, the ritual establishes the path.

The letting-go ritual could have been included in the rites of passage chapters. It's a healing ritual for broken ties, broken relationships primarily, but also for friendships gone sour. It can be used to release grieving for someone who has died, or to heal an abused childhood, and can be used with a group, a couple or alone. The intent is to release what no longer is viable, freeing the women to go forward with their lives and establish new bonds. It can be used as a public notification to the circle that a union is dissolved, but is first off a healing for the women involved, a boost to their self-image and an attempt to make the break as gentle as possible. A hope for gentleness and love goes with the ritual, including gentleness and love for oneself.

In all of the rituals of this book, a list of needs and tools is given at the beginning of each ritual outline. These are guidelines for assembling the items easily, so that something is not discovered missing in the middle of the ritual. The list is not limiting; the women can add to it whatever they choose, and adapt or change it as they want to. In the house blessing ritual, for example, the list includes enough flowers for each room and for the corners of the house outside. Flowers can be replaced with crystals or gemstones, pentacles or other meaningful objects. They can be deleted totally if the woman doesn't want them. So it is with the items listed for any of the rituals. In the case of song and food suggestions, they are also a matter of individual choosing. By this point in reading and using this book, women are ready to design rituals in their own way.

House Blessing

Moving is a chaotic situation. A woman takes apart the very fabric of her daily life and packs it into boxes. She buys things and throws things away, needs different things in a new house than in the old, and comforts or things needed may be temporarily out of reach. The disorder and the physical labor, the change into an unknown new house or apartment, a new neighborhood, are all highly stressful. If the woman is moving in with a lover, the emotional intensity is heightened. Not only a new home but a new life together are beginning; the changes are desirable and exciting, but also scary. Sometimes a move is because of a new job, a change of location, promotion or new situation. The addition of other factors, other life changes, adds to the stress of moving. A young woman moving into a college dorm, leaving home for the first time, is making a rite of passage into her first independence and adulthood.

Rituals help to put order into life changes, and moving is an occasion to do ritual. By setting the intent early that the new space, new living situation, new passage/relationship/job/school are positive and fulfilling, the woman helps them to be. By clearing out the old vibrations of her new space, she also clears out the chaos of her entrance there. By making the affirmations and invoking into the new home what she wants there, she establishes those things in her life from the beginning of her moving in.

The tarot card for a house blessing ritual is the Three of Discs, "building the house of the Goddess." The women in the Motherpeace deck are pictured creating safe and sacred space to live and work in. Goddesses for a house blessing are protection Goddess, who are usually Crones, and earth and abundance figures. Some of them include: Demeter (Greece), Hestia (Greece), Vesta (Rome), Benten (Japan), Habondia (Italy), Isis (Egypt), Obatalla (Africa), White Buffalo Calf Woman (Native America), Gaia (Greece), Ceres (Rome), Baba Yaga (Russia), Kwan Yin (China), Rhiannon (Wales) and Ala (Africa). Foods for after the ritual include a potluck dinner that the women bring to help the woman moving, and particularly any foods that can be made in the new home.

Colors for the ritual are chosen to symbolize what is wanted in the new house. Use green for abundance, rose for peace, friendship and love; red for sexual love; light blue or light green for healing; or purple for spirituality and psychic opening. For the banishing portion of the ritual, black candles can be lit, as black dissolves negativity; for the invoking portion, use the chosen colors or white.

House Blessing Ritual

The ritual can be done alone or with a group, and can also be used to remove negative entities or vibrations from an established house or living space. Begin the house blessing by setting up a permanent altar and dedicating it, then using the new altar as the foundation point for the house blessing ritual. If a permanent altar cannot be made for the time of the ritual, use a temporary one, but don't forget to dedicate the permanent altar when it's built. See Chapter 2 for the altar dedication ritual.

Need

Altar — Permanent house altar, already dedicated if possible, or dedicate as the first thing in the ritual.

Candles — Choose colors for the attributes wanted: green for abundance, rose or light blue for peace, purple for spirituality, light green or blue for healing, etc. Use black candles for banishing, white for invoking.

Incense — Smudge stick of sage or sage/cedar, or bowl of loose incense of sage, rosemary, frankincense or lavender for the banishing portion of the ritual. They are scents for purification and protection. In banishing negative entities, use sage.

For invoking — Use rose for love and peace, sandalwood for protection, spirituality, healing or exorcism, amber for clarity and illumination. Less optimally, invoke with sage or smudge stick.

Flowers — One flower for each room and each corner of the house outside. Use chrysanthemums for protection, roses for love or daisies for peace. Cedar branches — one for each room and each doorway outside. Put these on or in front of the altar at the start of the ritual.

Food to share, preferably made in the new house, or potluck dinner contributions.

Matches to light candles and incense, charcoal block for loose incense, ritual wand.

Outline

Light candles — If using separate candles for banishing (black) and invoking (white), light them when they are needed in the ritual, and only light the general altar candles now.

Purify — With incense. Use sage, sage/cedar, rosemary, frankincense or lavender. As an alternative to smoke, use salt water.

Cast circle/Invoke house, protection and abundance Goddesses. When casting the circle, include the entire house and grounds inside it.

>Earth — Demeter, protector of women, children and the home (Greece).
>Air — Benten, Goddess of the kitchen (Japan).
>Fire — Vesta, Goddess of the house and hearth (Rome).
>Water — Habondia, mother of abundance (Italy).
>Spirit — Obatalla, creator of the Goddesses and earth (Africa). Or White Buffalo Calf Woman, protector of her people (Native America).

Invocation — "We are here to dedicate this house to the Goddess, and to protection, safety, peace and creativity for (*name/s*) who now live here. In this ritual, we banish anything that could be negative, and invite instead all prosperity and love."

Dedicate the altar, if it is not already dedicated.

Body of ritual — The women make a procession counterclockwise through the house, smudging every room thoroughly. To banish unwanted entities, smudge three times. In each room say:

"I banish from this house all pain and negativity. I neutralize the energy." If the ritual is to banish entities, say: "I banish all negative or mischievous entities from this house. I send you to the Goddess, to heal you and take you where you need to go." Place a cedar branch in each room before leaving it. Go outside and do the same in a procession around the outside bounds of the yard, house or property. Put a cedar branch in front of each doorway.

Still outside, turn clockwise in procession around the property. Change the incense to rose, sandalwood or amber. While smudging say:

"I invoke to this house protection, prosperity, peace, love, wellness, creativity, etc." Place a flower at each corner of the house, or a crystal, pentacle or other object.

Procession re-enters the house and repeats the smudging clockwise in each room, invoking positive aspects and blessings, and ending at the altar. Place a flower in each room before leaving it.

The women form a circle at the altar. Each woman in the ritual (or the woman working alone) invokes the Goddess names and qualities she wants for the house, blessing the house with:

"Yemaya, bring healing; Demeter bring abundance; Amaterasu bring power and warmth; Spider Woman bring creativity." (Or Yemaya bring running water and good plumbing; Amaterasu low heating bills; Habondia bring a full refrigerator always; Moneta bring lots of money.)

Raise energy — Use humming, drums and rattles, songs or chant: "This house is a blessed house. This house is a safe house. This house is a prosperous house" to raise the cone of power. Direct the energy to making the blessings manifest and the house a positive, good home.

Ground.

Open circle/Hugs.

Share food.

Some songs to use in a house blessing include:

> The earth is a woman and she is rising.
> The earth is a woman and she is rising.
>
> We all live in her.

or

Pentagram
by Shekinah Mountainwater

Earth witch, ear to the ground,
Listening to her heartbeat.

Water witch, arms in the stream,
Reflecting on reflection.

Fire witch, breath to the flame,
Kindles passion.

Air witch, throat full of song,
Spinning sweet spells.

Spirit witch, embracing stars,
Imagining her magick.

Meeting Spirit Guides

The basis for this ritual is the wonderful book by Laeh Maggie Garfield, *Companions in Spirit* (Celestial Arts, 1984). As women become involved in the wiccan craft, they begin to open psychically, and ritual work in particular is a stimulant to this opening. An important way to aid psychic development, to bring guidance and comfort into women's lives, as well as to promote further growth and awareness, is to help women connect with their spirit guides. These nonphysical Be-ings, spiritual ties to the other world and the Goddess, are helpers and guardians to each incarnate spirit.

We are born into the earthplane with spirit guides to teach, guide and protect us, and to be a connection with the other world. As women open psychically and become aware of that other world through the between-the-worlds space of the cast circle, connection with spirit guides becomes a key to further growth. When women are ready to meet these positive Be-ings who are so much a part of them, a simple meditation ritual makes the bridge between the worlds. Experiencing it and meeting one's guides, or using it to deepen connections already made, is beautiful and empowering. Since Women's Spirituality and women's rituals are based on power-within/women's consequence, a ritual for making this connection seems important to include in this book. By meeting one's spirit protectors, women experience Goddess-within.

Spirit guides are a part of us and have been there always. In the African concept of the *sekpoli*, a woman's Be-ing is a combination of her ancestor/guardian and her own spirit. That guardian, or in the West "guardian angel," inner self, higher self, or conscience-voice is women's spirit guide. In Native American culture, these guides are animal totems. Each woman living on the earthplane has a life guide and probably a number of other guardian spirit helpers. By connecting with these Be-ings, a woman finds entrance to a source of great comfort and information, learning, protection and companionship. We were not meant to come to earth alone.

First impressions on connecting with a guide through this ritual are, "Of course I know you. You've always been here." From that point, the woman can ask questions, find out who her guide is, what she looks like, why she is there to help her. Guides appear as female or male, of any age or race, as an aura of light, or as an animal spirit. Once the initial contact is made, reconnection happens easily and spirit guides enter a woman's life as an active force, an active way to bring other-plane information into daily consciousness and life. The ritual/meditation and contact with guides is a moving experience, surprisingly simple to do.

Decorate the altar with purple or white candles and flowers, crystals and a crystal ball. The ritual can be done easily with a single candle and no other formal setting. Do it in a dark room, where the space feels very safe, comfortable and good. Use optimal meditation conditions, candle light, the phone shut off, barefoot and skyclad or in loose clothing. Lie flat with legs drawn up so feet touch the floor, keep legs uncrossed. Get very deeply relaxed. A good incense for this ritual is sweetgrass, which draws spirits. Avoid any scent that banishes entities, like sage, as that prevents contact and defeats the purpose of the ritual. Cast the circle with the intent of warding against negative entities and admitting positive ones.

Motherpeace tarot cards for this ritual are The Hanged One or High Priestess, cards that tell women to trust the power and love of the universe/Goddess. Goddesses to invoke in casting the circle are Goddesses of gentleness, love and psychic opening. Some of them are serpent/python Goddesses, others are Goddesses of the elements of water or air. A few possibilities are: Yemaya (Africa), Gaia (Greece), Aido Hwedo (Haiti), Rainbow Serpent (Australia), Isis (Egypt), White Buffalo Calf Woman (Native America), Mari (Near East), Inanna (Sumer), Tiamat (Semitic), Chalchiuhtlique (South America), Kwan Yin (China), Kwannon (Japan) or Ceridwyn (Wales). Foods for after the ritual are herb teas and fruits in season. This is a very quiet, gentle ritual that can also be used for past life journeys and regression work. It is done as easily alone as with a group.

Ritual for Meeting Spirit Guides

Do this ritual in a room lit only by candle light and with optimal meditation conditions. In the meditation, the high priestess/leader makes sure to give the women time to experience each step before moving on. Choose for high priestess the woman in the circle with the best sense of meditation timing, or a woman who is already in contact with her guides. The high priestess usually remains outside of the action of the ritual. The meditation can be taped beforehand, but is less effective that way. When working alone, a woman prepared beforehand for the meditation can lead herself through it; she does not need to speak the directions aloud. A key for success in this ritual for meeting spirit guides is to be completely relaxed before beginning the affirmation to meet your guide. Do a full relaxation sequence at least twice.[1]

Need

Most of the needs for this ritual are optional. The ritual can be done with one lit candle in a quiet, dark space.

Candles — Use white or purple.

Flowers — White, optional. Place some crystals on the altar or held in the women's hands.

Incense — Use sweetgrass or rose, no banishing scents. Sweetgrass invites the presence of spirits, rose is for love.

Optional — Use a musical background, instrumental and played very quietly. Try Patricia Sun's *All Sounds and Meditation Tape* (P.O. Box 7065, Berkeley, CA 94707), 1987.

Matches to light candles and incense, charcoal block for loose incense, ritual wand (or use a flower to cast circle).

Outline

Light candles — Take phone off the hook.

Purify — With sweetgrass.

Cast circle/Invoke gentle, psychic Goddess aspects.

    Earth — Gaia, the python Goddess (Greece).

    Air — Aido Hwedo, serpent mother (Haiti).

    Fire — Rainbow Serpent, dreamtime mother (Australia).

    Water — Kwannon, gentle mother (Japan).

    Spirit — White Buffalo Calf Woman, protecting spirit (Native America).

Body of ritual — Meditation ritual. The women lie down on their backs, legs drawn up with feet on the floor. Keep legs uncrossed. Feel grounded, centered and very, very relaxed. Women who fall asleep in meditations may prefer to experience this one sitting up.

Begin with a full body relaxation sequence, relaxing every part of the body moving from feet to head. After completing it, do it a second time, then do the Tree of Life Meditation from Starhawk's *The Spiral Dance.*[2] Feel your feet rooted to the floor/earth. Feel roots emerging from the bottoms of your feet and growing deep to the center of the earth. Feel energy moving through you from your feet (the earth) to your head, and out.

Make the affirmation, "I am ready, willing and able to meet my guide," and ask for a guide to appear to you. Ask with love, and ask for one guide at a time to come, your life guide.

    Ask her name.

    Who is she?

    What does she look like?

Why is she your guide, why is she there for you?
Ask what she needs from you.
Ask if you have known her before and how.
Ask how it is easiest for you to contact her.
Are there other guides present?
Does someone else want to come forward?
Ask who she is.

Ask what else you need to know for this first time. Give time between each question to receive the answers. Give time at the end to ask other questions from within. Make this a slowly paced meditation, with a sense of how much space to wait between questions. The answers are profound, don't rush them.

If there are blocks to meeting your guide/s, see if a fear of the unknown is the reason, if you were stopped as a child from being with "invisible playmates," if you really feel ready for the contact. Ask for help from your guide in making the connection, clear your chakras by drawing energy from the earth to release through your crown and send love and readiness through your aura. Make the affirmation again, "I am ready, able and open to receive my life guide on the conscious plane."[3] Know you are in full control of the experience.

Come out of the meditation and come back to now. Move slowly at first, and return slowly and gently. Go found the circle sharing the results.

Offer thanks.
Open circle/ground.
Sharing food after the ritual helps to ground.

Group Bonding

When a group of women begin meetings to form a coven, they usually start with a large number of women. As time goes on and the meetings continue, the number of women that come to each subsequent meeting starts to lessen. Over time, those with less commitment and those who feel this particular group is not meeting their interests and needs drop out. By the time the women have been together for six months, the numbers have dropped from perhaps twenty or thirty to five or six. These five or six women are the core group of the coven. They continue working together, meeting and planning, doing rituals and study sessions. At some point they close the membership, occasionally adding or losing a member until a solid working coven has developed. This is the coven-forming process of most Women's Spirituality ritual groups, those that form covens instead of open gatherings. In a coven, the same women work together all the time. In an open gathering, anyone can come to any session or ritual, and the membership differs from gathering to gathering. In traditional witchcraft, the coven-forming process is different; the high priestess chooses the new members, sometimes from an outer circle that meets as above.

Once the process has begun of forming a women's coven, the process of group bonding has also begun. As the less interested women drop out, the more committed ones become more aware of each other. They want to know who each other is, what each is like, what each brings to the group. Openness develops that increases to trust and friendship. As the women share the group together, their mutual experiences and shared activities result in group bonding. The women who came together as strangers develop into intimates, friends who know each other well and who come together for a mutual, important reason. They become a chosen family, a small matriarchy.

The following ritual is a good beginning ritual for a new group. It is best done on a waxing or full moon, but can be done at any time and in any season. It's a simple enough ritual to be a group's first one, and serious enough to have consequence in the developing group process. One woman may cast the circle, five others each invoke an element and spirit, another can lead the meditation, and someone else opens the circle. By involving all the women, everyone is the high priestess for the coven's first ritual, and the group begins learning to work together. Plan the ritual in advance, decide who is to bring what and who is to do what part/s. Do the ritual on an evening when no other business is planned, and when everyone can be there. The potluck dinner at the end, or some form of communal food sharing, is an important part of the ritual and evening.

Decorate the altar together, women bringing to it things that are meaningful for them. Each woman brings a candle and holder in her own personal or Goddess color. Flowers are optional, but always nice; bring what feels right. Have a candle for each direction and a central spirit/Goddess candle: use green for earth, indigo for air, red or orange for fire, light blue for water, and white or purple for spirit. Choose Goddesses that are meaningful for the women of the group, remembering to include names from nonwhite cultures. Use a European Goddess, an African Goddess, a Native American Goddess and an Asian one to invite and make welcome a diversity of women and as an affirmation of the group's intent.

The Motherpeace tarot cards for this ritual are The Magician and The Chariot, depicting desire, will and manifestation of change through women's inner work. Try also the Three of Cups, women coming together to share joy and spirituality. In the potluck dinner that follows the ritual, the women cooperate to not duplicate energy. One brings dessert, another a beverage, others main courses, salads or side dishes. Coordinate the effort to prevent a series of desserts or side dishes with no main meal or beverage, or all main meals with no dessert.

Group Bonding Ritual

The following ritual is best done with a small- to medium-sized group, more than four but less than ten women. It can be done earlier in the size reduction process, with a larger group, and repeated later when the group is reduced to the serious coven core. Discuss and plan the ritual in advance, decide what each woman is to do and bring for the ritual and potluck. The women may want to have outline cards of the process for doing this first ritual together. Notecards work well for this. Be careful not to over-plan or rehearse in advance answers to the go-round-the-circle questions. Too much is lost when a ritual becomes a script; keep it spontaneous, relaxed and natural. If there is critiquing afterwards, be gentle with each other; the mistakes matter less than the effort and intent, and the Goddess won't mind them at all.

Need

The women make an altar together, each bringing items for it. Arrange them before the start of the ritual.

Candles — Each woman brings a candle and holder, candles in her chosen color. On the altar, use a green candle for earth, an indigo one for air, red or orange for fire, light blue for water, and white or purple for spirit.

Flowers — Whatever the women bring are welcome.

Incense — Use sandalwood for healing and love, lotus or heliotrope for spirituality, lilac or rose for harmony. Or purify by stroking auras with a flower or whisk broom.

Invocation/Poem — Use the "Charge," the following poem, or choose others.

Chalice of spring water or fruit juice.

Plate of cookies, crescents or pentacles, enough for everyone.

Oils and mirrors for Self-blessing. Use olive or vegetable oil if fragrant oils are unavailable.

Potluck dinner contributions.

Matches to light candles and incense, charcoal block for loose incense, ritual wand (or use a flower).

Outline

Candles are not lit yet.

Purify — With aura-stroking or incense.

Cast circle/Invoke the four elements and spirit. Light a candle for each direction on the altar while invoking that element, and a larger spirit candle in the center. The women's candles are not lit yet.

> Earth (Green) — Mawu, mother of growth and women's bonding (Africa).
>
> Air (Indigo) — White Buffalo Calf Woman, mother of women's creativity (Native America).
>
> Fire (Red/Orange) — Amaterasu, Goddess of the sun and women's power (Japan).
>
> Water (Light Blue) — Isis, mother of harmony and peaceful group relations (Egypt).
>
> Spirit (White or Purple) — Ceridwyn, Goddess of women's working together and change (Wales).

Go round the circle and chant each woman's name three times. Move clockwise, the direction of invoking, for all parts of this ritual except opening the circle.

Invocation. On Full Moons read "The Charge of the Goddess." At other times, try the following poem or choose another.

Invocation Poem
by Lee Lanning and Nett Hart

We honor the energy of the elements within us.

We are earth. We are dark, we are heavy, we are substantial. We are grounded.

We are water. We are fluid, we are clear, we are vital. We are renewed.

We are fire. We are bright, we are hot, we are intense. We are aroused.

We are air. We are light, we are movement, we are open. We are changed.[4]

Meditation — The women sit in the circle holding hands for this. Go through the full relaxation process, then do a meditation on the group. Visualize the group's goals, future, growth and women.

Allow free-form ideas and images to come, and follow them where they lead. Ask for a Goddess to be a guide for the developing group. Notice what she looks like, what she says or does. Ask her for a message or a gift to take back. Come back to now.

Body of ritual — Go round the circle and have each woman talk about what she saw for the group in the meditation. She describes the Goddess/guide she saw and her message or gift. She talks about her own ideas for group goals.

Go round the circle again. Each woman says what she wants from the group and what she brings to it. Responses are more than one sentence, but are not overly long. When she finishes speaking, the woman lights her candle and places it in front of her or on the altar. Candles remain lit for the rest of the ritual.

Raise energy — The women hold hands, and raise energy by humming or songs. Direct the cone of power to the group's harmony, bonding and success.

Ground.

Self-blessing/mirror.

Share food — Pass around the chalice, each woman making a toasted blessing for the group, then taking a sip from the chalice. Pass around the cookies, each woman feeds the one next to her.

Open circle.

Ground again.

Everyone hugs everyone else.

Potluck dinner. (Don't forget to blow out the candles.)

Some song suggestions for this ritual are:

> We all fly like eagles,
> Flying so high,
> Circling the universe,
> On wings of pure light.

> Oo, witchy-I-O
> Oo-E-I-O.
> Oo, witchy-I-O
> Oo-E-I-O.

or

> Chorus:
> A river of birds in migration,
> A nation of women's with wings.

> Find the heart of freedom,

Buried in the ground.
Mother Earth is calling you
To lay your burden down. (Chorus)

Find the heart of changes
Deep within your soul.
Your inner self is calling you,
A story to unfold. (Chorus)

or

She's been waiting, waiting,
She's been waiting so long.
She's been waiting for her children
To remember to return. (by Paula Wallowitz)

Letting Go

The focus in modern culture is on beginning and building relationships, on romance and moving-in or marriage. There is an illusion that once two people come together, they will stay together for life and live "happily ever after." The fact is that few relationships are lifelong. The partners have come together at a time in their individual lives when that coming together is right for them. For whatever reasons, positive or negative, the relationship gives them both something they emotionally want or need. Over time, as the individuals grow they change or their life situations change, or their emotional/spiritual/psychological needs change. This change is a part of living, and as it happens the partnership may no longer be right for one or both of them. Over half of heterosexual marriages end in divorce, and while there are no statistics, the same is true of lesbian relationships.

Since the 1987 Harmonic Convergence, I've watched dozens of long-term relationships dissolve, with more or less pain to the partners. One may be ready to end the relationship, but the other is devastated. Anything that is not working in women's lives is being challenged; the problems must be faced and resolved or the partnerships end. As nonfunctional pairs separate, women go through serious periods of loss and revaluation before new bonds form. The new bonds beginning to happen now seem free of old problems, old baggage that made the earlier ones untenable. Many soul mates or karmic lifemates are finding each other again, and helping each other heal to new wholeness. False starts are still happening for some women, but will be temporary; new fusions are beginning to occur.

There is also a growing number of women with chronic lower back pain, often serious disability. Every one of these women's pain, with whatever direct physical cause, began at a time when their long-term relationships broke up or reached the no-return deterioration point, and the women have not yet come to emotional terms with the hurt. Emotional pain manifests physically, and lower back pain is a belly chakra issue, caused by retained anger, hurt, low self-image and loss of personal power connected to a sexual relationship. The relationships that ended, sometimes years ago, seem to be negative ones — the partners fought with each other constantly, one felt submerged and dominated by the other, one felt she did all the work of holding it together, one partner grew, and the other didn't. After sometimes more than a decade of holding it together, the relationship ended, and the woman who suffered within the relationship suffers after it. When her physical/emotional damage is released and her consequence is rebuilt, she can go on to the new fusions, new and positive relationships, free of pain. The healing is physical, emotional, mental and spiritual — and sexual. It involves letting go, and choosing and accepting inner power.

Little public recognition is made at a time of breaking up of the pain of the partners separating. If one partner decides to leave and the other doesn't choose the split, the one left is devastated and holding all the hurt. She is the candidate for the back problems. When a couple has friends together and the relationship ends, one or both partners lose their support system and community. The partner left may feel she did something wrong or "wasn't good enough," or she may be very angry and/or suppress the anger. If her partner takes a new lover soon, it hurts even more. One or both partners may take on blame, when usually no blame can be assigned. No support is given in modern culture for the courage it takes to realize a relationship is no longer working and to end it and go forward. No cultural attempts are made to release enough pain and anger so that the partners can be friends, and so that neither develops back problems in her attempts to suppress the emotions, hurt and anger.

The following ritual is to unbind a relationship, and to do it in a circle-supporting, healing, pain-releasing way. It is best done in the coven and with both partners, but can be done alone as well. Use it for separating from a lover or ending a friendship or other relationship without recriminations. Use it as a release from a long-ended relationship not let go of, or by an incest or child-abuse survivor, as a way of clearing old ties and going forward. The recognition in the circle is on loss, and on healing the loss to move on.

Do the ritual on a waning moon, the time for unbinding. The colors are black for endings, white for new growth, and red for transformations. Use sage or cedar incense, purification and renewal scents, and an unbinding cord of black or purple. The Motherpeace tarot cards for this ritual are The Tower, for major change, Death, for shedding and renewing, and The Star, for rebirth and trust in the Goddess/universe. Put a bowl of salt and a bowl of honey on the altar, for the bitterness and sweetness of life and love, and serve sweet foods in the food sharing after the ritual.

Goddesses for a letting go ritual include both Crone and love Goddesses, for the Goddess of love has her other side of transformations. Some of the Goddesses include: Aphrodite (Greece), Venus (Rome), Freya (Scandinavia), Oshun (West Africa), Igaehindvo (Native America), Vega (China), Hecate (Greece), Oya (West Africa), Ceridwyn (Wales), Astarte (Semitic), Inanna (Sumer), and Ishtar (Mesopotamia). Remember the healing mothers, too — Kwan Yin (China), Kwannon (Japan), Isis (Egypt), Yemaya (Africa), Mari/Mary (Semitic), Sarasvati (India), and Chalchiuhtlique (South America).

Letting Go Ritual — Unbinding a Relationship

This is a ritual for ending a relationship, or for a woman who has been unable to let go after a relationship's end. It's a clearing for going forward, a ritual both of recognizing loss and opening to new beginnings. Expect a release of tears in the circle, not to be prevented by the high priestess. The two women on whom the ritual is focused agree to behave civilly with each other and to leave animosities outside the ritual space. The high priestess holds them to that promise.

Women seated on each side of the pair in the circle should be close friends, ready to soothe and comfort. The goal of the ceremony is that the pair release enough hurt to eventually retain a friendship, and that both partners are able to move forward in their lives — alone or with new lovers later. Hold the ritual with both partners if possible, or focus it on the healing of one of them. Place the Motherpeace tarot cards — The Tower, Death and The Star — on the altar, as a reminder of the healing process.

Need

Candles — Use black, white and red candles on the altar for endings, new growth and transformation.

Incense — Sage or cedar for purification and renewal. Or stroke auras with a dried corn ear shuck.

A bowl of honey and a bowl of salt are on the altar, for sweetness and bitterness in love.

Tarot cards — The Tower, Death, and The Star, for the process of change, endings and renewal.

Flowers — Evergreens for endings and renewal.

Cord for unbinding — Black or purple, about three feet long.

Scissors — To cut the cord.

Invocation/Poem — Use the one that follows or choose others.

Oils/mirror for Self-blessing.

Optional — Drum for raising power.

Matches to light candles and incense, charcoal block for loose incense, ritual wand.

Outline

Light candles.

Purify — With sage or cedar incense, or use aura stroking with a whisk broom (not tryst broom) or dried corn ear leaves.

Cast circle/Invoke Goddesses of love and change.

> Earth — Hecate, for endings and beginnings (Greece).
>
> Air — Aphrodite, the ephemeral one, that she come again (Greece).
>
> Fire — Oya, Goddess of change and transformations (Africa).
>
> Water — Kwan Yin, for healing and compassion (China).
>
> Spirit — Ceridwyn, for immortality and peace (Wales).

Invocation — The high priestess says:

"We are here tonight to recognize the unbinding of (*name*) and (*name*), to help them to go their separate ways in love and peace."

Invocation
by Carol Christ

Pausing at the threshold of the temple, I pour out the water and wine. All of a sudden I hear what I can only describe as the laughter of Aphrodite, as clear as a bell. I hear Aphrodite saying through her golden laughter, "Whoever told you that you could know sexual ecstasy without pain?" And then she begins to laugh again, saying, "What can you do but laugh?" I begin to laugh with her. I laugh with joy and pain.[5]

Body of ritual — The high priestess binds the cord loosely around the two women's hands, binding the women together.

The two women take turns making pairs of short single-phrase statements, one good and one bad about their relationship. Remind the women to remain honest, but also polite and civil with each other. Go back and forth till all is said, keeping the statements very short. If working alone make a list. The women do not interrupt each other or respond to each other's statements; there are no recriminations, no guilt, no meanness. Women on each side put arms around the pair, if needed. Expect tears, it's part of the healing.

The two women make a verbal gift to each other, each says something very caring and loving about the relationship or her ex, or offers her a blessing for the future.

Each woman in the circle goes to the pair, hugs each, and offers each a verbal gift (clarity, peace, new love, healing, etc.). The couple last offers each other such a gift and they hug.

Meditation — The whole group does a meditation on chakra cords/ties to others. Visualize the ties that cord you at your belly chakra. Identify and evaluate each tie or cord and choose to keep it or pull it out. Gently remove or cut those cords to people/relationships no longer in effect or positive. Fill the cord wounds and whole aura with blue light for peace, healing, serenity and clarity. Recognize what cords still bind you, and what cords re-attach after pulling. Know that you choose them to be there, and that some cords are harder to pull than others. Come back to now.

The high priestess asks:

"Are you ready to break what binds you?" When both partners say yes, she cuts the cord that ties their hands.

Self-blessing/mirror.

Raise energy — Use drums, humming, songs, or chant; "She changes everything she touches, and everything she touches changes."[6] Direct the cone of power to the women for clarity, peace, healing and going on to new goals, new relationships when they choose them.

Ground/Open circle.

Ground again.

Group hug — The pair hugs each other first, then everyone hugs everyone else in the ritual.

Share food.

Some songs to use for this ritual include:

The Goddess rises within me,
I am she who ever would be free.
From troubles she can lift me,
I am she who ever would be free.

The Goddess in me,
Lifts me up and takes me to the sea
To cleanse and heal the wounds of
Chains that bind me.

The Goddess in me, I am
She who is free.
The Goddess in me, I am she.
She is we. We are she.

or

Shine on, darling shine on.
Remember I love you, shine on.
And wherever you go,
Let your sweet spirit show.
You are loved in the universe,
Shine on, shine on. (by Karen Mackay)

or

Born of water,
Cleansing, powerful,
Flowing, healing —
We are.

Notes

1. Suggested by Laeh Maggie Garfield and Jack Grant, *Companions in Spirit* (Berkeley, CA: Celestial Arts, 1984), pp. 38-39.

2. Starhawk, *The Spiral Dance: A Rebirth of the Ancient Religion of the Great Goddess* (San Francisco: Harper and Row, 1979), p. 44.

3. Laeh Maggie Garfield, *Companions in Spirit*, p. 39.

4. Lee Lanning and Nett Hart, *Awakening: An Almanac of Lesbian Lore and Vision* (Minneapolis: Word Weavers, 1987), p. 48.

5. Carol Christ, *Laughter of Aphrodite: Reflections on a Journey to the Goddess* (San Francisco: Harper and Row, 1987), p. 191.

6. Starhawk, *The Spiral Dance*, p. 175.

Chapter Ten

—————————○—————————

Candle Magick

Many women work alone at ritual all or most of the time. They have not found other witches, or not found a coven, have not found the right women to do ritual with, want to do ritual work more often than their group does them, or simply choose to work alone some or all of the time. Some women limit their solitary rituals to the Sabbats, the Full Moons or to important occasions in their lives, while others connect with Goddess and Goddess-within energy every day. That connection can take several paths. Meditation is one way to work alone on a regular basis, and is also the key to most spiritual and psychic development. Affirmations are another way to do solitary rituals, and they can be combined with meditation. In affirmations, a woman makes positive, present-tense statements about qualities and things she wants to add to her life, and the statements come true and the qualities or things manifest. Another way to do solitary rituals is with candle magick, a technique that combines meditation and sympathetic magick for manifesting.

In meditation, women go into a quiet, psychic space and use that altered state to manifest what they design through visualization. To visualize is simply to imagine, to create an image in any sensory way (sight, sound, hearing, touch, scent or a combination of these). Psychic healing is based on meditation and visualization, entering a quiet place and visualizing oneself or someone else receiving light, colors or healing. Another form of visualization/ meditation is the guided journey, where a woman goes to another place, real or idyllic. She experiences something or meets someone there who gives her a message or gift, or shows her what she needs to know or do. This form of meditation is used in rituals, as in guided meditations to experience one's own birth, or to meet a Goddess who will guide the formation of a coven.

There are two other important forms of meditation used by women in the Goddess craft. In one, meditation is done by taking the random thoughts that come into one's mind and following them where they go. The thoughts can be directed to what one chooses and creates or just followed where they will. The other form is the opposite process of eliminating thoughts, pushing them out of mind until there is total stillness within. In India, this form of meditation is considered the road to enlightenment, but it is also the hardest type to do. Meditation in any of its forms is the basis for virtually every aspect of craft practice.

Affirmations are another way to do solitary rituals. If a woman wants a new job, for example, she goes to her altar and lights a candle (green for prosperity), and makes positive, present tense statements about the job she wants. She says "I have," rather than "I am looking for" or "I will find," since by visualizing it as being here now, she makes it happen in the now. Putting the image off until later by "I *will* have," puts its manifesting off until some time in the indefinite and always moving-away future. The technique can be used for any number of ideas.

If a woman wants a particular quality in her life, she uses affirmations for things like inner power, psychic development, a career break, prosperity, healing, a new house or apartment, to find a coven, or a lover. In the case of a lover, direct it at a specific lover only if you know she is in agreement, otherwise just ask for the quality of love, or "the right lover." By combining "I have" statements with clear visualization in the meditative state, the ritual becomes more powerful. When asking for a new apartment, for example, don't just ask for any apartment, but specify and imagine the ideal one. When asking for a new job, imagine the best one and what working at it is like. By visualizing along with going out and job or apartment hunting, the right thing comes quickly and to specifications. This form of affirmation ritual is a form of candle magick.

True candle magick carries the techniques of visualization and meditation further, and combines them with sympathetic magick. Sympathetic magick is a way of using symbols to make a small model/microcosm of what you want to manifest in the larger/macrocosm world. An example of sympathetic magick is using a candle to represent the element of fire, or a candle at each element to represent the four elements and spirit. A candle is a small example of a larger concept, or is used as a representative of that concept. Another example is with a healing doll. What the healer wants to create for the person she is healing is shown on the doll.

The doll represents the woman being healed, and if it's a broken leg that needs healing, the doll is shown with her leg mended. The idea is that the magick transfers to the woman, whose leg will also mend. Candle magick, as its name indicates, uses sympathetic magick with primarily candles as its symbols.

The art of magick is defined as the art of shaping consciousness at will, and magick is central to the Women's Spirituality craft. "Consciousness" and "will" are the two key words here. By being aware of the reality of the power of magick — which is women's ability to have consequence in the world, to create a world as they choose it — women can and do create anything they want. Being aware of the power of will, the power of desiring something and knowing you can have it, women use that consciousness to create their world and what they want to happen in it. The energy that is the universe/Goddess can be used in a variety of ways, and women's use of that energy in their lives becomes the structure of their lives. Much of the Goddess religion is based on these concepts: every ritual act in the cast circle is designed to create and to empower by consciousness and will. The cast circle is a microcosm of the larger world, as the candle symbols are in a candle magick ritual.

The world's consciousness has been badly abused in the patriarchy. Men have created for themselves an image of a world at war, choking in its own pollution and poisoned by greed. Women visualize and create a different world, a world of peace, of ecological sanity and reforestation, and a world where people help each other to survive. The choice is up to us as to what sort of world we create, on the personal or political level. On the personal level, a woman can visualize herself in a life of poverty, struggle and pain (which is probably where she started out), or use her consciousness and will to change that image. Even with as strong a force as the patriarchy going against her to prevent her positive image from manifesting, she accomplishes great changes by her efforts.

This is not ever to say, as the New Age sometimes does, that any misery or dis-ease in women's lives is there by their own choosing or because they haven't worked to change it. Women enter the world with several strikes against them, simply by being born female. If they are additionally born as a woman of color, or disabled, or belonging to a minority group, or lesbian or poor, they have that many more obstacles to overcome, that many more oppressions to survive. That a woman survives at all in some instances is a modern miracle of will in itself. The idea that women choose their circumstances and even their illnesses may possibly be so on the karmic level, but if so it is in a nonconscious, non-earthplane way. That a woman from a highly downtrodden background becomes a great success is a tribute to her ability to manifest will and consciousness. That another woman in downtrodden circumstances has not done so, however, puts no stigma on the other woman. No two walk the same path, and blame is unfortunate, unproductive and cruel. No woman has the right to judge another in any way.

Ritual magick, the structure and intent of the Sabbats, moon, rites of passage and other rituals, creates a world inside the circle that is used to transform the world outside it. This is sympathetic magick, creating an idealized world or chosen positive events, then carrying the image and reality out to the physical plane. When a woman visualizes and ritualizes the job she wants, she finds it on the earthplane waiting for her. When a woman visualizes and ritualizes world peace, she creates a thought that helps it happen. In sympathetic magick, the microcosm is chosen carefully; energy is a neutral thing, to be used by women for whatever they choose. In choosing what to manifest, women create their wills by consciousness, by conscious use of their power to shape reality. In a group ritual or a candle spell, the idea is the same.

Energy is a neutral thing, neither positive nor negative. Like water or any element, it has its positive and negative sides and can be used or misused. Water is the stuff of which life is made, and no living thing lasts long without it. On the other hand, the power of tidal waves or torrential hurricanes can destroy life with water, too. The African Goddess pair Yemaya and Yemaya-Olokun demonstrate this idea. Yemaya is the gentle water of life, while Yemaya-Olokun is the angry, destructive side of the ocean, held in chains at the bottom of the sea, lest she destroy the world. In sympathetic magick, the energy is also neutral and can be used for good or not. The patriarchy has created a negative world by its negative world view; women do the opposite and work to heal the damage.

Candle magick has a bad reputation for misuse and manipulative ethics, but its energy is neutral and can be used in highly positive ways. Women are aware of the laws of the craft and the laws of the universe/Goddess: 'Harm none,' and 'What you send out comes back to you three- (or ten-) fold.' Interfering with another's free will is considered harm in the strongest degree; women have fought for too many centuries for autonomy from men and patriarchy to allow negative use of energy on themselves or others by manipulative magick. The books on candle spells often contain negative work, with no discussion of the ethics or consequences.

217 Candle Magick 217

This chapter on candle magick follows the Goddess religion's clear ethics — its energy is used for the good of all, according to free will, harming or manipulating none.[1] When this simple ethic is observed, candle magick can add much to women's solitary rituals and women's lives in a highly positive way. No book on ritual can ignore its power or positive potential for women's Goddess-within consequence.

Marion Weinstein's *Positive Magic* (Phoenix Publications, 1981), offers good grounding in the use of ethical work and clear delineation of what is positive and what is not. If a form of magick affects anyone else's free will in any way, it is negative. If it harms anyone, or is not good for someone, it is negative. Positive magick is good for all involved, harming none, manipulating none, and done totally according to free choice. Since what is sent out comes back, and has karmic consequences even beyond this life, only positive magick makes any sense at all, and is women's way. Hexing, the sending out of negative or manipulative energy, even to a rapist or murderer, is not to be considered. The energy's return to its sender makes it just not worth it. Let the rapist's own karma deal with him, and it will. (Women take power by fighting him through the legal system, however.)

Some forms of candle magick are definitely negative, even though not meant to be. The classic one is the love spell, which is also a classic example of manipulation of another's free will. A woman related this story: She and her lover of several years were having difficulties in their relationship, and the lover was having an affair. The woman bought two image candles, red for sexuality/sexual love and shaped in female forms. She wrote her name on one and her lover's on the other, tied them together and lit them, visualizing the couple drawn together again. Then the candle she had designated for her lover went out, and she couldn't relight it. The woman phoned me in great fear, asking if that meant her partner's love for her had gone out and couldn't be relit. I told her I thought it was a warning about manipulation, to stop doing such magick. It turned out that while the candle spell was happening, the lover developed an intense headache, knew something was wrong, and her own energy had doused the candle. The relationship has not mended, though the woman who did the spell is still holding on. She is avoiding further candle spells done without her partner's permission.

With women's consciousness to do positive work and will to create a world that is good for all, candle magick can have powerful positive effects and good karma. The woman who uses candle magick (or meditation/visualization/psychic healing) to help in the healing of someone who requests it or astrally accepts it is doing positive candle magick. The woman who manifests for herself the perfect apartment or job, or asks for love in a nonmanipulative way and receives it is doing positive magick that helps herself, helps others, harms none and is according to free will. This powerful form of ritual work, generally done alone, can be used to manifest great good in women's lives and to better the conditions of the individual and the world. Use it with ethics and conscious awareness for the good of all.

Candle magick is based on a series of correspondences that establish the symbols of the candles as precisely as possible. Colors are a basic symbol correspondence system, as in using green candles for prosperity, purple for spirituality, or rose for love and peace. Candle colors used throughout this book, based on the chakra colors and correspondences, use this system. Though most candle magick books declare black a negative color, it is not, but instead is used for banishing, grounding and to dissolve negativity. White, so overused in Women's Spirituality, is all the colors of light together, as black is all the colors of pigment together. Rather than depending on "white light" (a somewhat racist concept), it is better to know what color is the best for the intent and to use that instead. The candle colors below are good correspondences for women's candle magick work.

Black	Grounding, banishing, dissolves negativity, dark moon energy.
Red	The life force, red blood cells, passion, survival energy, heat.
Orange	Sexuality, fertility, power, pride, vitality, mood-raising, emotions.
Yellow	Manifesting, intellect, psychic development, self-confidence, power.
Green	Prosperity, healing, harmony, renewal, success, money, growth.
Rose	Healing, self-love, love, trust, friendship, peace, emotional peace.
Blue	Peace, blessings, healing, speech, expansion, fidelity, creativity.
Indigo	Spirituality, psychic opening, karma, connection with others, meditation.
Purple	Meditation, connection with Goddess, spirit contact, protection, calming.

White/Clear   All-aura, all-colors, all-healing, contacting the other world, focusing.

Some other candle colors are:

Silver   Lunar energy, dissolves negativity, psychic development, the Goddess.

Gold   Fast luck, overcoming obstacles, healing, intuition, understanding.

Magenta   Penetrates the planes, healing, change of luck (burn with other colors).

Brown   Earth energy, financial success, business, earth spirits/elementals.[2]

The days of the week each have their designated planets and colors, and each day is used for a specific type of candle magick work. For example, in doing a prosperity ritual, the color of the candle is green or gold and the day is either Thursday (Jupiter) for expansion of what is already there, or Sunday (The Sun) for new money. For stimulating new ideas and projects, burn yellow candles on Wednesday, using the power of the planet Mercury, which represents ideas, communications and intellect. Where color suggestions seem to conflict, use either color on the correct day of the week for that attribute. Various writers' color lists may differ; use what is personally meaningful.

Sunday
(Sun)
Gold/Yellow   Success, luck, new money, action, healing, leadership.

Monday
(Moon)
New, Silver/White
Full, Red/Green
Waning, Black   Birth, inspiration, travel, generation, fertility, psychic ability, secrets, the sea, women, love.

Tuesday
(Mars)
Red   Courage, victory, struggle, aggression, strength, protection, anger.

Wednesday
(Mercury)
Yellow/Violet   Communications, intellect, creativity, science, ideas, adaptiveness, business, memory.

Thursday   Expansion, groups, power, leadership,

| (Jupiter) | wealth, business, success, acclaim, |
| *Bright Blue* | more of any quality. |

Friday	Love, harmony, friendship, attraction,
(Venus)	sexuality, pleasure, natural order.
Green/Indigo/	
Rose	

Saturday	The unknown, binding, obstacles,
(Saturn)	death, time, breaking habits, limits,
Purple/Black	patriarchy, the labyrinth.[3]

The phases of the moon are followed in candle magick, as in other rituals. Use the new moon for beginnings, the waxing phase for rituals of increase, the full moon for fulfillments, and the waning moon for banishings, changing habits and disintegration. Energy increases in the waxing phase, peaks at the Full Moon, and wanes until the next New Moon date. To do a banishing ritual on the waxing moon or a prosperity ritual on the waning goes against natural flow and obstructs the energy from manifesting. Do prosperity rituals on the waxing moon and banishings in the last quarter, using the flow of the changing lunar cycle for maximum results. Add the factors of candle color and the best day of the week to the ritual.

When the moon is in the various astrological signs, use the correspondence of the transits along with the moon phases. When the color of the candles, the day of the week, the moon phase, and moon sign all correspond to the purpose of the ritual, the candle magick is given its most power and is at its best advantage. When working this type of ritual, use as many of the correspondent factors as possible, but don't avoid the ritual if the exact conditions are unavailable. Candle color and moon phase are priority considerations, the day of the week is next, and the astrological moon sign is the last factor. Women who wish to be even more exact can study and use the planetary hours, not discussed in this book. To find lunar and planetary information on a daily basis, use an astrological calendar; it lists the moon phases and astrological signs of the moon transits. Avoid doing manifesting work on the aspect known as a Void of Course Moon — it's a waste of energy to do the ritual, as nothing will happen from it. These aspects are also designated in astrological calendars.

The moon signs and what to best use them for in candle magick are as follows:

Moon Sign and Color / Type of Candle Magick

Aries
Red
Beginnings, banishing, exorcism, direction, change, near end of transit peace rituals, seven-day rituals.

Taurus
Green/Indigo/
Rose
Protection, stability. Projects begun in Taurus increase in value, not good for making changes.

Gemini
Yellow/Violet
Mind and intellect matters, writing, communications, ideas.

Cancer
Silver/White
Emotions, influence, fertility, lunar energy.

Leo
Gold/Yellow
Money from others, romance, ambition, recognition, performance, leadership, promotions, success, lawsuits if you know you are right.

Virgo
Green/Brown
Money, healing, animals, protection, intellect, details, romance at end of transit in waxing moons.

Libra
Rose/
Bright Blue
Partnerships, assistances, teamwork, attraction, beauty, balance, separations on waning moon.

Scorpio
Dark Red
Intensity, stability, making plans, merging, fertility, lust, secrets.

Sagittarius
Purple
Self-improvement, high ideals, increase, travel, independence, intuition, ideas, higher learning and achieving degrees.

Capricorn
Dark Green
Money, status, material needs, jobs.

Aquarius
Blue/
Multi-Colors
Innovative and revolutionary projects, psychic development, dealing with the public, freedom.

Pisces
Sea Green/
Mauve
Escapism, entertainment, confusion, spirituality, psychic development, past-life regression work.[4]

Besides the correspondences to maximize energy use, another aspect of candle magick that difffers from group rituals is the focus on oils and incenses. These are used in candle rituals to enhance the energy by designating scents that attract the qualities the ritual is asking for. While fragrances to do that have been suggested throughout this book, more attention is paid to them as a factor in candle magick. They are an additional reinforcing symbol of what the ritual is about, along with the color, planet/day, moon phase and moon sign. Oils put the woman's intent into the candle as another act of will, and the scent is also burnt as altar incense.

Oils and incenses are available from magick shops and Afro-Spanish botanicas with names describing what they do but contents unlisted. Some of these fragrances have names like: Cast Off Evil Oil, Altar Oil, Blessing Oil, Concentration Oil, Money Oil, Lucky Oil, Love Oil and Wishing Oil. Other less savory types are: Black Devil Oil, Break-Up Oil (in red or black), Do As I Say Oil, and Fiery Command Oil. (The names are from a botanica catalog.) Some scents in oils and incenses invoke the Seven African Powers, or single Goddesses such as Yemaya (Our Lady of Regla), Oshun (Virgen del Cobre), or the Mexican Our Lady of Guadalupe. Candles in seven-day glasses are usually available to match, and botanicas are one of the more fascinating places to explore and shop for magickal supplies. Remember the ethics of what you bring home, though.

The other type of oils and incenses are those listing a single herb, as individual herbs have magickal qualities that are made use of in candle magick rituals. The botanicas carry these, and individual herbs are available at food co-ops and herb or health food stores. Oils can be made at home, relatively simply, or purchased as natural or essential oils from a variety of sources. Incenses are made of natural loose herbs simply by sprinkling them on a lighted charcoal block (not a charcoal grill briquette) in an incense burner or other fireproof container. Scott Cunningham's books, *Magical Herbalism* or *The Encyclopedia of Magical Herbs* (Llewellyn Publications, 1983 and 1985) are good guides to herbs and oils for candle magick use. The following list of herb attributes is from *The Encyclopedia of Magical Herbs*, The Papa Jim botanica catalog,[5] and from magickal herbalist Elaine Movic:

> Agrimony — to reverse spells, protection, sleep
> Alfalfa — to keep poverty away
> Amber — for clarity and love
> Angelica — purification and dissolve negativity, exorcism
> Basil — love, Goddess Erzulie, wealth, astral projection
> Bay leaves — protection, psychic powers, healing, purification
> Bayberry — prosperity
> Benzoin — peace of mind, purifies (burn with other scents)

Bergamot — success, money attracting
Black Cohosh — protection, sexuality
Blue Flag — draws money, business
Blue Vervain — attracts love, quiets nerves, creativity
Carnation — power, healing, strength, protection
Cedar — clears negativity, purification, protection, healing
Celery Seed — psychic development, mental powers, lust
Cinnamon — protection of person, money, love
Clover — money, protection, red clover for love
Cloves — mediumship and psychic development, protection
Dandelion — makes wishes come true, clairvoyance
Dock — money, business, fertility
Dragon's Blood — strengthening, healing
Echinacea — strengthening, healing
Eucalyptus — healing, protection
Fern — exorcism, rainfall, luck, money, health
Frankincense — purification, protection, exorcism, power, spiritual opener
Galangal — court case success
Gardenia — love, peace, healing, spirituality
Gotu Kola — meditation (burn prior, but not during)
Heather — avoiding passion, protection, luck, rainfall
Heliotrope — psychic opening, exorcism, wealth, healing
High Joan the Conqueror — love, luck, health, money, success
Honeysuckle — money, psychic power, protection
Jasmine — love, money, prophetic dreams
Lavender — peace, love, money
Lilac — past lives, exorcism, protection
Lotus — meditation, psychic opening
Magnolia — psychic development, fidelity
Mimosa — healing, dreams, love, purification, protection
Mint — money, changes in life, protection, lust, travel
Mugwort — strength, psychic opener, healing, herb of Artemis
Musk — sex (non-animal scent)
Myrrh — purification, protection, exorcism, spirituality
Myrtlewood — love, peace, fertility, prosperity
Orris root — good magickal works, love, attraction
Patchouli — money, fertility, lust, love

Peony — success in business, protection, exorcism
Pine — healing, fertility, protection, prosperity
Rose — healing, love, trust, unconditional love (white
      rose — love in highest degree)
Rosemary — purification, protection, love, lust, mental
      powers, healing, sleep, prophetic dreams, fidelity
Sage — healing, prosperity, immortality, wisdom, wishes
Sandalwood — protection, wishes, healing, spirituality,
      love
Sweetgrass — calls spirits
Thyme — healing, love, purification, courage, psychic
      powers
Vanilla — sex, attracts women, love, mental powers
Violet — love, healing, peace, wishes, protection
Wisteria — higher consciousness
Wormwood (Artemisia) — psychic development
Ylang Ylang — attraction, lust, love, job hunting

Burn the incense as a loose herb and anoint the candles with either the essential oil of the same herb or another oil that reflects the meaning of the ritual. An example of this is a candle spell for psychic development, using mugwort for incense and Psychic Oil in the candles. In a prosperity ritual, use cinnamon incense and cinnamon oil, or myrtlewood incense with Money Drawing Oil.

Oils are used to "dress" or anoint the candles in the candle magick ritual. In a ritual to draw something to you, to bring an idea from the astral to manifest on the earthplane, or to cause an increase in a quality or energy, the method of "dressing" is as follows. Place a few drops of the chosen oil in your receiving (usually left) hand. Take the candle in your right (sending) hand, and rub the oil onto it moving in straight strokes from the bottom/base of the candle to the center. Then repeat, moving from the tip to the center. A way to do this in one step is to stroke the oil onto the candle from the tip to the base. In a ritual to banish, dissolve negativity, or exorcise rub oil onto the candle from the center to the bottom/base, then from the center to the top. To do it in one step, apply the oil moving from the base to the tip. For either type of ritual, visualize your purpose manifesting as you "dress" the candles.

Several types of candles are used in candle magick rituals and women are directed to use what's available, what they choose to, or what works. Seven-day candle glasses make wonderful Goddess candles for the center of the altar, and can be burned a section at a time to continue a ritual for a week. Some wishing candles, or the more familiar memorial ones, remain lit for a period of up to two weeks. Seven-knob candles are in seven segments and without the glass, and are mainly used for prosperity rituals (green), to attract love (red or rose), or for banishing (black). Image candles come in male or female to represent yourself or someone else in a ritual to reverse bad luck or for healing. Image candles also come shaped like witches (stereotyped), snake or cat candles to draw psychic power or luck, skull candles used in healing for serious illnesses, and yoni candles to invoke female/Goddess energy. Tapers that are half in a color and half coated black are used to reverse bad luck and dissolve negativity. Buy these specialized candles in botanicas or magick shops.

Most women who do candle magick use ordinary candles, tapers in the designated colors bought in card shops. These can be of any length or size, thick or thin, or small votives. Some women use a thicker pillar candle for the Goddess candle/spirit/center and small tapers or votives that burn down quickly for the others. Some candle spells require the focus candle to burn out, rather than be put out at the end of the ritual, and other than the Goddess candles, candles are only used once. Be creative in using candles. They are beautiful in their colors, varied in their shapes and sizes, and magickal to burn. There is no wrong or right in what kinds to use for a particular ritual, only personal choice and availability. Beeswax candles are wonderful for magick work but less readily available and are expensive. (Few candles today are made of animal fat anyway.) When adding scented oils and incense, most women prefer candles that are not already scented. Even when a corresponding scent is already in the candle, "dressing" it adds intent and power to the ritual. Women who make candles can add oils or herbs to the wax in the making, and visualize the intent as they do so.

Candle magick rituals have a basic structure that can be very elaborate or very simple. Two simple formats are given here. In one candle magick set-up, the altar is set with two Goddess candles at the back, one on the left and one on the right, sometimes called altar candles and usually white (or try candle glasses representing Goddesses from a botanica). At the front left and right sides are two more candles. One is a Personal candle, representing oneself by using one's zodiac color or a personally meaningful color, and the other is a Focus candle for the purpose of the ritual. The Focus candle for healing would be orange, light blue or green; for prosperity green or gold; for spirituality indigo or purple. When doing a ritual for someone else, the Personal candle represents them. In the

```
┌─────────────────────────────────────────────┐
│  Goddess Candle              Goddess Candle   │
│                                               │
│                                               │
│                Incense Burner                 │
│                                               │
│                                               │
│              Symbol Object:                   │
│              Photo, Gemstone,                 │
│              Dollar Bills, etc.               │
│                                               │
│                                               │
│  Personal Candle               Focus Candle   │
└─────────────────────────────────────────────┘
```

```
┌─────────────────────────────────────────────┐
│  Earth Candle                    Air Candle   │
│                                               │
│                                               │
│                Incense Burner                 │
│                                               │
│              Goddess / Spirit                 │
│                  Candle                       │
│                                               │
│               Symbol Object                   │
│                                               │
│                                               │
│  Water Candle                   Fire Candle   │
└─────────────────────────────────────────────┘
```

center of the altar is an incense burner, and in front of it a photo, gemstone, or whatever other symbols seem appropriate.[6] In a prosperity ritual place a large-denomination dollar bill there; in a healing ritual a photo of the woman being healed; in a ritual to find a new home, draw or clip a picture of what you are looking for. Try setting the candles in a circle, rather than a square, with the incense burner and symbol in the center. All the candles are "dressed" with oils for the intent of the ritual, and the incense is to match.

In another altar format, one used by herbalist Elaine Movic, there is one Goddess candle in the center, with four more candles (for the four elements) in a circle around it. The Goddess candle is always white, and the other four candles are the color of the ritual's intent or focus. The incense burner is behind the Goddess candle, and in front of the Goddess candle is the symbol object. She prefers gemstones to other symbols. In a prosperity ritual, for example, there would be a white center candle, four green ones, incense in a prosperity-drawing fragrance, and a prosperity/green gemstone like peridot, pyrite or aventurine. In addition, Elaine casts a circle with a thirteen-foot length of yarn in the ritual's focus color. She makes the circle around the altar with the yarn, enters within it, then closes it, drawing the trailing ends of the string toward the circle's center. Candles are "dressed" with oil — the Goddess candle with Altar, Blessing or Goddess Oil, and the element candles with an oil for the intent. In the prosperity ritual, that oil might be clover, bergamot or botanica Money Drawing Oil.

To do a candle magick ritual, cast a circle in a formal or informal way, yourself and the things needed for the ritual inside it. Make the altar as above, "dressing" the candles, and light the candles and incense as part of beginning the ritual. Focus on the ritual's intent throughout, particularly while anointing the candles. Add objects other than those specified if desired, but candle magick is best kept simple.

Some ritualists feel that matches should not be used to light the candles, but that an extra taper be lit with a match and then used to light the ritual candles. Others prefer lighters to matches. Some ritualists say to use a snuffer or wet fingers to put candles out, while others say to blow them out. Personally, I see no difference and use one long match for lighting all the candles, and blow them out at the end. I like to light the candles moving in a clockwise direction, and extinguish them moving counter-clockwise, blowing out first the candle lit last. Try various ways and see what works best for you.

Visualizing the intent in every aspect of the ritual intensifies the candle magick process. By choosing candle colors, oils, incense and symbols to reflect the focus, the focus becomes the ritual itself. By doing the ritual on the day of the week, moon phase and moon sign for the purpose, the intent and energy are heightened even more. All the factors are reflections of women's will and consequence; the focused intent and the action of employing it come from Goddess-within. By making the effort to consciously choose every detail, women put their will into the ritual, and women's will is the most vital factor in manifesting the results. The more focused, visualized, and detailed the candle magick ritual, the better the outcome received from doing it. In the body of the ritual itself, focusing is continued by using meditation, visualization, affirmations and/or sympathetic magick. Actions are done to create in the mind or microcosm/circle, what is wanted to happen/manifest on the earthplane.

Candle Ritual to Draw Prosperity

The following candle magick ritual is to manifest money or abundance. The ritual was created by Elaine Movic and uses her four elements and spirit altar format. Do it on a Thursday on a waxing moon, anytime from the new to full moon date. The best moon sign transits are in Leo (for money from others), Virgo or Capricorn. For increased or building energy, repeat the ritual for four, seven, or eight nights. As in other rituals, do this prosperity ritual at a time and place free of interruptions and take the phone off the hook. Use optimal meditation conditions. Wear loose clothing or work skyclad, and bathe before the ritual using seven drops of Prosperity Oil (or oil of clover, pine or bergamot) in the bathwater. Wear a pendant of a green prosperity gemstone, peridot, aventurine, malachite or gold pyrite.

Need

Goddess Candle — White (one candle), or Goddess candle glass.

Element Candles — Green (four of them), small tapers or votives.

Oil for "dressing" candles — Prosperity Oil, clover, pine or bergamot for the Element Candles, and Altar Oil, Blessing Oil, Goddess Oil (or frankincense oil, sage oil, heliotrope oil) on the Goddess Candle.

Incense — Prosperity Incense, clover, pine or bergamot, any money-drawing fragrance.

Symbol Object — A large denomination dollar bill or silver dollars. Aim high: the higher the bills, the more is attracted.

Optional — Thirteen-foot green cord for making the circle.

Matches to light candles and incense, charcoal block for loose incense, ritual wand (if used).

Outline

Light candles — "Dress" the Goddess candle and place it in the center of the altar; "dress" and place the four element candles. Light the candles. Use Prosperity Oil, and focus your intent on what you want to manifest.

Purify — Use Prosperity Incense, or clover, pine or bergamot as loose herbs.

Imagine a white light coming out of the top of your head and surrounding your whole body. Let it stay with you. Relax and know that you are protected from all harm.

Cast circle/Invoke a Goddess or Goddesses of abundance and prosperity. This can be done informally, or as in the full group ritual.

Invocation — "Yemaya, Great Mother, be with me in this ritual. Lend me your peace, healing, gentle emotions and love. Hear my prayer, rule my way. My life is free and of my choosing, I have and keep that which is mine. My finances are secure, and with plentiful gain to care for myself and those I love. I have the strength and wisdom to provide for myself and my loved ones. I have abundance of food, shelter, transportation and money, forever and ever. So mote it be!"

Meditation — Meditate on abundance and feel it has already worked through you and for you. Plant a positive feeling of abundance inside you, a permanent image. Stay in the meditative state visualizing abundance and prosperity for yourself for about twenty minutes.

Give thanks.

Open circle/Ground.[7]

Take the ashes from the incense, the wax drippings and/or candle remains (if the candles can't be left to burn until they go out) and bury them outside in the earth. If the ritual is repeated over a number of nights, mark the candles to divide them into that number, let them burn one division, extinguish them, and relight them again the next night. At the end of the number of days, the candles burn out of themselves. The Goddess candle is a larger candle and should never burn out before the element candles do. Some workers feel candles should be extinguished with fingers or a snuffer, not blown out. The candles are never reused for other rituals.

When you open the circle, let the energy go without dwelling on it or thinking about it. Let the magick do its work. Give thanks, as what you have asked for is already granted.

Two other spells — not candle spells — for prosperity are as follows. One is called "Candy at the Crossroads" and is a voudoun ritual. Get a bag of colored candies and take them to a busy inter-section/crossroads. While crossing the street, spill the candles without looking at them and cross the street not looking back. Walk or drive away, without looking back, and do not cross that intersec-tion again for at least a week. Visualize the abundance you want while spilling the candles.

The other spell, called "Magick Dimes," is even more fun. Take a dime and bless it for prosperity for whoever finds it, as well as prosperity generally or specifically for yourself. Leave the dime where someone can pick it up. Since what you send out returns to you three- or tenfold, the prosperity you've wished for someone else returns abundantly. Even very specific wishes manifest, sometimes in unexpected ways. My friend Renee, who shared this ritual with me, gets a roll of dimes at the bank every payday. For myself, I've tried both rituals and know they work. Do either spell on a waxing or full moon, on a Thursday for strongest energy. Try placing the dimes or candies on the altar in a prosperity ritual before using them, or outside in Full Moon Light.

Candle Ritual for Healing

This is a candle ritual for distance healing, to send healing energy to someone not present. If the woman who is to receive the energy cannot be asked permission, visualize her in the meditative state and ask her permission there. Honor the yes or no response. Do the ritual on a waxing moon with the intent of invoking good health, or on the waning moon to banish disease and achieve balance. The best days are Sunday or Monday and the best moon sign is Virgo. Though this ritual is presented as a candle ritual with optimal days and candle colors to use, distance healing can be done at any time, in any place where the healer can be centered enough to visualize. When healing is needed, do it — whatever the times or days,

Prosperity Candle Ritual

Element Candle   Element Candle

Incense Burner

Symbol Object:
Dollar Bills,
Gemstone,

Element Candle   Element Candle

Healing Candle Ritual

Goddess Candle   Goddess Candle

Incense Burner

Symbol Object:
Doll or Photo

Personal Candle   Focus Candle

whether there are candles or altars available or not. When there is time to wait and plan, use the optimal conditions, and put will and intent into maximizing the outcome.

Need

Goddess Candles — White (two candles), placed left and right on the back of altar.

Personal Candle — Zodiac color of the woman being healed, or a color that seems appropriate for her (see moon sign colors), placed at left-hand front of altar.

Focus Candle — Orange, light blue or green, placed at right-hand front of altar.

Oil for "dressing" candles — For Goddess Candles, use Goddess Oil, Blessing Oil, Altar Oil, or clear vegetable or olive oil. For Personal and Focus Candles use Healing Oil, sandalwood oil, sage oil, cedar or pine oil; for emotional healing use rose oil or vervain oil.

Incense — Sage, sandalwood, cedar or pine; rose or vervain for emotional healing.

Photo of woman to be healed, or a small doll with her name written on it. Photo or doll are lying down at front center of altar at the beginning of the ritual, sat or propped upright after the healing visualization.

Matches to light candles and incense, charcoal block for loose incense, ritual wand (if used).

Outline

Light candles — "Dress" the Goddess candles and place them to the back of the altar; "dress" the Personal candle and Focus candle with Healing Oil, placing them to the front of the altar at the left- and right-hand sides. Place the other objects on the altar, and light the candles, focusing your intent and will on healing.

Purify — Use incense for physical (or emotional) healing. Light the charcoal block, give it time to heat, and sprinkle the herbs onto it intermittently through the ritual.

Cast circle/Invoke the Goddess or Goddesses of your choice, or surround yourself with light in the color of your choice. Do this formally, as a simple verbal statement, or as a visualization.

Invocation — Great Mother of healing, White Buffalo Calf Woman, be with me in this ritual of healing for (*name*). Guide me to know what to do in helping her heal; help her to have what she needs for healing.

Body of ritual — Use the woman's photo or your ability to

visualize to make an image of the woman to be healed in your mind. Ask to see what is wrong; you may see it in symbolic ways and see her in silhouette or outline. Ask for a color to send her for healing, and using that color, fill her aura with that light. If something in her body needs to be "fixed," make an image of fixing it — these can be things like taping up a broken leg with "Goddess tape" or closing wounds with "magick zippers." It may mean sending light to a pain area until the pain or dis-ease fades and disappears. Women who do healing work are guided in what to do, follow your intuition as to colors and what to visualize.

When the healing part of the visualization is complete, surround the woman's full aura with color (use green or blue if no other color comes to you). Imagine/visualize her in perfect health. If she has a broken leg, see her playing softball; if she's had surgery, see her out in her garden weeding. See her better than ever. Then imagine her five years from now, also happy and in perfect health. Surround her with light again, and come back to now.

Surround yourself with light, and do not dwell on the woman, her illness, or what happened in the healing. Take the photo or doll and stand it upright, a symbol of the woman no longer "lying low," but in good health again.

Thank the Goddess/es you have invoked, and your guides, for their help.

Open circle.

Ground — Thoroughly. Place your hands palms down on the floor or earth, and let any pain you may have absorbed in the healing work leave you. Feel it flowing from your hands, changing to neutral energy for earth healing. Grounding is highly important after healing work.

Allow the candles to burn out, or extinguish them and bury the remains and drippings with the incense remains in the earth. Put the photo away, and erase the woman's name from the doll, or leave the doll on your permanent altar until the woman is well. Cleanse the doll thoroughly in sage smoke before using it for other purposes. In a crisis, do the healing meditation several times a day from anywhere, it only takes a few moments. Repeat the healing ritual nightly if needed. Always remember to see the woman well at the end of the visualization and to let the energy go, don't dwell on the woman's dis-ease after the ritual.

This simple candle magick ritual is the basis for all psychic healing work done for others or oneself. Develop skill by doing it, and trust your intuition and guidance to learn expertise as a distance/psychic healer.

Candle Ritual to Banish Depression

Banishings are done to rid your life of any negative quality, to break bad habits, and to clear old "stuff" or transform it. Anytime something is banished, something else must take its place, the energy changed to a positive quality. In banishing depression, replace the negative with joy and self-worth; in banishing a smoking habit, replace it with clear lungs; in banishing an abusive *situation* (never use banishing directed at a person, that is a hex), replace it with a positive situation. Banishings have the potential for manipulative or negative use, be aware of this and avoid it. But banishings also have the potential for positive work and life transforming, and this is the type of women's consequence to encourage.

Do banishing rituals on waning or dark moons. The day of Saturn (Saturday) is a good day for entering the labyrinth/unknown to change habits, and Saturn's colors are purple or black. A moon in Sagittarius, for high ideals and self-improvement; in Aries for change, banishings and beginnings; or in Cancer for the emotions and lunar energy are signs for the ritual. In a negative-emotions issue try invoking the Moon on a Monday in the sign of Cancer, to replace a negative emotion (depression) with a positive one (joy). Cedar, sage, rosemary or pine are good incense and oil fragrances for the banishing candle. For the invoking candle use a fragrance that draws the new energy, such as rose for emotional healing or amber for clarity and love.

For this candle magick ritual, use a white Goddess candle in the center, or two Goddess candles to the back of the altar. At the front left, use a black candle for banishing; at the front right, a candle for invoking the qualities you want to draw. In a ritual to banish depression and replace it with joy and self-love, use pink for the invoking candle or use red for the colors of the Maiden, Mother and Crone on the altar (white, red and black). The New Moon or the last night of the old is a very good time to do this ritual, or anytime in the waning moon phase. Follow it into the new and waxing by burning candles in the invoking color from the night of the ritual until the next Full Moon, and meditate nightly on the new qualities invoked.

Need

Goddess Candle — White, one at center of the altar, or two at the back.

Banishing Candle — Black, placed at the left front of the altar.

Invoking Candle — Pink or red, placed at the right front of the altar.

Incense — Sage, cedar, rosemary or pine at the beginning of the ritual, changed later to rose or amber. Burn loose herbs on charcoal block to do this.

Oils — Use Goddess or Altar Oil on the Goddess Candle; sage, pine or other banishing oil on the Banishing Candle; and rose oil on the Invoking Candle and for the Self-blessing.

Symbol Objects — Use a black gemstone for banishing, and a piece of rose quartz or a rose quartz pendant for invoking. Place the pendant on the altar and put it on before doing the Self-blessing.

Matches to light candles and incense, charcoal block for loose incense, ritual wand (if used) to cast the circle.

Outline

Light candles — "Dress" the candles with the oils, working base to tip (away from you) for the Banishing candle and tip to base (toward you) for the Invoking and Goddess candles. Visualize the intent, banishing depression when handling the banishing candle, and invoking joy and self-love while "dressing" the Goddess and invoking candles. Light only the Goddess candles at this time.

Purify — Start the charcoal block and give it time to heat up. Sprinkle loose herbs of sage, cedar, rosemary or pine on the hot coal and use the smoke for purifying. Visualize the intent of the ritual, at this point visualize banishing depression and emotional pain, while smudging with the smoke. Then light the black candle from the Goddess candle.

Cast circle/Invoke a Crone Goddess or Goddesses to help in banishing, and a Goddess of gentleness and peace for the invoking part of the ritual. Try Kali the Destroyer or Hecate for banishing, and Kwan Yin for gentleness and invoking. Use Goddesses for the five elements or these two aspects only, or whatever feels right. Do a full casting and invoking to make the circle, or an informal invitation to the aspects and elements.

Invocation — Dear mothers of wisdom and grace, I invite you here to ask your help. I refuse my depression and choose to banish it, and ask instead for joy and peace of mind. Help me in my work tonight, Kali and Kwan Yin.

Body of Ritual — Focus on the flame of the black candle, thinking of all the things that need changing. Remember fully all the reasons for depression and pain, acknowledge all your anger, all your rage, and all your fear. Dwell on every hurt, every feeling, every negativity. When you have focused them all onto the candle, shout "No!" and blow the candle out in a decisive, quick motion. Watch the smoke rise from the extinguished black candle, and feel all the negativity dissolving in the rising air. Breathe the banishing incense for awhile.

Now light the Invoking candle. Do it from the Goddess candle, and sprinkle rose incense on the charcoal block. Let the light of the pink candle and the fragrance of the rose incense fill you as you watch and breathe them. Breathe the energies in deeply, remembering the qualities of Kwan Yin, or other Goddess/es of mercy invoked to the ritual. Ask Kwan Yin for her presence and help.

Focus on the candle flame and think of all the good things in your life. Refill each banished item and negativity with some positive attribute; where there was pain before, replace it with love. For every wrong, remember something to give thanks for; for every pain remember something joyful. Remember your accomplishments in life, how good a woman you really are. Do a series of affirmations, "I am" or "I have," to list your good qualities and the qualities you choose to become or gain. Continue stating the positives and affirmations until you feel filled with pink light and the scent of roses.

Self-blessing — Put on the rose quartz pendant or hold the rose quartz stone. Do the Self-blessing ritual slowly and lovingly, anointing your chakras with the rose oil. Breathe the scent deeply and draw it into your body, emotions, mind and spirit.

Thank Kwan Yin for your joy and Kali for her energy of change. Open circle/Ground.

Allow the pink candle to burn out itself, or extinguish and relight it nightly (or others in the color) until at least the next Full Moon. Do affirmations nightly with the flame. Continue burning pink candles for as long as needed to remind you of new joy and positivity. Repeat the ritual on the next waning moon if needed; it will be needed less each time you do it. Each time, bury the remains of the black candle in the earth, along with the ashes from the incense; visualize your pain being buried and recycled with them. Repeat the Self-blessing at any time, and do it often, at least every New and Full Moon. Continue wearing the rose quartz pendant, or carry a piece of the stone with you at all times. Remember you are Goddess.

Candle Ritual for Love

This is a nonmanipulative ritual for bringing love to your life, for finding a lover, or for self-love. There are no names placed on the candles, both Focus candles represent yourself. If the ritual is done by two lovers together, both agreeing to it and wanting it, the candle

Banishing Depression Ritual

Incense Burner

Goddess Candle

Symbol Object:
Gemstone/s and
Pendant

Banishing Candle   Focus Candle

Candle Ritual For Love

Element Candle   Element Candle

Incense Burner

Focus Candle   Gemstone   Focus Candle

Element Candle   Element Candle

magick can be used to bless the beginnings of a relationship.In this case, write your name and your lover's on the pink candles. This is only done when both partners choose and agree to it. The four orange element candles can be placed on the altar or in the four corners of the ritual room. Orange is for sexuality, energy, attraction, friendship and pride. The two pink Focus candles represent yourself, you and your lover to come, "true love," gentleness, trust, self-love and spiritual fulfillment. The white candle is the Goddess, the love aspect of your choice. She is Freya or Oshun, Aphrodite or Venus, Ishtar, Astarte or Erzulie. Please use this ritual ethically, manipulating none.

Do candle magick to attract love on Friday, the day of Venus, or Monday for the Moon. Do it in the time from the New to the Full Moon (waxing). The seven days of the Full Moon are the most powerful for this ritual. Read "The Charge of the Goddess," and draw down the moon. Moon signs include Taurus for earthy and sensual love, Cancer for home and family love, Libra for romance and idealism, or Scorpio for a sexy, passionate love.[8] Oils for this ritual include Fire or Love, myrtle or rose on the pink candles; amber-rose oil on the orange four element candles; and Goddess, Altar or Blessing Oil on the Goddess candle. The incense is rose, jasmine or myrtlewood. The symbol object is a piece of rose quartz gemstone. Try image candles, shaped like women or woman and man, for the pink Focus candles. This ritual was designed by herbalist Elaine Movic, adapted for this book by the author, and used by permission.

Need

Goddess Candle — White (one), placed at center of altar.

Element Candles — Orange (four), placed at four directions of the altar or room.

Focus Candles — Pink (two), placed in front of and to the left and right of the Goddess Candle.

Oils — Amber-rose oil on the Element Candles; Fire of Love, myrtle or rose on the Focus Candles; and Altar, Blessing or Goddess Oil on the Goddess Candle.

Incense — Rose, jasmine or myrtlewood.

Symbol Object — A piece of rose quartz gemstone, placed between the two Focus candles.

Matches to light candles and incense, charcoal block for loose incense, ritual wand.

Outline

Light candles — "Dress" the four element candles (orange) with amber-rose oil, set them on the altar or at the corners of the room and light them. Then "dress" the Goddess candle with Altar, Blessing or Goddess Oil, place it in the center of the circle or altar and light it. Next, "dress" the two pink Focus candles with Fire of Love, myrtle or rose oil, place them in front of the Goddess candle and light them. All candles are dressed in the invoking manner, from tip to base. Place the rose quartz gemstone between yourself and the pink candles.

Purify — Light your charcoal, giving it some time to heat. Put a pinch of rose, jasmine or myrtlewood incense on the coal, use the smoke to purify, then place the burner behind the Goddess candle. Add more incense herbs as needed.

Cast circle/Invoke Goddesses of the elements and spirit. Use love Goddesses for each element, or one Goddess. Be as formal or informal as you choose. Aphrodite, Oshun, Venus, Astarte and Erzulie are some choices.

On Full Moons — Read "The Charge of the Goddess" and/or draw down the moon. These steps are optional.

Invocation — Imagine a cone of beautiful pink light coming from the top of your head and surrounding your whole body, filling the circle. Let it stay with you. Meditate on your intent. Move your pink candles a little closer together and say:

> I invoke Aphrodite, Goddess of Love, to join me in this circle. Hear my request for a perfect mate, true lover, fulfillment in love, and a meaningful love relationship. I have the strength, wisdom and logic to know true love, according to free will and for the good of all. So mote it be.

Body of ritual/Meditation — Meditate on your intent for twenty minutes or so, exploring all the aspects of love and designing/visualizing your ideal lover (without name or face). Imagine her with you. Know your request has been granted, and your love is a reality that will manifest. The magick is done and has worked.

Do the Self-blessing.

Thank the Goddess for being with you and helping you have what you desire.

Open circle/Ground.

Allow the candles to burn out or extinguish them. Take the candle remains and drippings, the incense ashes and remains (add a little water to them to extinguish), and bury them in the yard or throw them into moving water in a river or stream.[9] Never put them in the garbage, they were your altar. Keep the stone in your pocket and carry it, or place it at your bedside. The gift of peace, self-love, and the right lover come to you through this ritual. Repeat it again with your lover. Blessed be!

Marion Weinstein's "Words of Power for a Love Relationship" in *Positive Magic* can be used as the Invocation for this ritual. The "Words" go like this:

> There is One Power,
> Which is perfect love.
> And I (your name), a complete individualization of the Power,
> Hereby draw to myself the most appropriate, fulfilling, perfect love-relationship, which is right for me.
> This takes place in a perfect exchange of love with the right person,
> And for the good of all,
> According to the free will of all,
> And so it must be.[10]

She suggests inserting the following: "I hereby release all loneliness, despair, negative emotional patterns, etc."[11] I highly recommend her work.

I thank my friend Elaine Movic of Earth Magic for her help on this candle magick chapter.

Notes

1. Derived from Marion Weinstein, *Positive Magick* (Custer, WA: Phoenix Publications, 1981), Chapters III and VIII.

2. Charmaine Dey, *The Magic Candle, Facts and Fundamentals of Ritual Candle Burning* (New York: Original Publications, 1982), pp. 27-29.

3. *Ibid.,* pp. 51-56, and Starhawk, *The Spiral Dance: A Rebirth of the Ancient Religion of the Great Goddess* (San Francisco: Harper and Row, 1979), pp. 204-208.

4. Charmaine Dey, *The Magic Candle,* pp. 51-62, and Jim Maynard's *Celestial Guide 1989* (Ashland, OR: Quicksilver Productions, 1989), pp. 10-12. Zodiac colors from Leo Vinci, *The Book of Practical Candle Magic* (Great Britain: Aquarian Press, 1981), pp. 105-107.

5. Papa Jim and Co., 5603 S. Flores, San Antonio, TX 78214, (512) 922-6665.

6. Anahita-Gula, "Coloured Candles: To Use or Not to Use," in *Harvest* (P.O. Box 228, South Framingham, MA 01701), Vol. 9, No. 6, June 1989, p. 18.

7. Ritual and invocations by Elaine Movic, adapted for this book by the author. Used by permission.

8. Starhawk, *The Spiral Dance*, p. 209.

9. I am concerned about the ecology of this means of disposal, though these methods are traditional.

10. Marion Weinstein, *Positive Magic*, p. 228.

11. *Ibid.*

Afterword

In a private channeling session on Beltane, 1989, just before starting this book, I asked for advice on writing it and for ideas to include. I was advised to add the music and chants that are part of all the full rituals, something I probably would not have emphasized. I was also told to tell my readers that in every aspect of spirituality, be it ritual, healing or anything else, they must go ahead and do the work themselves. Reading about it is not enough, nor is waiting for someone else to lead, teach or do it for them. Everyone must do her own work, take what she's learned and use it, apply it, expand and continue it. Everyone of us is important, and while teachers or books can present what they know, it is up to everyone to do the work and carry the information forward for use in her own ways. There is no "right way" in Women's Spirituality, only what works for the individual. This is how change is made in women's consequence and in the world, by individual work, action and choices.

This book is only a bare beginning of the possibilities of Women's Spirituality rituals. Be very free in using it, adapting the rituals to individual needs and writing new ones. Adapt the rituals for groups or individual work, using what feels meaningful for any given time or occasion. Follow ritual structure and create your own; the outline makes a framework for creativity. The rituals in this book are my own ideas and are meaningful to me. Other things may be meaningful to other women. Everything in this book is open to question and change.

Learning about Women's Spirituality and writing about what I've learned has been the core of my life for almost ten years. I am highly grateful to the women who have taught me along the way, the women who have come to my workshops, whose rituals I have experienced, and whose books have changed my life. I am highly grateful to the women's networking system, the support and caring that have been a mainstay in my work and everyday Be-ing. I am grateful and thankful for all the women who have offered love in its many forms to me along the path.

I offer this book as a beginning of Women's Spirituality rituals and a step along the way in reclaiming women's consequence, Goddess-within, and matriarchal values. I see these qualities as the best real hope for saving our earth and the people on it from war, ecological poisoning and destruction, and from world death by the loss of real values, women's values, wiccan values. Women in spirituality are learning their worth, learning to heal themselves from the ravages of patriarchy, learning to heal others and learning to heal the planet. We are the hope of our time, perhaps the last hope. I offer a blessing to women everywhere to carry on this work. You are needed, your work is needed, your hope and joy are needed. Begin with this book, and carry on.

Blessed be.

Appendix

───────────○───────────

Women and the New Craft

Women's Spirituality has developed some major differences from traditional wicce or witchcraft, but their beginning origins are the same and their ultimate goals and practices are similar. The central difference is Women's Spirituality's focus on women and the Goddess, and traditional wicce's use of male and female together — the Goddess and God dualism. In a Women's Spirituality coven or ritual group, the membership is women-only and the male aspect is neither mentioned nor invoked, whatever the sexual preferences of the members. A few gay male covens consider themselves Women's Spirituality, also, and invoke female energy. In a traditional wiccan coven or ritual group, the membership is both male and female, sometimes couples only, and the Goddess and God have either equal roles or there's a stronger emphasis on the Goddess. Women's covens and the women's religion as a whole have much less hierarchy and authority than traditional wicce, and more focus on the individual. There are fewer rules or requirements for membership and little emphasis on initiation.

Traditional wicce and Women's Spirituality both trace their beginnings to remnants of the non-Christian (Pagan) religions decimated by the Church Inquisition. The Burning Times of the thirteenth to seventeenth centuries in Europe killed nine million people, most of them women, partly for not being Christian and for practicing their religion underground. It was the final ending of matriarchy, though this is a highly simplified analysis of the politics of that time. British author Gerald Gardner, claiming membership before 1939 in an underground coven, published his first novel, *A Goddess Arrives*, in 1938 mentioning the Goddess and the craft. Three later books, two of them published after the British witchcraft laws were finally repealed in 1949, became the most public basis for what is today's wiccan religion. The books were *High Magic's Aid* (1949), *Witchcraft Today* (1954) and *The Meaning of Witchcraft* (1959).[1] Gardner had studied spirituality in the East and had been on Goddess archeological digs, besides going through his own wiccan initiation. His books and influence began the neo-Pagan (and probably the New Age) movement.

Though he is highly regarded, Gerald Gardner's claim of early initiation has come under scholars' controversy. Attempts to prove that there really was a pre-1939 coven that he was part of and learned from have met with confusion. Evidence of the Goddess being dominant in The Burning Times underground religion or since the Inquisition's end have also been questioned by some researchers. Did Gerald Gardner create what is becoming a world religion, or was he actually trained by a surviving coven? In an interesting article by Aiden Kelly, "The Invention of Witchcraft" (In *The Great Write*, Issue 4, 1984),[2] Kelly offers evidence that the craft was created and the major writing was done less by Gardner than by two women. One was the original high priestess of the first coven Gardner started, identified only as Dafo, and the other was Doreen Valiente, second high priestess of that coven and well-known today. Kelly shows that no early documentation existed for Gardner's Book of Shadows, that Gardner's dyslexia affected his writing too much to make him the author of the material (or sole author), and that these two priestesses were the actual authors and creators of Gardnerian witchcraft.

Says Kelly:

> Gardner met Dafo in some sort of magical group during World War II and they decided to found a religion of "witchcraft," which they would claim dated from the Middle Ages. They collaborated on the writing of *High Magic's Aid* and on creating the BAM ('Ye Bok of Ye Art Magical,' 1944-53) manuscript, which is clearly intended for liturgical use in rituals. Apparently they met with very little success until they initiated Doreen Valiente in 1953. She promptly put her very real talents as a writer to work for the new religion, rewriting the rituals in existence and creating new ones, probably doing the majority of the writing in *Witchcraft Today*.[3]

The idea of recreating what cannot be otherwise retrieved is not new to wicce or to Women's Spirituality, and is not to be condemned. How much was created and how much was traditional will probably never be known. Kelly traces the Gardnerian Book of Shadows, the book that is the basis for Gardnerian wiccan practice, to Doreen Valiente and states:

> There was no emphasis on the Goddess as the major deity and on the
> High Priestess as the central authority in the coven until after 1957,
> when Doreen Valiente became the first such "Gardnerian" High Priest-
> ess and began to adopt the White Goddess myth invented by Robert
> Graves as the official theology of her coven.[4]

That Robert Graves "invented" the White Goddess as a "myth" is
another question.

But if Aidan Kelly's research is even partly correct, wicce from
both the traditional side and from the Women's Spirituality side had
female origins. Gardnerian wicce was brought to the United States
from England in the 1950s by Ray and Rosemary Buckland and
Donna Cole, among others, who went to Britain to be initiated by
Gardner or his students, and who spread the teachings here. The
open and inquiring atmosphere of the 1960s brought an upsurge in
spirituality among American youths and a rebellion against the
dogma of standard politics and religions. In this atmosphere wicce
grew strong, to what Kelly estimates as "100,000 serious adherents
worldwide" today.[5] I believe that number highly conservative, and
not inclusive of Women's Spirituality, and his view of the origins less
important than the results.

The Women's Spirituality movement began in the late 1960s,
partly originated and much influenced by traditional wicce, but with
additional sources. The 1960s upsurge in inquiry and nontradi-
tional thinking was also the beginning of the women's movement.
Surrounded by a variety of unconventional spirituality forms, from
the Jesus freaks to Hari Krishnas to Buddhism and the tarot,
women were also surrounded by various radical freedom movements. The early 1960s Black Civil Rights movement, the anti-
Vietnam War/Peace movement, the back to the land and later
women's self-care movements were all influences on what became
women's rights and Women's Spirituality. Many women who are
middle-aged today grew up surrounded by both politics and spirituality, and connecting the two became an everyday thing. Matriarchy
was initially a political concept, not a spiritual one. While the
politics became public and angry, the spirituality remained personal and quiet. Though "the personal is political" became the by-
word of the late sixties to mid-seventies women's movement, spirituality in that movement remained unexamined for awhile. This had
been true in the 1848 First Wave of Women's Liberation, where
spirituality also became important later. Spirituality emerged in
these years through women's literature and as a vehicle for women's
political anger. The words "Goddess" and "witch" in these contexts

became familiar.

WITCH, an acronym with changing meaning but originally standing for Women's International Terrorist Conspiracy from Hell, began on Halloween, 1968. It was a group of radical political women in New York City, whose first Coven inspired others in at least seven large cities, and whose actions and demonstrations made frequent news. They were women's liberation radicals, and their position papers and jubilant actions made women look at the word "witch" in a new way. Some of us adopted it and wanted to know more.

An early position paper from WITCH's New York Coven states:

> WITCH is an all-women Everything. It's theater, revolution, magic, terror, joy, garlic flowers, spells. It's an awareness that witches and gypsies were the original guerrillas and resistance fighters against oppression — particularly the oppression of women down through the ages. Witches have always been women who dared to be: groovy, courageous, aggressive, intelligent, nonconformist, explorative, curious, independent, sexually liberated, revolutionary. (This possibly explains why nine million of them have been burned). . . .
>
> WITCH lives and laughs in every woman. She is the free part of each of us, beneath the shy smiles, the acquiescence to absurd male domination, the make-up and flesh-suffocating clothing our sick society demands. There is no "joining" WITCH. If you are a woman and dare to look within yourself, you are a Witch. You make your own rules. You are free and beautiful . . . You can form your own Coven of *sisters* Witches (thirteen is a cozy number for a group) and do your own actions.[6]

What made a woman a witch (or a WITCH)?

> You are a Witch by saying aloud, "I am a Witch" three times and *thinking about that.* You are a Witch by being female, untamed, angry, joyous and immortal.[7]

A WITCH position paper from the Chicago Covens brought to many women's attentions, possibly for the first time, information about the witch burnings and who the nine million dead really were. The Goddess and matriarchy were discussed, and the political misogyny of Europe of the time, along with the losses in freedom women experienced under Christianity everywhere. The witch as a political revolutionary was the theme of the paper, but to women already refusing male religions along with patriarchy and seeking alternatives, it was just a beginning. Women began claiming the identity, often not yet understanding the practice, "saying aloud, 'I am a Witch' three times and *thinking about that.*" The concept of

Women's Spirituality witchcraft was begun.

Defining that spirituality also began and still continues. *WomanSpirit Magazine* started in Autumn, 1974, begun from a *Country Women* special issue on spirituality that same year. For ten years, editors Ruth and Jean Mountaingrove published poetry, stories, news and information submitted by women worldwide on Women's Spirituality wicce. Other publications followed, and several women's movement political and literary journals published special issues on spirituality and the Goddess. Z. Budapest, a hereditary witch from Hungary, taught by her mother, began leading women's rituals in California. She started the first Women's Spirituality book and magick shop, The Feminist Wicca. The women's cultural festivals that began in 1973 discovered a concentration of wiccan information in the women's volunteered workshops. The number of early festivals, conferences and gatherings grew and women began to form covens.

Books were and are the major sources of information influencing the growth of the Goddess movement. Except for some underground publications, these began in the seventies. Judy Chicago's art piece *The Dinner Party* (1969) and the book that followed it encouraged women's herstory with information on Goddesses, matriarchies and the Inquisition. The earliest books were probably Helen Diner's *Mothers and Amazons* (1965) and Elizabeth Gould Davis' *The First Sex* (1971), both discovering the Goddess religion in ancient cultures. Merlin Stone's *When God Was A Woman* (1976) and *Ancient Mirrors of Womanhood* (1979) were a beginning in Goddess archeology and matriarchal thought for many women. Mary Daly's *Gyne/cology* discussed the radical politics of witchcraft in 1978. Starhawk's *The Spiral Dance* and Z. Budapest's *Holy Book of Women's Mysteries* (both 1979) were early germinal guides to women's craft practice. Marion Weinstein's *Positive Magic* (1978 and 1981) and *Earth Magic* (1980) followed, using traditional wiccan practice, and Vicki Noble's *Motherpeace: A Way to the Goddess Through Myth Art and Tarot* (1983) came later. My own books began with *The Kwan Yin Book of Changes* (1985) and *The Women's Spirituality Book* (1986). The movement was already well established by that time, and expressing its own style and creativity.

Although the Women's Spirituality movement has been strongly influenced by traditional wicce, and the two are complementary, they are not totally the same. These branches of the craft have a similar structure, but a different focus and emphasis. The two groups' world views, from which they originate, differ. Traditional wicce bases much of its purpose and philosophy on the male/

female duality, the God and Goddess, while Women's Spirituality uses the Goddess and female only. In traditional craft covens, there is a high priestess and high priest, who are usually a couple. They are experienced teachers who direct every facet of the coven and coven members' training and participation in the craft and group. At the most positive, they make the coven into an extended family through their expertise and leadership, and their training for the high priestess/priest role takes several years and two to four initiations.

In Women's Spirituality there is a high priestess, but she is high priestess only for the purpose of leading a specific ritual. She often has no formal training, but is chosen by the group and/or self-taught (or sometimes she has had training through a traditional coven). No one runs the coven, it is run by consensus of all the members, and hierarchy is abhorred. Each woman with a skill to teach is given time to teach it to the group, but most learning and training are self-pursued. A women's coven enforces the idea of leadership shared equally by the members, and this in reality is sometimes hard to make function. Consensus is a slow process, and real leadership is often necessary.

In traditional wicce, a woman who wishes to become a witch must study with a coven for a year and a day to be initiated. She must first be accepted by the high priestess and high priest of a coven, and prove her seriousness and sincerity in the training period. In Women's Spirituality, any woman who chooses to be a witch and names herself as such is a witch. No training or initiation is required, and few covens do initiation rituals. No one's authority is needed for membership in the craft, and no validation but one's own. Women who lack commitment drop out sooner or later, and those with it learn in every way they can. Many women wish for formal training that is rarely available.

Joining a Women's Spirituality coven usually requires consensus of the group. Where no group is established or is open to new members, women form their own. Being a witch in Women's Spirituality does not require membership in a coven. A solitary witch, a woman who works in wicce alone, is as much a craft member as a woman who works with a group. The coven system is much tighter in traditional wicce than in Women's Spirituality, where probably most women who want to be in covens can't find them. A working coven is not easy to locate in either form of witchcraft, and the woman is no less a witch if she is isolated from others who are "of a like mind."

Unlike Gardnerian wicce, women's craft bases its emphasis on

matriarchy and the early Goddess religions, the way things may
have been not only before the Burning Times but before patriarchy
and the patriarchal religions began. Aidan Kelly's research leads
him to state that there was no Goddess movement in Europe left
over from the Burning Times, and he may be right — it may have
been wiped out by then. (I believe that Kelly is incorrect.) But
archeology by a number of women courageous enough to speak out
has established that the Goddess was present in virtually all pre-pa-
triarchal cultures. Women's Spirituality goes back to envision those
cultures, discover what they were like, and apply and recreate their
lifestyles for today.

The Women's Spirituality movement also takes its development from the political women's movement. The fact of women's
oppression and of women's refusal to accept any more of it under
patriarchy is a central theme in women's wicce. Fewer women would
list Gerald Gardner as their craft roots than such women activists
and philosophers as Mary Daly, Starhawk or Z. Budapest. While
Gerald Gardner's (or was it Dafo and Doreen Valiente's?) work has
been a beginning influence in Women's Spirituality, it has not gone
back far enough in time or far enough ahead in political analysis.
Gardnerian wicce has not been the sole influence on what women do
in the craft today.

Both women's and traditional wicce work with such skills as
crystal and gemstone work, healing, herbs, psychic develoment,
astrology and various forms of divination. These have always been
women's skills and continue to be in Women's Spirituality, and are
important skills for the members of traditional craft covens. Skills
like working with high magick and Kaballah are not emphasized in
Women's Spirituality, but are important for some members of
traditional witchcraft. Both use rituals, and the structure is similar,
but the rituals are very different.

Women's Spirituality rituals usually employ a changing high
priestess, and often all the members of the group take part. Ritual-
making is seen as important for everyone to learn, both for women
in covens and individuals working alone. Planning for a ritual is
usually done by the group and by consensus. New rituals are
created for each occasion, though records of what was done before
are often kept. If a woman writes and/or leads one ritual, someone
else does it for the next one. Women's rituals are designed to
celebrate the occasion, and are also designed for the empowerment
of the women who participate.

In traditional witchcraft, the high priestess and high priest of
the coven lead all of the rituals as a permanent job. They have

personally passed three initiations, sometimes taking as long as ten years work and training to prepare for the role. In some traditions, they do not write the rituals themselves, but obtain them from a Book of Shadows, handed down to them in their training, that is their coven's "Bible." Once the Book of Shadows is established the rituals are set, and the same ritual is done for each Sabbat every year. Creativity and spontaneity in rituals is less valued than tradition is, and the traditions are designed to be handed down. The coven's members participate in rituals as much as the ritual or high priestess includes and calls for them. There is more hierarchy and the high priestess is definitely in authority, with the high priest slightly behind her. Rituals are more focused on celebrating the occasion than on individual empowerment.

Vows of secrecy are often required in traditional covens as one of the requirements for initiation. Laws against witchcraft and the not-so-long-ago Inquisition, not to mention the crazy right-wing today are some of the reasons, along with personal safety and confidentiality. But secrecy is rarely a practice in Women's Spirituality, or at least not as a rule or requirement. The number of books describing craft practice, beginning with Gerald Gardner, indicates the loosening of the secrecy strictness in traditional craft as well. While the confidentiality of individuals is secure in women's wicce, the structure of last week's Full Moon ritual is something to discuss. When a group is looking for ideas for their ritual, they often ask members of another group, "What did you do?" Sharing and openness are valued.

Most women today feel that education of non-wiccans about the positive nature of Women's Spirituality and wicce is important. Openness about their involvement is a way to prevent discrimination, prevent future Burning Times. Too many women who are lesbians have lived "in the closet" for some portion of their lives, afraid to be known for who they are, to be willing to accept the damage of that again. While the "broom closet" exists, it exists much less often in Women's Spirituality than might be expected. Today's New Age movement, another outgrowth of the sixties, has made spirituality in general acceptable to mainstream society; wicce is seen as a branch of it, another outgrowth of the New Age (which it is not). A little bit of explaining and educating go a long way in reducing stereotypes.

For Women's Spirituality, the most troubling aspect of traditional craft is its occasionally still-existing homophobia. Some male/female wiccans refuse to acknowledge Women's Spirituality as part of the craft, because women invoke the Goddess only and/

or because many Women's Spirituality members are lesbians. Traditional craft secrecy and the concept that there must be a male aspect to have fertility seem to encourage this homophobia and misogyny, a factor that separates the two branches. Women wiccans would probably participate more in traditional craft, particularly in traditional craft initiation training, if this were not so and some women's wariness of traditional craft stems from it. Traditional craft women and their covens could also gain from women's perspectives and ways of doing things. This is not to say that homophobia is universal in traditional craft, it is not. It is true, however, that some women have experienced homophobia in traditional wiccan settings.

Another emphasis that Women's Spirituality has that traditional wicce does not is its outreach to all women. The women's movement learned early that any woman's oppression is all women's and that every woman, from whatever experience, is every other woman's sister. That attitude is held in strong regard in Women's Spirituality. In matriarchy, the Goddess was worshipped everywhere, in every culture. In Women's Spirituality, knowledge of all cultures and outreach to women of every culture is important. Women's real values and principles of peace refuse racism, ageism, fatism, ableism and all the other -isms as a major tenant of the movement. Goddesses in all colors and from all cultures are invoked at rituals, the Maiden, Mother and Crone are honored equally. If a woman can't attend a second floor ritual because she can't get her wheelchair up there, the women move the ritual. This awareness is only beginning in traditional craft and where it is beginning, it is largely because of Women's Spirituality's influence. Both women's and traditional wicce are aware of earth and ecology issues, and the concept that "the earth is our mother, we must take care of her." Many craft people of both types are political or environmentl activists. Women's Spirituality members are especially active in women's rights, gay rights, anti-apartheid, ecology and peace work.

Margot Adler in her book *Drawing Down the Moon* (Beacon Press, 1979) describes the many types of traditional wiccan groups and covens in the United States. Covens of both traditional and Women's Spirituality wicce are fully autonomous, answering to no central or regional authority, and therefore can vary greatly. This is so in both types of craft. Wiccans are independent, highly intelligent people, resistant to authority and primarily working from within. No two women's views of Women's Spirituality will be the same, and probably no two members of traditional wicce, either. Unlike traditional wicce, women's covens happen when enough like-minded women choose to start one and they continue for as long as the women feel they are getting what they need from the group. Groups come and go, though some are long-term, and it is not unusual to hear about a women's coven that has been functioning for fifteen years.

There has been no emphasis in Women's Spirituality on the hereditary coven, as there has been in traditional wicce. In this type of family-descended coven, the rituals are handed down, and great grandma was the high priestess until she handed the job over to the daughter she had trained. As time goes on and Women's Spirituality matures, this type of coven is very possible; many women are raising their daughters in the circle and the craft. Most women who are interested in the Goddess were not raised in the tradition, and so women are starting their own traditions as best they can. Most women's covens are not perceived to be life-long entities. The women come together to fill a need of the members, and dissolve the group when that need is fulfilled or no longer being met. This is not to say that the women in such covens, the work they do in them, or their intent in starting and maintaining them are not serious. As time goes on, women's views on heredity and longevity of craft groups will move closer to those of traditional craft, but hereditary covens will never play a large part in Women's Spirituality. They are only a small number of traditional wiccan covens, also.

Women's self-empowerment and self-esteem, and the return of both Goddess and matriarchy are central issues in Women's Spirituality and in women's covens. Other than their focus on the Goddess, these are not primary issues for traditional wicce. The Goddess in traditional craft is paired with the male aspect at all times, with the God, as reflected in the high priestess/high priest pair. The Goddess is the dominant figure, but much of the coven's rituals and activities are based on maintaining and portraying the male/female duality. Women's self-esteem is a byproduct of the role models of Goddess and high priestess. Women's Spirituality's emphasis on Goddess-within, women's consequence, and "You are Goddess" is less in traditional wicce, simply because of the male presence. In a patriarchal society men lead; they are trained to do it, and women are trained to let them. Though they take a back seat to the female in most wiccan craft covens, they are still there. Where there are no males, as in Women's Spirituality, women take leadership and discover their own powers and abilities, often for the first time, and probably for the first time since 5,000 years of patriarchy began.

Women-only groups are not man-hating, but are woman-affirming instead. A few women are separatists, but man-hating is seldom the reason for the women-only stance. With the emphasis on women's self-empowerment in the circle, women working with each other becomes essential. They need a totally safe space to explore female realities, to discover other women and themselves. Some women have a deep lack of trust of men — they have been abused by men sexually, physically or emotionally — and the circle has to be a place of trust. Some women go home to husbands, but need a space for women-only in the coven. Where there are men present, the focus moves away from women. Men are trained for leadership and automatically take over; women need that training for themselves, and need it unimpeded. Some women feel they have to nurture men, or step aside for them. Male presence in the circle changes the energy dramatically, and women need women-only space.

When women work together in women-only groups, they learn about each other, about working together, about their own potentials for leadership, and about who they are inside. In a women-only space, individuals are free to be who they are without defenses or fear. When the group operates from that level of honesty and trust, real magick happens in the ritual, in group dynamics, and in women's Be-ing from within. The changes and transformations that happen in a Women's Spirituality ritual would not happen where there are men present. Other things, other transformations, may occur, but not the ones that happen in women-only space. By invoking the Goddess as women's ultimate role model, women empower themselves. By invoking a Goddess and God, separating the energy into a duality, the possiblity for healing women's damage from patriarchy is lost. Healing women from this damage is a focus of Women's Spirituality; in traditional wicce the focus is on balancing the duality by including women and men, rather than focusing on women alone.

There are more similarities than differences between women's and traditional witchcraft. Both types of craft have the same beginnings, both worship the Goddess, and members of both come together as peaceful people to heal each other and the earth. There is a difference in some of the emphasis, and some differences in practices, but each have things to teach the other. Traditional wicce is more highly structured than Women's Spirituality, and this is its weakness and its strength; Women's Spirituality is nonhierarchal and nonexclusionary, and this also is its weakness and its strength.

Traditional covens are usually made up of heterosexual people with good intentions and a lot of knowledge. They have worked hard to be admitted to the craft, to find a coven and a high priestess and high priest to teach and admit them. They have worked for a year and a day for initiation. They often have no knowledge of what the Women's Spirituality movement is, or the reasons why women do things differently. Women's Spirituality covens are groups of women-only who have come together to worship the Goddess and reclaim women and women's values and herstory. They feel deeply that everyone has the right to the Goddess, that no one should be excluded, and that leadership is to be shared. They work in women-only groups to affirm and empower women, and to meet women's needs for safety, trust and privacy.

Both traditional and Women's Spirituality wiccans are descendents of those burned to death for witchcraft, and many have past life remembrances of this. We are the descendants of people from anywhere in the world that faced forced conversions to Christianity. Both groups trace at least partial beginnings to Gardnerian wicce, whether Gerald Gardner or Doreen Valiente and Dafo originated or saved from extinction the old Craft. Both groups owe early influence in this country to the atmosphere of the 1960s for impetus and ideas. It was only from this point that Women's Spirituality began to do things differently, choosing different focuses, and adapting to the needs of a specialized community. The two branches of wicce coming together have much to share and learn from each other. A merging of skills and ideas would especially benefit women, whose craft is, after all, less than twenty years old.

It will be interesting to see what happens in the next few years.

Full Moon in Sagittarius
July 16, 1989

Notes

1. J. Gordon Melton, "The Neo-Pagans of America," in *The Great Write* (Epiphanes, P.O. Box 25129, Chicago, IL 60625), Issue 2, 1981, p. 6.

2. Aiden A. Kelly, "The Invention of Witchcraft," in *The Great Write* (Epiphanes, P.O. Box 25129, Chicago, IL 60625), Issue 4, 1984, pp. 5-19.

3. *Ibid.*, p. 11.

4. *Ibid.*, p. 12.

5. *Ibid.*, p. 6.

6. Robin Morgan, Ed., *Sisterhood Is Powerful: An Anthology of Writings From the Women's Liberation Movement* (New York: Vintage Books, 1970), pp. 605-606.

7. *Ibid.*, p. 606.

Bibliography

Adair, Margot. *Working Inside Out: Tools for Change.* Berkeley: Wingbow Press, 1984.

Adelman, Penina. *Miriam's Well: Rituals for Jewish Women Around the Year.* Fresh Meadows, NY: Biblio Press, 1986.

Anahita-Gula. "Colored Candles: To Use or Not to Use." In *Harvest Magazine*, Vol. 9, No. 6, June 1989.

Andrews, Lynn. *Flight of the Seventh Moon, The Teaching of the Shields.* San Francisco: Harper and Row, 1984.

Budapest, Zsuzsanna. *The Holy Book of Women's Mysteries, Vol. I and II.* Los Angeles: Susan B. Anthony Coven No. 1, 1979-1980.

Budapest, Zsuzsanna. *The Rise of the Fates, A Mystical Comedy in Eight Acts.* Los Angeles: Susan B. Anthony Coven No. 1, 1976.

Christ, Carol. *Laughter of Aphrodite: Reflections on a Journey to the Goddess.* San Francisco: Harper and Row, 1987.

Cunningham, Scott. *Cunningham's Encyclopedia of Magical Herbs.* St. Paul: Llewellyn Publications, 1985.

Cunningham, Scott. *Magical Herbalism.* St. Paul: Llewellyn Publications, 1983.

Charmaine Dey. *The Magic Candle, Facts and Fundamentals of Ritual Candle Burning.* New York: Original Publications, 1982.

Durden-Robertson, Lawrence. *Juno Covella, Perpetual Calendar of the Fellowship of Isis.* Erie: Cesara Publications, 1982.

Durden-Robertson, Lawrence. *The Goddesses of Chaldea, Syria and Egypt.* Erie: Cesara Publications, 1975.

"The Eleusinian Mysteries." *The Crescent*, Vol. 1, No. 3, Sept. 1988.

Emerson, Deanna. "Inanna's Ascent." *The Beltane Papers' Octava*, Vol. 4, No. 4, Beltane, 1989.

Falanga, Julia and Helen Farias. "The Maypole: Dance and Feast."

The Beltane Papers' Octava, Vol. 3, No. 4, 1988.

Farias, Helen. *The College of Hera: The First Seven Lessons.* Clear Lake, WA: Juno's Peacock Press, 1988.

Farrar, Janet and Stewart. *Eight Sabbats for Witches.* London: Robert Hale, Ltd., 1981.

Flowers, Felicity Artemis. *The P.M.S. Conspiracy.* Marina del Rey, CA: Circle of Aradia Publications, 1986.

Gamal, Anisa. "Mothering and Nurturing." *Thesmophoria,* Vol. 7, No. 8, May Eve 1986.

Garfield, Laeh Maggie and Jack Grant. *Companions in Spirit.* Berkeley, CA: Celestial Arts, 1984.

Gonzalez-Wippler, Migene. *Santeria: African Magic in Latin America.* New York: Original Publications, 1981.

Johnson, Buffie. *Lady of the Beasts, Ancient Images of the Goddess and Her Sacred Animals.* San Francisco: Harper and Row, 1988.

Joyce, Norma. "Ritual Planning and Making." In Diane Stein, Ed. *The Goddess Celebrates: Women and Ritual.* Freedom, CA: The Crossing Press, 1991.

Kelly, Aidan A. "The Invention of Witchcraft." *The Great Write,* Issue 4, 1984.

Langsoeur, Lynn. "Holiday Foods." *Sage Woman Magazine,* Vol. II, No. 7, Fall 1988.

Lanning, Lee and Nett Hart. *Awakening: An Almanac of Lesbian Lore and Vision.* Minneapolis: Word Weavers, 1987.

Lanning, Lee and Nett Hart. *Dreaming: An Almanac of Lesbian Lore and Vision.* Minneapolis: Word Weavers, 1983.

Lanning, Lee and Nett Hart. *Ripening: An Almanac of Lesbian Lore and Vision.* Minneapolis: Word Weavers, 1981.

Mariechild, Diane. *Mother Wit: A Feminist Guide to Psychic Development.* Trumansburg, NY: The Crossing Press, 1981.

Maynard, Jim. *Jim Maynard's Celestial Guide 1989.* Ashland, OR: Quicksilver Productions.

Melton, J. Gordon. "The Neo-Pagans of America." *The Great Write,* Issue 2, 1981.

Monaghan, Patricia. *The Book of Goddesses and Heroines.* New York: E.P. Dutton, 1981. Reprinted by Llewellyn Publications, 1989.

Moody, Jr., Raymond J. *Life After Life.* New York: Bantam Books, 1975.

Morgan, Robin (Ed.). *Sisterhood is Powerful: An Anthology of Writings from the Women's Liberation Movement.* New York:

Vintage Books, 1970.

Mountainwater, Shekinah and Lunea Weatherstone. "Goddess Has Risen." *Sage Woman Magazine*, Vol. III, Issue 9, Spring 1989.

Noble, Vicki and Karen Vogel. *Motherpeace: A Way to the Goddess through Myth, Art and Tarot.* San Francisco: Harper and Row, 1983. Book and tarot deck.

Sjoo, Monica and Barbara Mor. *The Great Cosmic Mother: Rediscovering the Religion of the Earth.* San Francisco: Harper and Row, 1987.

Starhawk. *The Spiral Dance: A Rebirth of the Ancient Religion of the Great Mother.* San Francisco: Harper and Row, 1979.

Stein, Diane. *All Women Are Healers.* Freedom, CA: The Crossing Press, 1991.

Stein, Diane. *Stroking the Python: Women's Psychic Lives.* St. Paul: Llewellyn Publications, 1988.

Stein, Diane. *The Goddess Book of Days.* St. Paul: Llewellyn Publications, 1988.

Stein, Diane. *The Women's Book of Healing.* St. Paul: Llewellyn Publications, 1987.

Stein, Diane. *The Women's Spirituality Book.* St. Paul: Llewellyn Publications, 1987.

Stein, Diane. *The Kwan Yin Book of Changes.* St. Paul: Llewellyn Publications, 1985.

Stone, Merlin. *Ancient Mirrors of Womanhood.* Boston: Beacon Press, 1979.

Stone, Merlin. *When God Was A Woman.* New York: Harcourt, Brace, Jovanovich, 1976.

Teish, Luisah. *Jambalaya: The Natural Woman's Book.* San Francisco: Harper and Row, 1985.

Vinci, Leo. *The Book of Practical Candle Magic.* Great Britain: The Aquarian Press, 1981.

Walker, Barbara G. *The Women's Encyclopedia of Myths and Secrets.* San Francisco: Harper and Row, 1983.

Wambach, Helen. *Life Before Life.* New York: Bantam Books, 1979.

Washburn, Penelope (Ed.). *Seasons of Woman.* San Francisco: Harper and Row, 1982.

Waters, Frank. *The Man Who Killed the Deer.* New York: Pocket Books, 1971. Originally published in 1941.

Weaver, Kelly. "Wiccaning Ritual." *Circle Network News,* Winter 1988-89.

Weinstein, Marion. *Positive Magic.* Custer, WA: Phoenix Publishing, 1981.

Wynne, Patrice. "Practical Wisdom: An Interview with Luisah Teish."

In Patrice Wynne, Ed. *The Womanspirit Sourcebook*. San Francisco: Harper and Row, 1988, pp. 37-44.

Tapes

Barrett, Ruth and Felicity Flowers. *Invocation to Free Women*. Circle of Aradia Publications (4111 Lincoln Blvd. #211, Marina del Rey, CA 90292), 1987.

Ferron. *Testimony*. Lucy Records. 1980. (Order from Ladyslipper, P.O. Box 3124, Durham, NC 27705.)

Gardner, Kay. *Avalon: Solo Flute Meditations*. Ladyslipper Records (P.O. Box 3124, Durham, NC 27705), 1989.

Mackay, Karen. *Annie Oakley Rides Again!* West Virginia Woman Records, 1984. Also *West Virginia Woman*. (Order from Ladyslipper.)

Madsen, Catherine and the East Lansing Spinster's Guild. *The Patience of Love*. Wormwood Productions (P.O. Box 6167, E. Lansing, MI 48823), 1982.

Mountainwater, Shekinah. *Songs and Chants of the Goddess, Vol. I and II*. Moonspell (P.O. Box 2991, Santa Cruz, CA 95063), 1983.

Murphy, Charlie. *Catch the Fire*. Good Fairy Productions (P.O. Box 12188, Broadway Sta., Seattle, WA 98102), 1986.

Sun, Patricia. *All Sounds and Meditation Tape*. Patricia Sun Tapes (P.O. Box 7065, Berkeley, CA 94707), 1987.

Moon Phase Rituals - 28½ day Menstrual cycle / Lunar cycle

Candle Magick - short rituals

pg. 12